Law and Society
Recent Scholarship

Edited by Eric Rise

A Series from LFB Scholarly

News Piracy and The Hot News Doctrine
Origins in Law and Implications for the Digital Age

Victoria Smith Ekstrand

LFB Scholarly Publishing LLC
New York 2005

Copyright © 2005 by LFB Scholarly Publishing LLC

All rights reserved.

Library of Congress Cataloging-in-Publication Data

Ekstrand, Victoria Smith, 1966-
 News piracy and the hot news doctrine : origins in law and implications for the digital age / Victoria Smith Ekstrand.
   p. cm. -- (Law and society)
 Includes bibliographical references and index.
 ISBN 1-59332-075-2 (alk. paper)
 1. Journalists--Legal status, laws, etc.--United States. 2. Copyright--Newspaper articles--United States. 3. Piracy (Copyright)--United States. 4. Copyright and electronic data processing. 5. Internet--Law and legislation. I. Title. II. Series: Law and society (New York, N.Y.)
 KF2750.E38 2005
 346.7304'82--dc22

2005001035

ISBN 1-59332-075-2

Printed on acid-free 250-year-life paper.

Manufactured in the United States of America.

Table of Contents

Acknowledgments		ix
Chapter 1 **Introduction: The Scope of Piracy**		1
Copyright Versus Hot News		4
The Hot News Doctrine		6
Hot News in the Digital Age		8
Adopting Legislation to Protect Fact-Based Works		10
The Debate About Hot News		12
Chapter 2 **The Origins of the Hot News Doctrine**		15
Building the AP		16
The Rise of INS and Coverage of World War I		25
The Progressive Era		32
Corporate Due Process		33
The Effects of Antitrust Law		34
The Rise of Unfair Competition Law		36
Early Copyright Law		38
History of Statutory Copyright and Protections for News		39
History of Common Law Copyright		41
Case Law Leading Up to *INS v. AP*		43
Summary of Findings and Conclusion		47
Chapter 3 ***INS v. AP***		49
The Claims and the Evidence		50
The District Court		60
The Second Circuit		64
The Supreme Court		66
A Property Right in News		67
The Duration of a Property Right in News		72
INS's Actions and Extent of Protections		74
Discussion		76

The Dissent	77
Response to the Decision	78
Summary of Findings and Conclusion	80

Chapter 4   Interpreting *INS v. AP* — 83

The Advent of Radio and the Expansion of Misappropriation (1920s-1960s)	84
The Broadcast of Printed News	86
The Broadcast of Performances and Recordings	88
The Broadcast of Sports Events	91
Rewriting Copyright Law and Questions About Misappropriation (1960s-1976)	95
The Cable Television cases	97
The Tape Recording Cases	100
Other Cases of the Period	104
New Law, New Technologies, and Narrowing Misappropriation (1976-1996)	106
Stocks, Databases, and the "Extra Element"	108
News and Sports Information	114
Summary of Findings and Conclusion	116

Chapter 5   NBA v. Motorola and the New Boundaries of Hot News — 119

Corporate Histories	120
Motorola	120
The National Basketball Association	123
The Facts	127
The Legal Claims and Arguments	132
Preemption	133
Application of *INS*	134
The First Amendment	136
The Decisions	139
The District Court	139
The Second Circuit	140
Hot News After NBA	143
Application of the Five-Part NBA Test	143
The Free-Riding Element	145
The Threat Element	148
Summary of Findings and Conclusion	150

Table of Contents vii

Chapter 6   Conclusion **153**
Hot News and New Communications 154
Hot News and the Judicial Forum 156
The Parameters of Hot News 160

Endnotes 165

Bibliography 205

Index 211

Acknowledgments

In a book that directly addresses notions of property and ownership – and which supports the free flow of ideas and facts – it would be seriously remiss not to mention those individuals who freely and graciously offered their ideas and expertise in this endeavor.

I'm especially indebted to Cathy Packer, associate professor at the University of North Carolina at Chapel Hill, who helped to inspire and cultivate my love of intellectual property law and who provided extraordinary intellectual and emotional support. I am also grateful to Margaret Blanchard, Ruth Walden, Laura Gasaway, Paul Jones, and Pei-Ling Lee for their assistance.

Thanks also go to the lawyers who represent The Associated Press, Motorola, Stats, and the National Basketball Association: Bob Penchina of Clifford Chance Rogers & Wells; David Tomlin and George Galt of The Associated Press, Jeffrey Mishkin, formerly of the NBA, now with Skadden, Arps, Slate, Meagher & Flom; Herbert Schwartz of Fish & Neave; and Andrew Deutsch of Piper, Marbury, Rudnick & Wolfe LLP. They generously gave their time to discuss the hot news doctrine with me and add the kind of context not found in the texts of the case decisions.

The Park Program at UNC's School of Journalism and Mass Communication allowed me to explore this topic. The extremely generous Park Fellowship, of which I was a recipient, is due to the generosity of Roy H. Park, who died in 1993, and his family.

I am also grateful to Michael Sproule, former director of the School of Communication Studies at Bowling Green State University, and to the faculty of the Journalism Department, for their support of my research.

My interest in intellectual property was born out of my experience as an Associated Press employee for nine years at the AP's headquarters in New York City. I'm indebted to the AP for making me a stronger writer, researcher, and manager, and I'm grateful to those who trained me in those pursuits: Kelly Smith Tunney, vice president and director of Corporate Communications; Michael Bass, director of the News and Information Research Center; and Elaine Hooker, Hartford chief of bureau.

On a personal level, my parents, my brother, and in-laws provided encouragement at every turn. My husband, Chris, was and continues to be a source of strength and loving guidance. I am fortunate to be part of such a nurturing and supportive family.

CHAPTER 1
Introduction
The Scope of Piracy

The age of digital piracy – the unlawful taking of creative works by computer file sharing, usually across the Internet – reached one of its most critical moments in September 2003. The Recording Industry Association of America (RIAA), a trade association whose members create, manufacture, and/or distribute approximately 90 percent of all sound recordings produced and sold in the United States, began a wave of lawsuits against individual users illegally swapping songs across the Internet. The action brought enormous publicity to the issue of digital piracy and elevated the debate over the rights of individuals who buy creative works versus the rights of the creators to protect random and unregulated copying of those works.

On a daily basis, however, digital piracy usually involves much less exciting – though no less valuable – content. In some cases, the debate is over the piracy of material as seemingly insignificant as scores, prices, and voting results. A few examples:

• In 2002, a media company named Morris Communications sued the PGA Tour for prohibiting it from gathering and reselling the real-time scores from major golfing events.[1] The PGA gave Morris press access to PGA events for the purpose of covering its events, but prohibited the resale of real-time scores because the Tour produced these results for its own Web site, pgatour.com. The PGA argued these scores were valuable property whose use the Tour had a right to control; Morris and others initially argued the scores were in the public domain and therefore, free to use. Morris later argued that the PGA

1

engaged in unfair trade practices. The Eleventh Circuit eventually ruled for the PGA.[2]

• In 2000, eBay, the Internet powerhouse that lets users sell and trade their wares by online auction, fought for and later won an injunction to stop Bidder's Edge, an online company that compared prices across multiple online auction providers, from using eBay data on its site.[3] "The eBay site certainly is open to the public, but we have rules about how you can use the site, how you can access it, whether you can copy and what use you might make of the information," eBay counsel Jay Monahan told National Public Radio. "If you permit third parties to take content from other entrepreneurs, simply misappropriate it and capitalize it and commercialize it themselves, it is absolutely inevitable that the incentives for creation of such content will be eroded over time, and in some cases, destroyed."[4]

• Also in 2000, Voter News Service (VNS), a consortium of The Associated Press, CBS News, NBC News, Fox News, and CNN, threatened to sue several Web site operators who were leaked the results of VNS exit polls in the tight U.S. presidential race between former Vice President Al Gore and then-Texas Governor George W. Bush. These sites, including the *Drudge Report* and *Inside.com*, reported the data before VNS did and revealed the tight battle between Bush and Gore before polls closed.[5] Michael Hirschorn, *Inside.com*'s editor-in-chief, argued the information was factual and fairly obtained by news gatherers in his organization. "The genie is out of the bottle, and it's wishful thinking that you could put it back in," he said. "Once this information is out, thanks to e-mail and the Internet, it becomes incredibly easy to distribute."[6]

This specific kind of news and information piracy — what some view as news and information sharing — has a long history in the United States. During colonial times, the free exchange of newspapers[7] encouraged the practice of lifting news and information from other publications. Throughout the eighteenth century and for the first half of the nineteenth century, the general belief was that news and information belonged in the public domain.[8] The free flow of raw news and information was critical to the success of the new nation and the ability of the people to govern.

The introduction of technology, particularly the telegraph, upset this belief. With the ability to deliver immediate news and information, news providers used the "scoop" as a "weapon" of business.[9] News became a commodity; the first news offered the most value to publishers and readers. Publishers prosecuted those who took their product without permission and fought for new legal protections for their publications.[10]

Today, the battle against piracy has been renewed in the face of new and infinitely faster technologies. The Internet and other digital media not only reduce the costs of creating new works, but they also dramatically reduce the costs of redistribution. And the scope of pirated works has expanded. The Business Software Alliance (BSA), an international organization representing leading software and e-commerce developers in more than 60 countries, estimates that in 2002 the software industry lost more than $6 billion in revenue in the United States to software theft.[11] A study of database pirates suggested that although the number of database producers has grown since 1991, growth has slowed considerably over previous decades, in part due to piracy.[12] And a recent internal study by the *Wall Street Journal* during a 30-day period found 36,000 instances of copyright infringement, in which "Journal articles were reposted on the Internet without permission."[13]

Piracy is now rampant, a fact of the digital age. Solutions for controlling the problem (though not all digital piracy is a "problem")[14] are far from perfected. This study looks at one small but critical slice of the piracy issue – the law that protects against the piracy of breaking news (the newsman's "scoop") and real-time information. It examines the historical and legal factors that have influenced this law, known more commonly as the "hot news" doctrine.

In its simplest form, the doctrine, which originated in the 1918 U.S. Supreme Court case *International News Service v. The Associated Press*,[15] gives the creators of factual news and information a property right in that information for a limited period after publication. This doctrine has received renewed attention because of digital technologies that quickly and creatively package, sort, and deliver factual information – and just as simply pirate such data. The hot news doctrine can offer the creators of such fact-based works legal protections against such piracy. But there is significant disagreement about whether the doctrine goes too far by protecting facts that U.S. copyright law dedicates to the public domain – that body of free material such as facts, data, systems, methods, ideas, theories, and other uncopyrightable material from which new intellectual creations are born.

This book is the story of the doctrine. It examines the origin, application, and development of the hot news doctrine and its continued ability to preserve the balance between a vibrant public domain and a healthy market for fact-based works in the digital age. It is primarily an historical study of the doctrine and the cases that have refined and redefined the doctrine since 1918. As such, it provides a traditional review and analysis of the original case, *INS v. AP*, and major cases since. But unlike other studies of the doctrine, it offers an in-depth examination of primary source materials in the case record and the specific facts behind *INS* and the most recent appeals case on the doctrine, *National Basketball Association v. Motorola, Inc.*[16] The histories of these organizations – the AP and INS in 1918 and the NBA and Motorola in 1997 – are also addressed. In addition, a review of copyright law, unfair competition law and advances in technology is provided. This combined approach to studying the hot news doctrine offers a comprehensive picture of the historical influences on the doctrine's development and more information on which to base an opinion about its viability in the digital age.

COPYRIGHT VERSUS "HOT NEWS"

Ordinarily, those seeking to prosecute digital pirates first turn to copyright law for relief. Copyright law was designed to "promote the progress of science and the useful arts" by giving to creators exclusive rights in their work for "limited times."[17] While copyright offers protection for original expression — a sound recording or a computer program, for instance — it does not protect the underlying facts or information within a work, such as auction listings and prices on eBay or exit polling data. "The primary objective of copyright is not to reward the labor of authors, but 'to promote the Progress of Science and the useful Arts,'" wrote Justice Sandra Day O'Connor in *Feist v. Rural Telephone Inc.*,[18] a 1991 U.S. Supreme Court case that denied copyright protection to a telephone book compilation. "To this end, copyright assures authors the right to their original expression, but encourages others to build freely upon the ideas and information conveyed by the work. This principle, known as the idea/expression or fact/expression dichotomy, applies to all works of authorship."[19]

The 9-0 opinion in *Feist* reinforced three fundamental tenets of copyright law that have influenced current discussion about the hot news doctrine. First, *Feist* made originality a constitutional requirement.[20] For a work to receive copyright protection, the Court said, it must not only owe its origins to the author, but it must also display originality, which the Court defined as "some minimal level of creativity."[21] Thus, the facts of news do not reach that minimal threshold.

Second, *Feist* rejected the "sweat of the brow" or "industrious collection" doctrine, a principle followed by some courts that rewarded authors with copyright protection for the labor expended in creating their work.[22] In rejecting the "sweat of the brow," the *Feist* court cited *INS v. AP* as standing for the principle that effort alone was not enough to copyright the "news element." The news, it said, is "*publici juris*; it is the history of the day."[23] Just because a newsman has worked hard for his scoop does not entitle him (or more likely, his employer) to claim a copyright in the facts of the scoop.

Finally, by requiring originality and rejecting the "sweat of the brow," the Court reinforced a longstanding principle that no author may copyright his ideas or the facts he uses within a work:

> This is because facts do not owe their origin to an act of authorship. The distinction is one between creation and discovery: The first person to find and report a particular fact has not created the fact; he or she has merely discovered its existence. . . . The same is true of all facts — scientific, historical, biographical, and news of the day. "They may not be copyrighted and are part of the public domain available to every person."[24]

Furthermore, the Court said that copyright serves both to protect expression and to fuel it:

> Copyright assures authors the right to their original expression, but encourages others to build freely upon the ideas and information conveyed by a work. . . . This result is neither unfair nor unfortunate. It is the means by which copyright advances the progress of science and art.[25]

Thus, the copyright holder may not control every element of a copyrighted work.[26] Compilations such as a telephone directory or a database receive copyright protection to the extent that the "selection, coordination, and arrangement"[27] of the whole work are original, but the data within are "part of the public domain available to every person"[28] to reuse. Likewise, the expression of a news story may be copyrighted, but the facts within the story are not and remain available to others to reuse. The ruling in *Feist* reminded observers of these core copyright principles, but also rekindled debate about some obvious contradictions between the decision and the hot news doctrine.[29]

THE HOT NEWS DOCTRINE

If fact-based businesses like newspapers are unable to claim a copyright in facts or data, they may risk what economists call "market failure": An invasion of second-comers who pirate or "free-ride" on the investment made in the collection of facts or data, claim the information as their own, and destroy the compiler's incentive to produce (if not also destroy his business). Where some perceive this as a failure of or gap in copyright law, others see it as proof of copyright's holy grail: Facts and ideas must be left free to roam.

The U.S. Supreme Court first addressed this dilemma in *International News Service v. Associated Press*[30] and introduced a common law rule to protect fact-based compilers: those who free-ride on the labor of a competitor may be liable for *misappropriation*. The Court based its ruling on principles of unfair competition in business. (Unfair competition law, now primarily a part of state common law, protects businesses from economic injury due to a deceptive or wrongful business practice.) While the doctrine of misappropriation may be used in a wide array of unfair competition actions,[31] its particular application to the taking of news and information is more commonly referred to as the "hot news doctrine."[32]

In its original claim, the AP sued INS for paying an employee at an AP member newspaper to furnish AP news to INS as quickly as it came in over the wires; for obtaining news from another AP member by taking it off a machine over which AP news was distributed; and for procuring early editions of some AP member papers and from them, and from member newspaper bulletin boards, transferring the news into its contributions to its own customers.[33] The AP argued that it should have a limited property right in the facts of news and the particular "scoops" it obtained. INS argued that as soon as AP news was distributed, the facts, which were unprotected by copyright, were free to use.

The Supreme Court undoubtedly struggled with the unique facts of the case. In 1918, AP news was not copyrighted.[34] Indeed, wire services at the time claimed that it was impossible to register their thousands of dispatches.[35] The Court, therefore, did not entertain a discussion of copyright, but instead based its ruling on the principles of unfair competition in business, expanding these principles to include a new tort of misappropriation. In a 5-3 vote,[36] the Court ruled that between the public and news organizations there was no property right in news, but between rival newsgathering organizations, a "quasi-property" right existed.[37] In his opinion, Justice Mahlon Pitney admitted the case had no clear precedent. The Court appeared most influenced by the argument that the incentive to produce news was lost when rival organizations took news after publication, permitting organizations like INS to "reap where it has not sown":

> Stripped of all disguises, the process amounts to an unauthorized interference with the normal operation of complainant's legitimate business precisely at the point where the profit is to be reaped, in order to divert a material portion of the profit from those who have earned it to those who have not; with special advantage to defendant in the competition because of the fact that it is not burdened with any part of the expense of gathering the news. The transaction speaks for itself, and a court of equity ought not to hesitate long in characterizing it as unfair competition in business.[38]

Although the Court granted a limited property right in news vis-à-vis a competitor, it did not attempt to define the length of time such a right would last, saying "only to the extent necessary to prevent that competitor from reaping the fruits" of the organization's labor.[39]

Justice Oliver Wendell Holmes concurred in the opinion, but was not convinced there was a limited property right in news. Instead, he suggested "stating the truth" — that the effort in news collection should be acknowledged by those who use it after publication.[40] In this case, he wrote, INS needed merely to credit AP on its own wire. The majority criticized this rationale and wrote that a simple credit would still put AP members at a distinct disadvantage.[41] There would be little incentive to pay and subscribe to AP if one could simply take its news and give credit.

In his dissent, Justice Louis Brandeis rejected the notion of a property right in news, disputed that INS had obtained AP's news in an unfair manner, maintained that the Court was ignoring established principles of common law copyright, and questioned how the courts would be able to interpret what reasonable length of time the quasi-property right should endure.[42] He argued that although "a product of the mind has cost its producer money and labor, and has a value for which others are willing to pay," it is "not sufficient to ensure to it this legal attribute of property. The general rule of law is, that the noblest of human productions — knowledge, truths ascertained, conceptions, and ideas — become after voluntary communication to others, as free as the air to common use."[43]

He suggested that the ruling left the door open to misinterpretation and recommended that protections for news be solved by the legislature, not the courts.[44] Furthermore, he worried that the case would unduly reinforce AP's prominence.[45] He expressed concern that left without the use of AP's news, INS had no other means to obtain international war news.[46] "The facts of this case admonish us of the danger involved in recognizing such a property right in news, without imposing upon news-gatherers corresponding obligations," he wrote.[47]

More than 80 years later, Justice Brandeis' concerns seem prescient. The principles of misappropriation as established in *INS v. AP* have challenged the fact/expression rules of copyright, the rejection of the "sweat of the brow" doctrine in *Feist*, the expansion of copyright law since 1976, and the purpose of proposed legislation designed to protect the labor and investment of digital database providers. Thus, the doctrine is properly studied today within the context of both unfair competition and copyright law.

HOT NEWS IN THE DIGITAL AGE

Stealing news in 1918 required planning. To take AP's news, INS had to recruit and pay reporter thieves, gain access to AP news, take notes on what was found, and then file to the INS wire — and do all of it in secret. Today, a thief need only gain access to news sites distributing AP news, such as Yahoo, and understand how to "cut and paste." Within seconds, AP news can be pirated and redistributed.

The hot news doctrine has regained attention because it provides publishers an important weapon against those who steal fact-based works using these new technologies. When a competitor uses a "bot"[48] to troll the Internet and retrieve information, the hot news doctrine may provide relief to an online fact-based publisher whose information is taken. But it is exactly the ease of searching and exchanging information that built the Internet, and some critics contend anti-piracy actions are ultimately futile because the Internet's design is built on principles of open architecture and sharing.[49] Others worry that if the success of the Internet was its openness, the campaign against piracy will drastically change that success and the Internet's design, and in the process, inhibit innovation.[50] Against the backdrop of these disputes, courts today must decide the extent to which fact-based compilers — news organizations, realtors, movie theaters, legal publishers, sports leagues, stock markets, and other data providers — can successfully pursue a hot news claim.

The most recent case to address some of these issues and current interpretation of the hot news doctrine was *National Basketball Association v. Motorola, Inc.*[51] In that case, the NBA filed a hot news claim against Motorola for misappropriating up-to-the-minute scores and information about its professional basketball games and transmitting them to Motorola's "SportsTrax" pager customers. A U.S. district court[52] found Motorola liable for misappropriation, but the Second Circuit reversed. The appeals court first addressed whether the NBA's claim was preempted by copyright law, which under the 1976 revision prohibits the states from enacting "legal or equitable rights that are equivalent to any of the exclusive rights within the general scope of copyright . . . and come within the subject matter of copyright."[53] Simply stated, preemption means no state law can substitute rights that the law of federal copyright already addresses. The *NBA* court ruled the claim was not preempted, but whether hot news claims should be preempted by copyright law is still the subject of significant debate.[54]

The court created a new test for plaintiffs claiming hot news protection. To win a hot news claim, it must be shown:

(i) a plaintiff generates or gathers information at a cost;
(ii) the information is time-sensitive;
(iii) a defendant's use of the information constitutes free riding on the plaintiff's efforts;
(iv) the defendant is in direct competition with a product or service offered by the plaintiffs; and
(v) the ability of other parties to free-ride on the efforts of the plaintiff or others would so reduce the incentive to

produce the product or services that its existence or quality would be substantially threatened.[55]

The court concluded that Motorola did not engage in misappropriation based on its five-part test. The court said that the Motorola pager did not threaten the "very existence" of the NBA's product, which the court defined as its 29 teams that compete regularly in basketball games.[56]

ADOPTING LEGISLATION TO PROTECT FACT-BASED WORKS

NBA marked the beginning of a new era of hot news cases and contributed to the introduction of congressional legislation designed to federalize misappropriation — that is, to offer fact-based compilers federal statutory protection against piracy. Since 1996, federal legislators have proposed five bills to protect the content and labor put into databases that range from NASDAQ for market information to LEXIS-NEXIS for news and legal information. The first bill, The Database Investment and Intellectual Property Act,[57] was introduced by the House Judiciary Committee in 1996 and called for the protection of databases that were the product of significant investment. The bill, which died in committee, was attacked by scholars[58] and database users because it lacked a fair use[59] exception for researchers.

In October 1997, Rep. Howard Coble (R.-N.C.) introduced The Collections of Information Antipiracy Act.[60] The CIAA created a broadly defined property right in "collections of information" and prohibited the use of "all or a substantial part of a collection of information gathered, organized, or maintained by another person through the investment of substantial monetary or other resources, so as to harm that other person's actual or potential market for a product or service."[61] The bill passed the House in May 1998 and was included in the proposed Digital Millennium Copyright Act (DMCA).[62] However, continued debate prompted the Senate to delete it from the DMCA before that bill was passed in October 1998. Critics objected to the absence of a time limit on protection and a fair use exception for researchers.[63]

In January 1999, Rep. Coble reintroduced the bill under the same title with a traditional fair use exemption for research institutions and libraries and a protection limit of 15 years. The penalty for a first

Introduction: The Scope of Piracy 11

offense under the CIAA was a fine of up to $250,000, five years in jail, or both. A second offense was punishable by fines of up to $500,000, ten years in jail, or both. The new CIAA[64] was discharged by the Commerce Committee in October 1999 and was pending consideration by the Senate in 2000 but failed to become law because critics charged that the bill overprotected data collections.[65]

A competing Commerce Committee bill, the Consumer and Investor Access to Information Act,[66] attempted to provide protection for database producers, "while ensuring that public access to information will not be limited by publishers' asserting a proprietary right over facts and information, which historically have been part of the public domain."[67] It more narrowly defined a database as a "collection of discrete items of information that have been collected or organized in a single place" and that required a substantial investment.[68] It relied on a traditional misappropriation model; misappropriation would occur when an unauthorized duplicate of a database or a part of that database "displaced substantial sales" and "threatened the opportunity to recover a return on the investment of the first database."[69] It included exceptions for news reporting, scientific, and educational purposes, and it excluded government-produced databases. Furthermore, the measure contained a special amendment to the Securities Exchange Act that would prohibit the misappropriation of real-time market data and established liability for offenders and various exceptions.[70] Finally, the act required the Federal Trade Commission to enforce the measure and punish offenders. The bill passed the House Commerce Committee in 1999, but failed to go further.[71]

In 2003, Rep. Coble presented yet another version of a database protection bill, now titled the Database and Collections of Information Misappropriation Act.[72] This bill adopts the *NBA* court's test for hot news, providing relief to database providers if the harm done "causes the displacement or the disruption of the sources, of sales, licenses, advertising, or other revenue"[73] and if the database is "time sensitive," which is left to the courts to define.[74] The bill includes exceptions for educational institutions and research labs that may use data for nonprofit education, scientific or research purposes.[75] Critics charge that despite the "time sensitive" provision, the bill still gives database providers perpetual protection.[76] Opponents also question Congress' ability to legislate databases under the Commerce Clause of the U. S

Constitution.[77] Nonetheless, the bill has been referred to the House of Representatives for a vote.

THE DEBATE ABOUT HOT NEWS

Most observers are critical of the hot news doctrine in its current form, though they disagree about how it should be adapted to suit modern demands, if at all. The current debate over the doctrine's scope boils down to three key issues:

> 1. In view of the changes in copyright law and in technology, is the doctrine still good law?
> 2. If the doctrine is still viable, what form should it take? Should it remain as part of state unfair competition law or does Congress need to adapt its principles to fit modern circumstances, as the five database bills attempted to do?
> 3. In proposing a modern hot news doctrine, what should its parameters be? In other words, just how much protection should fact-based businesses receive against news and information pirates?

On the first point, scholars are generally divided. Some observers, including the American Law Institute, say changes in the law since 1918 forced the *NBA* court to significantly narrow the doctrine in 1997, making it useful only to a very small segment of fact-based content providers.[78] Others contend that though imperfect and significantly narrowed, the hot news doctrine, as common law, continues to provide important protection for those new works left unprotected by copyright law, such as digital databases.[79] Still others argue that the doctrine has the potential to threaten the public domain.[80]

In a recent essay on the hot news doctrine, Richard A. Posner, a prominent judge for the U.S. Court of Appeals for the Seventh Circuit, wrote that the doctrine should be "jettisoned,"[81] because "it is too sprawling a concept to serve as the organizing principle of intellectual property law."[82] Among numerous other criticisms, Posner condemns the doctrine's reliance on courts to decide whether some form of intellectual property receives the doctrine's protections or not: "Society has dealt with this problem primarily though not exclusively by specifying intellectual property rights statutorily rather than by leaving it to the courts to decide on a case-by-case basis whether the incentive-access trade-off favors protection or nonprotection."[83]

Introduction: The Scope of Piracy

Not surprisingly, scholars are also divided about whether a hot news protection should become statute. Those who support "federalizing" the hot news doctrine argue that such a move is simply smart business, particularly because it would harmonize United States law with European law.[84] Others argue that the *Feist* decision opened the door to the piracy of fact-based works by leaving such compilations more vulnerable to piracy and that the *NBA* ruling demonstrated the limitations of the doctrine.[85] Those opposed to the specific statutes proposed by Congress since 1996 sympathize with the need but caution that technology continues to evolve and makes the creation of a specific statute protecting data very difficult.[86] Other critics worry that legislation would unduly regulate speech, creating First Amendment concerns.[87] Some argue that database providers already have many others avenues of legal protection, most especially contract law, to protect their investments.[88]

Regarding the parameters of a modern hot news doctrine, some observers have proposed expanding the number of requirements to meet a hot news claim, with more specific requirements to meet modern business concerns.[89] In expanding the number of requirements, observers hope to protect that information which should be part of the public domain but still offer some reasonable incentives to those producers of fact-based works. Some of these proposals are addressed in more detail in Chapter 6.

In this book, these questions are addressed from an historical perspective. The study first examines the histories of The Associated Press and International News Service, their leaders and the state of the nation at the time the two companies arrived in court. It then offers a detailed look at the *INS* case and subsequent rulings, along with interpretations of the doctrine that followed during three technological periods: the rise of radio, the rise of television and the rise of the computer. Then, the study turns to an in-depth analysis of the most recent appeals case to address the doctrine, *NBA v. Motorola*. In that chapter, the histories of both organizations are addressed and an in-depth look at the case record in the dispute between the two companies is provided. The influence of *NBA* on hot news cases since is also discussed. Based on this history, this book argues that the hot news doctrine still serves a valuable purpose and does so best as common law. It supports proposals to modernize the doctrine's parameters, but recognizes the necessity for the doctrine to remain flexible.

CHAPTER 2
The Origins of the Hot News Doctrine

The story of the hot news doctrine is first the tale of a jilted employee and his revenge. In October 1916, Fred Agnew, manager of the INS Cleveland bureau, was denied a raise.[1] Agnew grew fearful that he was losing clout with INS management, who criticized him for poor coverage of a serious bridge disaster in Cleveland earlier that month. Colleagues observed that Agnew became increasingly angry and upset.[2] He told colleagues that he wished INS would lose all its clients and threatened to "do them all the dirt" if he lost his title.[3] On Nov. 17, 1916, Agnew made good on his threat. He was demoted to telegrapher, and not long after, he revealed to AP a secret arrangement by which INS received AP news from a telegraph operator at the *Cleveland News*.[4] On Jan. 8, 1917, the AP filed suit in U.S. district court, charging INS with unfair competition.[5] Within a year, the U.S. Supreme Court ruled against INS in the case.[6]

While Agnew planted the seeds of *INS v. AP*, the roots of the case are deeper than the unfair practices of one competitor and more intricate than the Court's decision in *INS v. AP* would suggest. Using a combination of both primary and secondary sources, this chapter traces those roots from the late nineteenth century, when the AP emerged from nearly a quarter century of internal strife and competitive turmoil, to 1917, when the case was first heard by the district court. It addresses the history and development of AP, INS, and their leaders, and it considers the events unfolding in the United States and Europe as the case went to court. Finally, it evaluates the law at the time and leading up to the *INS* case to gain a greater understanding of the foundations for the hot news doctrine. It concludes that the hot news doctrine was the result of several unique developments in the histories of AP, INS, and newsgathering in general, and was also the result of key developments in the law.

BUILDING THE AP

Founded by six New York City newspapers in 1848,[7] The Associated Press was formed on the basis of this simple business principle: A pact to share resources, particularly news from overseas, reduced individual newspapers' expenses and assured access to news and news facilities, particularly the telegraph. The early history of the AP reflected efforts to "centralize the gathering, assembling, and distributing of news stories."[8] As the AP grew, ownership of an AP franchise was largely considered a ticket to publishing success.[9]

Before the advent of the telegraph and the growth of cooperative newsgathering organizations like AP, the postage-free news exchanges encouraged news sharing and borrowing. Newspapers were exchanged by mail, and editors routinely lifted items of interest from other areas for local readers. For much of the nineteenth century, news was thought to be in the public domain, and the use of each other's news was considered an accepted practice.[10] The penny-papers often stole news from each other, but "in that era the tendency was to look upon piracy as an oblique compliment."[11] *New York Tribune* publisher Horace Greeley once told a British parliamentary commission in 1851 that he didn't mind when others used his news. "On the whole," he said, "I would rather that those who do not take it, should copy than not. All the evening journals copy from us and we rather like it."[12]

Much of that changed as the technology to deliver news improved, and news agencies like the AP added structure to the system of exchanging news. Following the Civil War, the growth and consolidation of the telegraph industry encouraged more newspapers to use telegraphed news and to deliver their news in smaller, continuously updated stories.[13] The "scoop," the more common term for what the courts later labeled "hot news," took on increasing importance, and "exclusive rights to news became weapons in the battle for subscribers and street sales."[14] This change fueled the demand for late-breaking news, and AP's business would be forever linked to the rapid delivery of such information.

As publishers increasingly relied on the telegraph for fresh news, the views on exchanging news also changed. News became a commodity — what AP's first general manager Daniel Craig preached as the industry's "string of onions."[15] The news, in Craig's view, should be sold like a string of onions was sold. Freshness mattered. Delivering the first news was each newsman's primary goal. Piracy, therefore, was viewed as an attack and an effort to unfairly benefit from another's labor and expense.

The AP was particularly vulnerable to piracy. Historian Barbara Cloud's research indicated that one-half of the news distributed by other news agencies during the latter half of the nineteenth century was stolen from the Associated Press.[16]

With the growth of the telegraph and the demand for hot news, the latter half of the nineteenth century was a period of tremendous growth for the New York AP. But differences arose among the founding organization in New York and its regional counterparts, particularly the Western Associated Press (WAP), based in Chicago. The WAP complained to the New York AP that the news it received focused only on the needs of the New York papers and that the WAP was paying far more than its share for that news.[17] These differences resulted in an agency war between the two regional APs in 1866. The WAP sought wire news from a new agency run by Daniel Craig, who had been dismissed by the New York AP. In response, the New York AP passed a bylaw that prohibited members from doing business with rival wire agencies. Newspapers across the country chose sides. In the end, Western Union forced the two sides toward resolution, as the strain of delivering two wire reports was just too much in some parts of the country.[18] When tensions flared again in 1882, the two sides formed a joint executive committee of New York and Western AP members. That arrangement would last until the discovery of joint executive committee fraud in 1892.

The struggle to manage and maintain a rapidly growing service, meet the demands of the regional APs, and navigate the tensions among many of its members — compounded by the growing realization that piracy meant lost revenue — led the New York AP to introduce increasingly stricter rules about the use of its news by its membership.

While a series of AP bylaws were in place as early as 1856, the AP continually revised them in an effort to protect the news report and its value.[19] The key and most controversial provisions prohibited AP members from doing business with "antagonistic" news agency services and from sharing member-generated news with any other news organization besides the AP.[20] Later versions of the bylaws prohibited the inclusion of new AP members within a 60-mile radius of existing "A members"[21] and gave "A" members exclusive veto power over admitting new members. Violators risked suspension or fines of up to $1,000.[22] Prior to *INS*, the AP relied primarily on these bylaws and individual contracts with members to control the use of AP news.

AP's increasingly stricter rules on use of its news did not go unnoticed. Competing publishers and the public expressed concern that AP's bylaws and its contracts with the telegraph companies gave it unprecedented control over the flow of news in the United States. Several U.S. Congresses from 1866 through the late 1870s considered regulation of the telegraph and the national flow of news but "failed to determine the adverse effect of a telegraph monopoly on press freedom and on the public good."[23] That did not deter investigators from examining the full picture, however, and legislators focused on the power the AP exercised over the flow of national news. Congress examined the practices of both Western Union and the AP. Business historian Menahem Blondheim wrote that the government was disturbed by what it found:

> It discovered that seven dailies in New York virtually controlled the national supply of news. It learned that this was done by having the nation's news "edited" or, to use a term that legislators were more comfortable with, "censored," in one office, by one man. It was told that Associated Press newspapers were not allowed to receive telegraphic reports from any competing news service. And it also found out that newspapers receiving the wire service's news were forbidden to criticize the Associated Press publicly, on pain of losing their franchise. . . . But the legislators' main discovery was the privilege of receiving Associated Press reports was restricted; certain newspapers could get them, others could not.[24]

While Congress chose not to act, competitors stepped in to challenge the AP's dominance. The first United Press (UP), which emerged out of a smaller agency in 1882, was by far the most significant competitor faced by the AP after the Civil War. AP's joint committee responded to increased competition from UP in several ways.

First, a committee of AP members lobbied Congress for legislation to establish a property right in news. In 1884, Henry Watterson of the *Louisville Courier-Journal* led the effort. Historian Barbara Cloud wrote:

> Watterson went to the heart of the issue when he noted that items in a newspaper office such as the press and the paste pot were protected by laws concerning theft, "but that which constitutes the real value of a newspaper property — its news franchises, costing vast sums of money and years of special enterprise, training, and labor — has no legal status whatever."[25]

Four bills were introduced in Congress to protect news content from theft. One was designed to protect news for several hours after publication.[26] That bill gave newspapers the "sole right to print, issue and sell for a term of eight hours, dating from the hour of going to press," the stories in the newspaper that exceeded 100 words. The bill allowed plaintiffs to sue for damages.[27]

Congress considered that bill, but it did not pass.[28] Cloud concluded that such efforts by the AP and its member newspapers "represented a prioritizing of values that undermined the principle of news as a public service."[29] She also wrote that by rejecting the bills, Congress recognized news "played an important role in the political process" and should remain a public good.[30]

A handful of smaller papers, led by publishers from New England to the Mississippi Valley,[31] were particularly opposed to the bills. Most of these papers were still largely dependent on the sharing of news by mail exchange and believed that a property right in news would end this practice and grant AP an unfair advantage.[32]

The AP's joint committee also addressed the competitive threat from UP by reaching individual regional contracts with UP that limited its growth in areas such as New England.[33] When Western Union threatened to increase rates for use of its wires and compete with both AP and UP, both organizations also signed two trust agreements[34] to limit competition between them in 1885 and 1887. In these agreements, UP stock was sold to individual members of the AP executive joint committee in exchange for the delivery of AP news to UP members. In addition, restrictions were imposed on what newspapers UP could serve, keeping the growth of UP in check.[35] The effect of these agreements discouraged competition and led to UP's demise. A new generation of WAP members, upon discovering the joint committee's "reckless game of gentleman's agreements and stock pools"[36] with UP, dissolved the joint committee and the regional APs and formed a singular Associated Press in Illinois in 1892 under the leadership of General Manager Melville Stone. Members of the former New York AP joined what remained of the first United Press, but that organization eventually folded in 1896. Of that tumultuous period in AP's history, historian Richard Schwarzlose wrote:

> The ensuing battle and victory over UP eliminated after a quarter of a century or more all vestiges of regional auxiliaries and brought the AP under a single national board and management. Paradoxically, this national unity was accompanied by a stronger emphasis on local publisher rights and protections than had existed under the joint executive committee.[37]

Such a new emphasis on national unity and control of AP news from one headquarters remained at the forefront of AP's agenda well into the beginning of the twentieth century. The AP began its new era of leadership determined to let neither internal corruption nor competition stand in its path. Stone and the new AP board "gave no ground, dispatching attorneys into courtrooms in many regions of the country wherever members and non-members challenged AP's bylaw authority to admit or reject membership application to restrict members' affiliations with other newsbrokerages."[38] For Stone, controlling the use of AP news was simply a matter of AP's right to protect its property, and AP's bylaws and member contracts were the primary means to assert that right.[39]

Between 1888 and 1914, AP's bylaws were challenged in more than a dozen court cases around the country.[40] The key claim was that AP restrained trade by restricting the resale of member-generated news and prohibiting affiliations with "antagonistic" news organizations. Plaintiff news organizations argued that the bylaws violated various state laws against trusts as well as the Sherman Antitrust Act, which Congress passed in 1890 to prevent trusts from creating restraints on trade or commerce and reducing competition.[41] AP won nearly all of the cases. In cases involving non-members who sought AP membership, the courts found that as a private business, AP wasn't obligated to provide service.[42] In cases involving AP members who wished to do business with agencies AP declared "antagonistic" or who themselves were declared "antagonistic" by AP, the courts rejected arguments that such provisions violated antitrust laws. In these cases, the AP argued that news could not be regulated as trade under antitrust laws because news was not property — it was unprotected by copyright law, and trade laws could regulate only property. The courts agreed.[43] Courts refused to interfere with private AP contracts,[44] but they also refused to grant AP additional remedies, such as an injunction, if a member contract provided for remedies such as fines and suspension.[45]

The major exception to these cases was *Inter-Ocean Publishing Co. v. AP*.[46] In *Inter-Ocean*, an AP member newspaper in Illinois sought to do business with the *New York Sun*,[47] which the AP had declared antagonistic. The *Inter-Ocean* claimed that AP's bylaws were an unlawful restraint of trade. In an unprecedented decision, the Illinois Supreme Court reversed a lower court decision and ruled that trade laws could regulate AP's business. The court wrote that because AP's business revolved around the purchase and sale of telegraph and telephone lines and its news was "of vast importance to the public," it was a public utility with a public interest and could therefore be regulated.[48] The court wrote that the AP bylaw on antagonistic news organizations "tends to restrict competition because it prevents its members from purchasing news from any other source than from itself," creating a monopoly.[49]

As a result of *Inter-Ocean*, the AP moved its headquarters in 1900 to business-friendly New York, where a new corporation was formed and the AP became a not-for-profit cooperative. The AP reworded its prohibition against doing business with "antagonistic" agencies, instead leaving it up to the board of directors to decide whether the use of competitor services by members was "seriously prejudicial to the interest and welfare" of the AP and would require the member to stop its association with that service.[50]

Under the leadership of Melville Stone in New York, the AP continued to rely on its bylaws and membership contracts to secure and protect AP news. With these provisions under continuous scrutiny and criticism, however, the AP looked for additional means of protecting its news. While the AP had previously argued that news was not property and not subject to antitrust regulation, the AP began to pursue a new and less defensive position under Stone. Stone proposed that AP news *was* property in which the AP had invested time and labor and which it had a right to protect from piracy. The law, Stone argued, was obligated to protect AP's business from pirates.

This move from relying exclusively on contracts and bylaws to seeking a legal property right in news represented a critical turning point in the development of the hot news doctrine, and Stone is largely to credit. As a newspaper publisher in Illinois, Stone thought the old custom of taking news from other published sources was "all wrong," and as a former law student, Stone actively reread the law and theory of property to find support for his view. His research convinced him that news deserved property protection:

> [I] dreamed a dream. There was a defect in the law which should, and perhaps might, be remedied. There were equities involved, and I had learned in the days when I studied the law that there was no wrong which the arm of the chancellor was not long enough to reach. I knew of the "tasteless" lawyers and their point of view. Precedent, as found in the books, with them was all-controlling. But, mayhap, there were others who could see beyond the books into the final authority of justice, and it was worth while to find out.[51]

Stone continued to lobby Congress for increased protections under statute, but failed to win support.[52] Stone was not surprised. "Relief must be sought at the arm of the Chancellor," he wrote.[53] Stone found such relief in the form of a friendship with Judge Peter S. Grosscup of the U.S. Court of Appeals for the Seventh Circuit, who shared the same residence at a Chicago hotel. Stone made his case to Grosscup, arguing that "to keep pace with the progress of the world there must be a revised definition of the word 'property' so that it should cease to cover simply 'movables' and 'immovables,' and should include everything having an exchangeable value."[54] Stone also argued that once news was published, the publisher did not abandon his right to the substance of the news. Stone wrote:

> One was justly entitled to buy the newspaper, to read it, to enjoy or regulate his conduct by the information thus obtained, but it was manifestly unfair that he should be permitted to use the telegrams in competition with one who had paid his money and exercised his ingenuity to obtain them. The publication in this case was a limited one, and the legal doctrine of animus domini — intent of the owner — should apply.[55]

Grosscup was evidently persuaded. In 1902, he ruled in *National Telegraph News Co. v. Western Union Telegraph Co.*[56] that although wire news was unprotected by copyright, it was entitled to protection under principles of equity.[57] *National Telegraph* involved the redistribution of Western Union sports news and financial information by the National Telegraph Company. National Telegraph argued the information was in the public domain. While agreeing with the National Telegraph News Company that such material was not copyrightable, Grosscup reasoned that its immediacy was "a method of making an enterprise succeed," which an equity court should protect, and that appropriation might result in "injury to, or total destruction of, the service."[58] Creating precedent, Grosscup wrote:

> Is the enterprise of the great news agencies, or the independent enterprise of the great newspapers, or of the great telegraph and cable lines, to be denied appeal to the courts against the inroads of the parasite for no other reason than that the law, fashioned hitherto to fit the relations of the public and this dissimilar class of servants? Are we to fail in our plain duty for mere lack of precedent? We choose rather to make precedent — one from which is eliminated as immaterial the law grown up around authorship — and we see no better way

to start this precedent than by affirming the order appealed from.[59]

In a tribute to Stone and his leadership of the AP, Grosscup wrote that Stone's views on news as property played a significant role in his decision:

> The [National Telegraph] case was assigned to me to prepare the opinion, in the course of which the service of The Associated Press came into my mind as a related subject-matter. Meeting Mr. Stone on the train, I started inquiries respecting his company which resulted in a revelation of the nature and extent of its work, of much of which I had been previously uninformed. I recall his interest, his earnestness, that revealed not only perception by the intellect, but the driving power of feeling. And when the [National Telegraph] case was decided on principles that have since upheld the right of the Associated Press to protection for its service, I recall his satisfaction and his expression of grim determination to some time bring its principles to the protection of news enterprise.[60]

While the circumstances of *National Telegraph* were different than those that would arise in *INS*, the Supreme Court would later cite *National Telegraph* in *INS* as support for the use of equity in its decision. The *INS* Court said *National Telegraph* showed that despite the lack of copyright protection, the news was "a legitimate business, meeting a distinctive commercial want and adding to the facilities of the business world, and partaking of the nature of property in a sense that entitled it to the protection of a court of equity against piracy."[61]

Thus, Stone's early crusade to create a property right in news would bear some fruit in *INS*. In another tribute to Stone, Frederic Jennings, who argued *INS* for the AP, wrote that Stone was largely responsible for the new protections:

> [A]ll honest news agencies and newspapers are largely indebted to him for the establishment of this principle, as applicable to news, so vital to the protection of their rights. It may well be doubted whether this decision would thus have

been obtained had it not been for his clear and positive views upon the subject and his pertinacity in maintaining them.[62]

When AP executive Kent Cooper first obtained evidence of INS's piracy of AP news in 1916, Stone presented his views on a property right in news to the AP board and "rather than out of courtesy to me than because of any faith in my endeavour, they authorized me to go ahead [in the case against INS] and voted to pay any expense involved."[63] With the Supreme Court's later ruling in favor of AP and its declaration of a limited property right in news, Stone wrote, "[T]hirty-six years after I had settled the equities in my own mind was the law finally revolutionalized."[64]

Thus, the history of the AP and newsgathering prior to *INS* contributed to the development of the hot news doctrine in several important ways. First, while the borrowing of news was an accepted or tolerated practice for much of the nineteenth century, the growth of the telegraph and the end of the Civil War ended notions of sharing and replaced them with concepts of news as a commodity that needed protection. Once the AP was established, the news agency wars of 1866 and 1882 and the development of trust agreements with the UP in the 1880s prompted AP to be extremely vigilant in its contracts with members and to adopt restrictive bylaws that prohibited members from dealing with competitors who might unfairly use AP news. Toward the end of the nineteenth century, AP actively pursued actions against members who violated those contracts or bylaws, and was, in most cases, successful in upholding those restrictions. But persistent criticisms that AP bylaws violated antitrust law encouraged the AP to pursue an additional and less defensive strategy to protect its report. Under the guidance of General Manager Melville Stone, the AP campaigned for a property right in news under the law, and in *INS*, achieved its goal.

THE RISE OF INS AND COVERAGE OF WORLD WAR I

The early history of the International News Service (INS) was much less storied than AP's, though no less important to the development of the hot news doctrine. The outcome of *INS* is in large part due to the politics and bravado of the news agency's controversial and colorful owner, publisher William Randolph Hearst, and coverage of World War I.

The foundation for Hearst's International News Service was laid in 1900 when Hearst leased wires to connect his newspapers in San Francisco, New York, Chicago, and Boston. By 1908, Hearst comics appeared in more than 80 newspapers in 50 cities, and Hearst began to develop an interest in distributing newsreel footage.[65] To facilitate the movement of Hearst's services among his own papers and other subscribers, he launched his own wire service, INS, in the spring of 1909.[66] By 1946, INS boasted well over 1,000 subscribers.[67]

From the beginning of World War I, Hearst supported U.S. objectives to stay out of the conflict. When in 1915 the Germans attacked the *Lusitania*, precipitating American involvement in the war, Hearst papers condemned the attack but also criticized the British and President Woodrow Wilson. In particular, his editorials attacked British censors who filtered news from the war. Hearst argued that the war was simply a "struggle for the mastery of the world's markets" between Great Britain and Germany and that "England and Japan were more menacing to [U.S.] neutrality than Germany."[68] He threw his support behind Jeremiah A. O'Leary's American Truth Society, a group of Irish and German Americans critical of U.S. support of Great Britain against Germany, and he publicized an exchange of nasty telegrams between O'Leary and President Wilson.[69] While Hearst was received favorably among German Americans and others who were critical of the British, the majority of Americans and their Allies were outraged, leaving Hearst "increasingly isolated." [70]

On Oct. 11, 1916, Great Britain denied INS use of the British mail and cable system unless Hearst promised that the news service's dispatches would be printed as British censors dictated. Scholars generally suggest that the British were angry at Hearst's pro-German views;[71] Hearst said the move was censorship. An affidavit in the *INS* case by Fred Wilson, INS general manager, pointed to three specific news reports that angered the British. The first was a news story printed by an INS subscriber with the erroneous headline "London in Flames." The story INS sent to the subscriber stated that fires had broken out in many parts of London after a zeppelin raid but not that the city was in flames, according to Wilson.[72]

The second story regarded the publication of a story in an INS subscriber newspaper regarding the Jutland Naval Battle.[73] Defending INS, Wilson said the subscriber combined INS reports with other sources that were erroneous and credited the entire report to INS. Finally, Wilson said the British government was angered that INS claimed the British had censored several news stories, including the sinking of the super battleship Audacious, the deposing of the Khedive (or viceroy) of Egypt, and the declaration that Great Britain would annex Egypt. According to Wilson:

> I verily believe that the British Government, either through misinformation or otherwise, has acted unfairly and unjustly in denying to the defendant the use of the cables from London. This stoppage of the use of the cables for the transmission of news has inconvenienced the defendant, and has compelled it on certain matters to use certain news after it had already been printed in other papers, which practice, however, is customary among all news service and among all newspapers. . . . [74]

Historian John K. Winkler wrote that Hearst was furious with the British order to prohibit INS's use of the mail and cable system:

> Hearst flushed and trembled with anger. He handed the message to his companion, who in years of association had never witnessed the faintest flutter in his chief's uncanny control.
>
> "What are you going to do?" asked the executive.
>
> "Do?" exploded Hearst. "I am going to tell them to go to hell."[75]

Publicly, Hearst insisted that INS's exclusion from Great Britain was a function of INS's "independent and wholly truthful attitude" toward the war, and he criticized British censors:

> I will not supplicate England for news or for print paper or for permission to issue. I will not permit my papers to be edited in the smallest degree by a foreign power. I would shut down

every publication I have first and I do not intend to shut them down. In fact, the more foreign powers endeavor to interfere in America's domestic matters, and the more these foreign powers try to control our American institutions, particularly our free press, the more necessary, it seems to me, that American papers for the American people shall continue to be published.[76]

Following Great Britain's lead, France, Canada, Portugal, and Japan also denied INS access to communication facilities.

Without access to war news, Hearst relied more heavily on his correspondents and connections in Germany and on resourceful INS editors to scrape together what they could from other sources, including AP reports printed in AP member newspapers and "tips" obtained by INS editors from AP member newspaper telegraph operators. Hearst's well-known penchant for sensationalism meant he "never much cared how his reporters got their stories. What counted was the final product."[77] That he didn't care whether his reports came from the Germans or from the AP would land Hearst in double trouble with the law: During the late fall and early winter of 1918, accusations of sedition would haunt Hearst in Congress, and accusations of piracy would land INS in the U.S. Supreme Court.

Hearst's connections to Germany became of increasing interest to rival legislators and his news competitors as it became clearer that the United States might have to intervene in World War I. During 1916 and 1917, Hearst stepped up his calls for peace in his newspapers, but he eventually toned down his rhetoric as the Germans began attacking U.S. ships.[78] As the tide turned against neutrality and toward United States involvement,[79] Hearst and his editors attempted to protect themselves by running patriotic mastheads and tributes in his papers, but their actions were too little, too late.[80] Officials in the War Department and Bureau of Investigation stepped up surveillance of Hearst, looking for any connections to the German government.[81] Several were found:

> Karl Fuehr, with whom (Hearst) had negotiated for German newsreel footage, was not the owner of an independent film company, but a German government employee. Bolo Pacha,

the French newspaper publisher whom Hearst entertained at a special dinner at Sherry's in March of 1916 and invited to his apartment to discuss newsprint contracts, was a German agent sent to New York to collect funds to establish a pro-German newspaper in Paris. William Bayard Hale, his chief International News Service correspondent in Germany, had been paid by the German government since the war began.[82]

While investigators were able to establish that Hearst conducted business with these men, they were not able to show Hearst knew of these men's activities or uncover proof of treason or disloyalty.[83] Nonetheless, suspicions against Hearst grew. After the war ended in November 1918, a subcommittee of the Senate Judiciary Committee held hearings on "foreign propaganda, espionage, and intrigue in the United States during the World War," accusing Hearst of ties to German spies.[84] His papers were boycotted, and he was burned in effigy in locations around the country. His competitors jumped on the bandwagon, with some, like the *New York Tribune*, keeping totals on how many pro-German, anti-war articles Hearst published.[85] Hearst actively challenged his critics and the investigation. Between Dec. 6, 1918, and Dec. 22, 1918, Hearst's *San Francisco Examiner* published seventeen articles and four editorials on the committee's investigation.[86] Many of these articles vigorously defended Hearst and his news organizations and accused congressional investigators of political deceit. Arguing that the majority of Americans were opposed to involvement in the war prior to 1917, Hearst said, "The course of my newspapers has been fair to Germany not because I am pro-German any more than I am pro-ally. I am merely patriotically interested in the welfare of my own country and altruistically interested in the progress of the world."[87]

Hearst's vigorous efforts to fend off public accusations of disloyalty and ties to the Germans during 1918 may have kept him from waging a more public battle against the AP's lawsuit and ultimately may have made it difficult for the Supreme Court to rule in INS's favor in the face of such anti-Hearst publicity. By the time the Court ruled in *INS* on Dec. 23, 1918, Hearst was at the height of battling the Senate investigation and appeared uncharacteristically quiet over the decision against INS. The *Examiner* carried just one article reporting on the decision, and no editorials from Hearst appear to have been written.[88] However, a day before the Supreme Court's decision was handed down, the *San Francisco Examiner*, seemingly aware of the unlikelihood of a decision favoring INS, announced the organization of a special foreign news service "surpassing in extent and in quality anything ever attempted by an American publication":

> [N]o other group of foreign correspondents for any publication, association or syndicate will equal that which "The San Francisco Examiner" will have posted at every strategic point in Europe. . . . It will not be the object of "The San Francisco Examiner" Foreign News Service to cover routine news. It will not attempt to duplicate the work of the Associated Press. But the staff will be held strictly responsible for at least one "bell ringer" each week — one exclusive story of such merit, both in material and in treatment, as unquestionably to deserve a leading place in any national magazine. . . . Even though each member of the staff were to produce only one such story each month, the result will be more than one hundred smashing headliner stories during 1919.[89]

Thus, during the late fall and early winter of 1918, Hearst and his businesses were hit hard from all sides: A Congress eager to prosecute spies and those disloyal to the government in the wake of World War I; a U.S. Supreme Court that was likely unwilling to support Hearst's INS in the wake of such negative press and alleged ties to the Germans; and a group of news competitors ready to see Hearst's enterprises suffer.

While AP's suit against INS may have been the immediate result of the British ban on the use of its mail and cables and of Hearst's policies, the origins of AP's animosity toward Hearst was already years in the making when it filed suit in 1916. Hearst's troubles with the AP dated back to before 1900, when Joseph Pulitzer, publisher of the New York *World* and a prominent AP member, looked to deny Hearst membership in the AP. In 1897, when the United Press folded, Hearst sought an AP membership for his *New York Morning Journal*, but was denied entry by Pulitzer.

Hearst, who routinely outspent Pulitzer and often stole his editors,[90] attempted to make a deal with his fiercest competitor: He would raise the price of the *Journal* if Pulitzer would similarly raise the price of the *World* and drop his opposition to the *Journal's* application for AP membership.[91] Pulitzer negotiated with Hearst, but nothing came of the talks. Hearst, who had previously admired Pulitzer and wished to emulate him, now characterized Pulitzer as the enemy. After being denied entry into the AP, Hearst called Pulitzer

> ...a journalist who makes his money by pandering to the worst tastes of the prurient and horror-loving, by dealing in bogus news, such as forged cablegrams from eminent personages, and by affecting a devotion to the interests of the people while never really hurting those of its enemies, and sedulously looking out for his own.[92]

Cleverly, Hearst purchased the *New York Morning Advertiser*, an AP paper, and secured an AP membership by merging that paper with the *Morning Journal*.[93] When Hearst later published an evening edition of the *Journal*, Pulitzer accused him of using AP news from his *Morning Journal* in the evening edition. Pulitzer dragged one of Hearst's editors into court over the matter, and forced an outraged Hearst to testify.[94] The AP also reprimanded Hearst for using AP news from his *San Francisco Examiner* in an edition titled *The Oakland Examiner*.[95]

Hearst felt unappreciated by the AP and its board. Instead, there "was deep antipathy toward him among some AP board members whose newspapers were competitive with his."[96] Years after the decision in *INS*, Hearst insisted that if the board had simply asked INS to stop using AP news, it would have done so, avoiding the lawsuit.

> But Mr. Stone had obsessed himself with the conception that he must establish legally the principle that there is a property right in news. He wanted to use the courts to legislate by means of a decision that would construe news as property. Then, if one of my nonmember papers or my news service used Associated Press news, the offender could be sent to

prison for theft of Associated Press property. Sometimes I have thought that they would like to put me there personally![97]

Thus, Hearst's relationship with the AP had been adversarial for more than twenty years by the time the Court heard *INS*. Furthermore, Hearst's anti-war, pro-German views during World War I contributed to Great Britain's decision to deny INS access to communication facilities for news coverage, forcing his editors to look to other sources, namely AP, for news and information, which his editorial policies condoned, but which led to the AP lawsuit. His pro-German, anti-war views also drew condemnation from the American public and criticism from Congress, which investigated his ties to Germany at the same time the Supreme Court decided *INS*. The public outcry against Hearst may have kept the Court from a decision more favorable to INS, and Hearst's fight to defend himself may have kept him from waging a more public battle against the AP.

THE PROGRESSIVE ERA

The AP's struggles and the Hearst controversies were very much a reflection of the times. The Progressive Era, which historians say began in 1890 and lasted until 1920, was a period of intense industrialization, immigration, and urbanization in the United States. New industries in steel, oil, transportation, and communications emerged, contributing to a twelve-fold increase in the gross national product by 1900 and more than tripling the value of U.S. exports.[98] Factories produced "steel girders for skyscrapers and bridges, metal tubing for bicycles, glass for large windows, copper wire for new electrical sources of light and power."[99] New technologies enabled faster and more comfortable travel and quicker communication, and the cheap mass production of consumer goods created a new consumer culture with new demands.[100]

But the enormous changes came at great social cost — including a depression in the 1890s, a world war, abusive working conditions, crime, and poverty. The progressive movement was an effort to address those costs and improve life for Americans. Government leaders, special interest groups, and other public figures who joined the progressive movement sought to "master the sweeping forces of change" by forcing government to intervene in the regulation of private business, which was responsible for so much of the change and which, during that time, grew from small, proprietary businesses to large corporations.[101] The watchword of the time was reform, and the primary issue was the relationship between public and private power, or more specifically, the role of the government in regulating the economy.[102] To institute change, legislatures passed new laws, formed new regulatory commissions, and created a modern government bureaucracy. The courts were called on to enforce and interpret the new reforms.

While the Progressive Era was initially thought of as a time when business was reined in and first regulated by government, historians have more recently argued that big business was closely tied to government in the development of reforms, many of which were more supportive of business interests than had been previously acknowledged.[103] The Supreme Court's decision in *INS* supports this latter view of the Progressive Era. The decision reflects three important contributions of Progressive Era reform in business: (1) the Supreme Court's recognition of businesses as "individuals" with due process rights to protect intangible property; (2) the Court's role in the interpretation of antitrust legislation designed to regulate business competition; and (3) the growth of unfair competition law. All three changes in the law would have important effects on the Court's decision in *INS*.

Corporate Due Process

The Fourteenth Amendment to the U.S. Constitution, adopted in 1868, prohibited states from depriving "any person of life, liberty, or property" without due process of law[104] and forced the Court to address the constitutionality of state property regulations. While the Amendment was designed to protect former slaves from discrimination, the Court would interpret it to "provide new protection for the right of property in an industrialized society," including property rights claimed by private individuals and corporations.[105] Thus, corporations were permitted to protect their property under the same due process procedures as individuals. The Court also expanded the notion of property to include intangible as well as tangible property. John R. Commons wrote of that time:

The definition of property is changed from physical things to the exchange-value of anything, and the federal courts now take jurisdiction. . . . [The] cases . . . have turned on a double meaning of property, and the transition is from one of the meanings to both of the meanings. . . . One is Property, the other is Business. The one is property in the sense of Things owned, the other is property in the sense of exchange-value of things. One is physical objects, the other is marketable assets.[106]

Between 1864 and 1917, the Court struggled to balance protection of the individual or corporation, his property, and his "lawful economic pursuits"[107] with the progressive goals of government to protect the public interest.[108] Increasingly, though, the Court sought to ensure that the individual's right to "pursue his happiness" was unrestrained and permitted government interference only in cases that were "affected with a public interest."[109] The Court interpreted this right as belonging to private corporations as well as individuals.

Thus, despite the Progressive Era's emphasis on regulating business for the benefit of the public, the Court created and retained a strong emphasis on protecting corporate property rights, both tangible and intangible. The Court's commitment to property rights for corporations played a significant role in *INS*.[110] By creating a limited property right in the facts of news for a short period after publication, the Court in *INS* reinforced its belief that corporations had a right to protect intangible property or "marketable assets," such as news, from theft. The Court's decision in *INS* was not possible without the recognition during this era that corporations possessed the due process rights of individuals.

The Effects of Antitrust Law

Antitrust legislation, specifically the Sherman Antitrust Act of 1890, addressed the issue of the federal government's regulation of trusts or monopolies. A trust was "a combination of companies in which the stock was controlled by a central board of trustees that could control prices and limit competition."[111] The Sherman Antitrust Act was designed to prevent trusts from creating restraints on trade or commerce and reducing competition.[112] While the Sherman Act helped to clamp down on trusts, some historians have argued that the restrictions against trusts drove businesses to consolidate and merge, creating larger corporations.[113] The AP is an example of this trend: After the Western Associated Press uncovered secret stock pool arrangements between the AP and UP to limit competition, it consolidated the regional AP's into one corporation based in New York and ultimately created a stronger and more successful business.

The Sherman Act created direct conflict between the Supreme Court's commitment to protecting corporate property rights and the new law, which articulated in statute the common law of restraint of trade.[114] Early interpretation of the Sherman Act by the Court, from 1890 to about 1897, followed common law understandings of competition and unfair restraints on trade. Under common law, the Court allowed agreements between corporations to restrict competition but intervened when the effect of the agreement was "unreasonable"; that is, when it was detrimental to the public interest. That changed in 1897 with the *Trans Missouri* case,[115] when the Court ruled that both reasonable and unreasonable agreements restricted competition and were a violation of the Sherman Act. The Court retained that view for more than a decade, despite objections from Progressive leaders such as Theodore Roosevelt. The Court changed its view in the *Standard Oil* and *American Tobacco* cases of 1911,[116] in which the Court outlawed only "unreasonable" restraints of trade. The Court ruled that the old common law interpretation applied: Imposing its "rule of reason" test, the Court weighed the "anticompetitive consequences of a trust . . . against the business justifications upon which it is predicated . . . and a judgment with respect to its reasonableness is made."[117] In doing so, the Court reassured early twentieth century businesses that antitrust laws could be enforced without destroying successful businesses.

By the time the Supreme Court heard *INS* in 1918, the struggle surrounding antitrust legislation had been resolved in a manner favorable to established business and strong corporate property rights. In the case, INS tried to argue that the creation of a property right in news would create "a most intolerable monopoly" because of AP's dominance over the newspaper market. INS argued that if a limited property right was awarded to AP news, it was also awarded to all the local news produced by the AP membership. With AP's stringent rules and agreements for obtaining and sharing the AP service, INS argued that a hot news right gave AP control not only over its wire but also over the news produced by its local member newspapers. This, INS argued, was unreasonable. The Court, however, did not agree. It said because the right it granted was limited in duration, it was not an illegal monopoly: "[T]he view we adopt does not result in giving to [AP] the right to monopolize either the gathering or distribution of the news ... but only postpones participation by [INS] in the processes of distribution and reproduction of news that it has not gathered, and only to the extent necessary to prevent [INS] from reaping the fruits of [AP's] efforts and expenditure...."[118]

INS's argument appears to have failed for two reasons. First, by 1918, the Court's position on monopolies was that only unreasonable restraints of trade would be outlawed — and a limited hot news right for the world's premier news organization was not an unreasonable restraint. Furthermore, INS did not argue that *AP* was an illegal monopoly with bylaws that unreasonably restrained trade but that the *granting of a hot news right* would have made it an illegal monopoly. Its argument hinged on criticism of the Court's response and not on the effect of AP's bylaws.[119] This was clearly a weakness in INS's defense strategy.

The Rise of Unfair Competition Law

In addition to the growth in antitrust law, the Progressive Era also saw an increase in common law restrictions on unfair trade methods and practices. The roots of modern unfair competition law are found in the Progressive Era, and *INS* reflected this law's expansion. The Court's decision in *INS* rested on a completely new interpretation of the boundaries of unfair competition.

Scholars and courts have had difficulty defining the common law of unfair competition, and many have rejected attempts to specifically define its boundaries because of a belief that the doctrine's strength is its flexibility.[120] Unfair competition is a commercial tort that courts have described in such wide-ranging phrases as "contrary to good conscience,"[121] "the decent thing to do in trade,"[122] and the "rules of fair play."[123] The U.S. Court of the Appeals for the Fifth Circuit has written: "The law of unfair competition is the umbrella for all statutory and nonstatutory causes of action arising out of business conduct which is contrary to honest practice in industrial or commercial matters."[124] J. Thomas McCarthy wrote that unfair competition "has developed as a flexible legal instrument to control the excesses of a market system in the throes of constant adjustment as it adapts itself to economic, political, and social changes."[125]

While unfair competition was born in British common law,[126] it evolved in the United States out of the common law of trademark, which was developed in the late nineteenth century to protect corporate marks.[127] At that time, trademark law protected "technical trademarks," which were arbitrary symbols or words that identified company goods.[128] Trademark law did not protect marks that were not distinctive, such as descriptive, geographical, or personal name marks. However, such marks came to be protected by unfair competition law because courts said such marks often acquired "secondary meaning" deserving of protection.[129] Early unfair competition cases normally involved "passing off" or "palming off," in which one competitor tried to "pass off" the product of another seller by means of similar labeling, packaging, or advertising.[130]

Unfair competition and antitrust law are sometimes confused because both attempt to regulate business practice, but they "spring from distinctly different ethical and social judgments as to what situation ought to exist in the business world. The fact that both sets of laws historically arose during the late nineteenth century tends to obscure their real differences. But different they are; for while antitrust law prohibits 'not enough' competition, unfair competition law forbids 'too much' competition."[131] Antitrust law regulates businesses that restrict competition; unfair competition law forbids business behavior that involves theft or fraud in an effort to gain an unfair advantage over a competitor.

The *INS* Court ruled that INS unfairly competed with AP by taking AP's news. In ruling for AP, the Court expanded the boundaries of unfair competition when it declared that "*passing off*" was not the only requirement for an unfair competition claim. In *INS*, INS did not attempt to "*pass off*" or *misrepresent* AP's news as its own; it simply took the news and redistributed it. This, the Court said, was *misappropriation*, another type of unfair competition:

Stripped of all disguises, the process amounts to an unauthorized interference with the normal operation of [AP's] legitimate business precisely at the point where the profit is to be reaped, in order to divert a material portion of the profit from those who have earned it to those who have not; with special advantage to [INS] in the competition because of the fact that it is not burdened with any part of the expense of gathering the news. The transaction speaks for itself, and *a court of equity ought not to hesitate long in characterizing it as unfair competition in business*. (Emphasis added.)[132]

Reaction to the Court's ruling by lower courts was mixed, with some accepting the new principle, but others less certain how it was to be applied. Much of that uncertainty remains today and is addressed in the case analysis in Chapter Four.

Thus, the Progressive Era's emphasis on business reform resulted in new statutory and common law that affected the Court's decision in *INS*. The Supreme Court's recognition of businesses as "individuals" with due process rights made it protective of corporate property, both tangible and intangible. The *INS* Court's development of a limited property right in news stems directly from this recognition. The growth of antitrust legislation and the Court's interpretation of it were in debate for many years leading up to *INS*, but that debate was settled by the time *INS* was heard by the Court. INS's allegations of AP's monopolistic practices fell short of the "unreasonable" standard the Court required. Finally, the growth of unfair competition law offered businesses such as AP a new weapon to protect company assets. The *INS* Court created a new unfair competition tort of misappropriation, forbidding businesses to reap where they had not sown.

EARLY COPYRIGHT LAW

At first glance, copyright law played a small part in *INS*. While the Supreme Court in the case acknowledged that news articles were eligible for copyright,[133] the practical difficulty in registering such works at the time was significant, and most news remained unregistered and therefore unprotected by copyright law. This was true in *INS* and was one of the main reasons AP pursued INS under unfair competition law and not copyright.

But on closer examination, copyright law is at the heart of *INS* and the debate over how far protections for news should extend. Because copyright law was significantly different in 1918 than it is today, the case, as precedent, is sometimes difficult to reconcile with modern copyright. This section addresses these historical differences in the law as important background for the Court's decision in *INS* and the current debate. It focuses on the history and development of statutory and common law copyright in the United States and its impact on *INS*.

History of Statutory Copyright and Protections for News

Copyright law in the United States was first enacted in 1790 after passage of the U.S. Constitution, which granted Congress the right to "promote the progress of science and the useful arts by securing for limited times" by giving "to Authors and Inventors the exclusive Right to their respective Writings and Discoveries."[134] This first version of U.S. copyright law was based on Great Britain's Statute of Anne, which had been designed to protect the public from publisher monopolies and government control of the book trade.[135] It granted authors of maps, charts, and books the exclusive right to print, reprint, publish, or vend their works for a period of up to twenty-eight years.[136]

News articles were not eligible for copyright protection under this first U.S. statute,[137] but at least one early U.S. copyright scholar commented that news articles had the same character as books, and in theory, should have been eligible for copyright if not for the "impracticable" task of registering daily news:

> [I]t may be said that the contents of a daily newspaper are too ephemeral and often too insignificant to be worthy of statutory protection. This is doubtless true of much that appears in a newspaper; but, on the other hand, among the contents of such publications are frequently found productions of great value and permanent literary merit. There is, then, nothing in the law of copyright, as made by the legislature or as expounded by the courts, to prevent valid copyright from vesting in a

magazine or a newspaper, as a whole, or in any of its contents that may be worthy of protection.[138]

The 1790 Copyright Act underwent several revisions during the nineteenth century, but none of those changes affected the copyright status of news articles. The next major change to copyright didn't occur until 1909, when Congress passed a new copyright act.[139] Under the new act, copyright protection was awarded to literary works and to artistic, musical, and dramatic works; the duration of copyright was also extended for up to 56 years.[140] Copyright in a work became effective when the work was published, included a notice of copyright, and was registered with the Copyright Office following publication.[141] And, for the first time, U.S. copyright law officially recognized a copyright in periodicals, such as newspapers, as well as their component parts.[142] Newspapers were required to pay $365 a year to register their copyright and to post a notice of copyright on their front page.[143] While the new law opened the door to protecting newspapers as compilations, it did not specifically grant copyright protection to news stories appearing on wire services, and such news organizations found it generally impractical to file for copyright protection on each dispatch. Thus, those stories remained uncopyrighted. Furthermore, the statute did not address the issue of whether the "matter" or "facts" of news could be protected.[144]

Thus, early copyright law in the United States was different from modern copyright law in two important ways. First, early copyright generally protected specific classes of works — such as maps and charts — from unauthorized copying.[145] While it also lists classes of works eligible for protection, modern copyright protects *all* "original works fixed in any tangible medium of expression" from unauthorized reproduction, distribution, and performance.[146] This means that "original" news stories today are automatically copyrighted from the moment they are "fixed." This was not the case when the Court heard *INS* in 1918.

Furthermore, eligibility for copyright protection in 1918 required several steps. A work had to be published, officially registered with the government, and printed with a copyright notice to receive protection.[147] Today, a work need only be "fixed" to receive copyright protection.[148] Again, this gives news stories immediate protection when they are first written or broadcast, a significant change from when AP and INS first sent their news by wire. The new elements of "orginality" and "fixation" in copyright give news stories greater protections today than they had in 1918. Had both elements been part of the statute in 1918, the *INS* case might have focused more directly on elements of copyright infringement rather than on unfair competition. (See Chapter Three for a complete discussion of the pirated dispatches.)

History of Common Law Copyright: The Issue of Publication

The 1909 Act required publication, registration, and notice for a work to receive copyright protection under the statute. Those works that were unpublished, published without registration and notice, or that were ineligible for copyright protection at that time came under the protection of common law copyright. Common law copyright in these works lasted up until the moment of publication, when it was thought that the author "abandoned" his work to the public, and then, provided the work was registered and contained a copyright notice, the copyright statute offered protection.[149] Thus, publication became an important criterion in deciding the kind of protection available to a work.

Common law copyright existed before copyright statutes were instituted by Great Britain, the United States, and other nations in the eighteenth century. Common law copyright generally awarded to the author a right to his work in perpetuity. In Great Britain, the earliest copyright statutes limited that right in an attempt to regulate the book trades by limiting copyright protection under the statute to 14 years. Once the statutes were instituted, however, British courts were forced to address whether the statute *created* an author's right or whether it *sanctioned* an author's existing right — his common law copyright or what some think of as his "moral right" — in his work once it was published.[150] After debate, both British and American courts during the eighteenth and nineteenth centuries held that copyright statutes *created* an author's right, and thus authors lost their common law rights once they published their works.[151] Thus, an author could not have a common law right in perpetuity when a statutory right was granted for "limited times." But this rule did not cover unpublished works or those works that failed to meet the requirements of the statute.

The dual existence of common law copyright and statutory copyright, particularly after the 1909 U.S. Copyright Act, raised two challenges for courts. The first challenge was protection for those works not specifically covered under the 1909 Copyright Act, such as wire service news. Because the new law specified certain classes of works for protection, it was often left to the courts to decide whether authors of those works *not* covered by the new law retained a common law right or some other protection. The second challenge was publication. Courts wrestled with defining the moment when a work was dedicated to the public. The intent of the author in publishing was often at issue. Richard Bowker, author of a key text on early U.S. copyright law, wrote:

> Publication depends upon sale or offer to the public, and it is a question whether the sale or offer of a copyrightable work, as the proceedings or publications of a society, to the members of that society only, constitutes publication, to be passed upon by the courts in view of the specific facts.[152]

Thus, while it was clear that unpublished works fell under common law copyright, courts were called on to decide what constituted publication.[153]

Both issues were crucial in *INS*. AP argued that its news was not protected by statutory or common law copyright but rather deserved protection under unfair competition law; INS agreed that AP's news was not protected by copyright but argued that the news possessed a literary quality and therefore fell under common law copyright. INS argued that when AP members posted AP news on bulletin boards or printed its news on the West Coast, the news was published and no longer entitled to protection under common law copyright. That meant the news was in the public domain and available to any and all to use. No similar distinction or argument could be raised in a similar case today: Because news is protected the moment it is fixed, there is no protection under common law and no issues surrounding the moment of publication and its dedication to the public. Despite these significant differences in copyright law, however, *INS* continues as precedent for the protection of news.

CASE LAW LEADING UP TO *INS*

Case law addressing whether the law protected the facts of news did not begin with *INS*, although *INS* represented the first time the U.S. Supreme Court ruled that news organizations had a limited right in the facts of news under unfair competition law. In their briefs to the Supreme Court, the AP and INS addressed the merits of nine federal and state court cases that bore most directly on the issue in *INS*.[154] The majority of these cases dealt with the property and publication of factual market quotations. These cases addressed two primary issues: First, whether the quotations were property owned by the markets that published them, and second, whether the quotations had been published and abandoned to use by the public. Market information providers generally received protection for market quotes if courts established that information providers had a property right in their quotes and that such quotes had not yet been published.

According to the *INS* briefs, the earliest case in the United States to address whether a news organization might possess a property right in its news and quotes was *Kiernan v. Manhattan Quotation*, an 1876 New York state case.[155] In *Kiernan*, the AP had an exclusive contract with the Gold and Stock Telegraph Company that gave the telegraph company use of all foreign financial news for 30 minutes after the AP received that news, which was sent in cipher. The Gold and Stock Telegraph Company, in turn, contracted with John Kiernan, who deciphered the news and who himself provided it to a group of his own clients. Kiernan sent that news back to the Gold and Stock Telegraph Company, which transmitted the news to his subscribers. The Manhattan Quotation Telegraph Company obtained copies of dispatches from Kiernan to his subscribers and used them for its own service, which led to the dispute.

The court addressed three questions in the case: (1) whether Kiernan had any property in the foreign news he obtained; (2) whether the Manhattan Quotation Telegraph Company took and transmitted that news; and (3) if Kiernan had a property right in the news, whether he abandoned that right when he transmitted that news to his customers.[156] The Manhattan Quotation Telegraph Company argued that Kiernan had no property right in the news because it was "public property and open to all the world."[157] The court ruled that while this news could have been taken from European publications, as was customary, once AP collected it at "great expense," the AP and those it contracted with possessed a property right:

> It would be an atrocious doctrine to hold that dispatches, the result of the diligence and expenditure of one man, could with impunity be pilfered and published by another. It is undoubtedly true that in respect to news, its publication cannot be interfered with where the party procures the intelligence by the diligence of its own agents; but if he seeks to profit by the superior diligence of his rivals, it is unjust that he should be allowed to do so until the right of property has been abandoned by publication. The mere fact that a certain class of information is open to all that seek it, is no answer to a claim of a right of property in such information made by a person who, at his own expense and by his own labor, has collected it.[158]

The court also ruled that the Manhattan Quotation Telegraph Company had clearly taken the news[159] and that the nature of Kiernan's arrangement with his customers did not constitute a publication or abandonment of that news.[160] Thus, *Kiernan* represented the earliest record of a court granting a news organization a property right in its news. However, because that news had not been published and was simply en route to its publisher, the case was not a clear precedent for *INS*.

Neither did subsequent cases serve as clear precedents for *INS*, although many of them, like *Kiernan*, revolved around the theft of financial news and stock market quotations.[161] Most of these cases involved the Chicago Board of Trade at the turn of the twentieth century, including one 1905 case, *Board of Trade v. Christie Grain & Stock Co.*,[162] that was appealed to the U.S. Supreme Court.

The Chicago Board of Trade grew out of a booming trade in grain in the Midwest in the mid-nineteenth century. By the early 1900s, the Board of Trade had emerged as the leading market for the trade of wheat, corn, and oats.[163] Its success, however, encouraged speculators, some of whom saw the market as a place to gamble. Many of these traders opened their own trading establishments, known as bucketshops, which gave the appearance of dealing in real delivery of grain, but in truth, were simply gambling houses. A bucketshop was "a place where wagers are made on the fluctuations of the market price of grains and other commodities."[164] The lifeblood of the bucketshops was the Board of Trade's market quotations, and the bucketshops resorted to all kinds of shady tactics to steal them. To stop the bucketshops, the Board of Trade first attempted to stop the flow of quotations. Later, the Board simply flooded the courts with lawsuits attempting to hinder bucketshop activities. Among the strongest arguments the Board brought to court was that market quotations were Board property.[165] This line of cases, although different from the facts and claims in *INS*, offered support to the concept of news as property.

The courts in these cases, including the U.S. Supreme Court, not only supported the notion that quotations were Board property but also that their transmission to subscribers did not constitute publication. In *Christie*, the Court upheld an injunction against C.C. Christie's Christie Grain & Stock Company, a broker known as the "king of the bucketshops," based in Kansas City.[166] In the case, Christie was accused of stealing the Board's quotations by tapping a wire to a legitimate Board client. Justice Holmes wrote that the transmission of information from information supplier to his client under contract did not mean such information was published:

> [T]he plaintiff's collection of quotations is entitled to the protection of the law. It stands like a trade secret. The plaintiff has the right to keep the work which it has done, or paid for doing, to itself. The fact that others might do similar work, if they might, does not authorize them to steal the plaintiff's. The plaintiff does not lose its rights by communicating the result to persons, even if many, in confidential relations to itself, under a contract not to make it public, and strangers to the trust will be restrained from getting at the knowledge by inducing a breach of trust, and using knowledge obtained by such a breach.[167]

Thus, the *Christie* case helped to establish an information provider's right to protect his information en route from supplier to client under contract.

National Telegraph News Co. v. Western Union Telegraph Co.[168] was the first and only case prior to *INS* to suggest that the taking of factual information gathered by another was a form of unfair competition. In the 1902 case, the National Telegraph News Company was accused of taking and redistributing sports and financial news sent to Western Union customers. The National Telegraph News Company argued that since wire news was unprotected by copyright, it was free to use. It also argued that such information, once distributed by Western Union, was published and available to the public. In his opinion, Judge Peter S. Grosscup – the same judge with whom AP General Manager Melville Stone pursued a friendship – agreed that such wire news was uncopyrightable.[169] But Grosscup held that the news was entitled to protection under unfair competition and introduced several key concepts later adopted by the Supreme Court in *INS* — including the concepts of misappropriation or "reaping where one has not sown," which Grosscup called the "parasite"; the notion that the harm to plaintiff might be so great as to destroy his business investment; and the idea that the value of the information is its immediacy.[170] Grosscup wrote:

> [I]f appellants may lawfully appropriate the product thus expansively put upon the appellee's tape, and distribute the same instantaneously to their own patrons, as their own product, thus escaping any expense of collection, but one result could follow – the gathering and distributing of news, as a business enterprise, would cease altogether. . . . The parasite that killed, would itself be killed, and the public would be left without any service at any price.[171]

Thus, the stock ticker cases established precedent for a property right in information and greater latitude in defining the moment of publication.[172] But the cases were factually different from *INS* in that information was taken en route to subscribers; in *INS*, INS took news from published editions of West Coast AP member newspapers and used that information for its East Coast wires. *National Telegraph* would have the most influence on the *INS* Court. That case introduced several important concepts the Court would adopt: that the plaintiff, who gathered the news at great expense, was entitled to relief if the defendant appropriated the commercial value of his time sensitive information and seriously harmed the plaintiff's business.

SUMMARY OF FINDINGS AND CONCLUSION

This chapter's study of the history leading to *INS v. AP* reveals several historical factors that contributed to the Supreme Court's decision to introduce the hot news doctrine. The unique convergence of these factors and circumstances led to the creation of the hot news doctrine and should be considered in any future discussion on the viability of the doctrine today.

First, the use of news from other publications was not labeled "piracy" until news became a commodity after the Civil War. What once was custom became theft, and news organizations with the most to lose, like AP, went after offenders, despite the persistent custom. The development of the hot news doctrine was the direct result of a successfully organized campaign by AP General Manager Melville Stone to establish a property right in news and to help prevent the theft of AP news which Stone thought threatened AP's stability. This included a friendship with an influential judge whose decision regarding a property right in information was eventually cited by the U.S. Supreme Court in *INS v. AP*.

Furthermore, INS Chief William Randolph Hearst was unable to match Stone's vigilance on the issue and convince the courts that published news was in the public domain, whatever the investment AP made to gather it. Hearst and INS were kicked out of Europe during World War I, leaving INS without a source for war news and prompting it to pirate AP's news. Both the Europeans and Congress thought that Hearst and his news ranks were pro-German. But Hearst claimed he was being censored for speaking the truth. Regardless, perceptions that Hearst was pro-German likely made it difficult for him to wage a campaign against AP and for the Supreme Court to find in his favor.

The Progressive Era's pro-business influence on changes in the law gave AP the chance to argue that its business was due special, new protection. The *INS* Court's development of a limited property right in news stems directly from the Supreme Court's recognition that businesses have due process rights and that unfair competition law protected business from a new tort of "misappropriation." By the time the Court heard *INS* in 1918, it had established its "rule of reason" in antitrust law, setting a higher hurdle for INS to jump in claiming that a hot news right would make AP "a most intolerable monopoly." In addition, news stories were unprotected by copyright law, keeping the subject of copyright at a distance in the case.

Finally, the stock ticker cases leading up to *INS* established precedent for a property right in news and greater latitude in defining the moment of publication, which offered information providers greater protection. With Stone's influence on Judge Grosscup, who decided *National Telegraph*, the *INS* court was persuaded that news, gathered at great expense, was entitled to protection under unfair competition law or else the information provider's business might crumble.

These historical factors suggest that the doctrine was far from being an independently constructed legal creation. But neither was it some kind of mistake in the Court's development of unfair competition law. The AP's ongoing campaign to establish a property right in news influenced the doctrine's formation, as did Hearst's inability to wage a successful campaign against it. The succession of "Ticker cases" lent credence to the idea of a property right in news and the Progressive Era and the limits of early 20th century copyright law saw a judicial movement toward greater protections for businesses who sought to protect their property. In hindsight, the convergence of these factors made the creation of additional protections for news inevitable, and the Court's conclusion, reasonable.

CHAPTER 3
INS v. AP

The legal record in *INS v. AP* is a detailed accounting of the highly competitive news agency business in the early part of the twentieth century. More than 50 individuals were interviewed under oath for the original district court case, mostly telegraphers for both wire services and for the newspapers who received and decoded the agency reports. The telegraphers who worked for both agencies often switched sides during the course of their careers, but were committed to "getting the story" no matter which agency they represented. At newspapers with both AP and INS, telegraphers were able to monitor both services and alert either service on breaking news, if they chose. Furthermore, the wire services often placed their own local operations at the member paper or paid a member telegrapher to act as an agent. This made it easier for wire services to have access to competitor news.

This part of the record offers specific examples of INS's theft of AP news by these telegraphers but also offers evidence that AP used INS reports. It demonstrates the loyalties of the telegraphers (mostly to each other and not necessarily to their employers) and the lengths to which they competed to get ahead. This chapter takes a closer look at this testimony, the court briefs and the case decisions to arrive at a greater understanding of the roots of the conflict and the development of the hot news doctrine.

THE CLAIMS AND THE EVIDENCE

The claims made by AP in the original case were claims that had been heard before in the ongoing news agency wars of the late nineteenth and early twentieth centuries. This time, however, the claims were presented to a district court for resolution, and AP came armed with mounds of evidence. First, the AP accused INS of obtaining AP news from a telegrapher at an AP member newspaper in Cleveland. Second, the AP said INS telegraphers copied AP news from AP receiving equipment at the *New York American* in New York City. At the *American*, an AP telegraph repairman saw an INS editor repeatedly walk into the paper's editorial room and read and make notes on news that had come in over the AP wire.[1] Two other AP repairmen corroborated that report.[2]

Finally, the AP accused INS of routinely taking early bulletins and editions of AP news printed in AP member newspapers and sending them to INS's clients. In this last instance, AP General Manager Melville Stone testified:

> By reason of the rapidity of telegraphic transmission, it frequently happens that these papers are able to publish the news of The Associated Press before it is possible for The Associated Press to deliver it to its own members. Telegraphic communication frequently is interrupted by storms or other causes. In such cases it is possible for the International News Service to send Associated Press despatches (sic), taken from the editions of Eastern papers, on their wires, if such wires are not interrupted, and those of The Associated Press are, and not infrequently these despatches are printed in the papers of their clients before it is possible for The Associated Press papers to use them.[3]

Stone detailed ten stories to demonstrate these three claims. Most of the examples showed strong evidence of piracy by INS. Many showed that INS not only took "hot news" from AP, but also took the expression of that news. The following excerpt was an example of the theft of hot news *and* the expression of that news. It also demonstrated how INS papers might publish before other AP members (particularly those on the West Coast) had received and printed such news.

> The Associated Press sent to its members the following report:
> "London, December 6—12:05 p.m.
> "Following is the official report of today from the Franco-Belgian front: 'Aside from intermittent enemy shelling in the Ancre area, there was nothing to report last night.'"
> On the same day, the said New York Evening Journal (a Hearst paper) published the following despatch (sic), which was evidently copied exactly from The Associated Press bulletin to its members:
> "London, December 6.
> "Aside from intermittent shelling in the Ancre sector of the Somme Front, there is nothing to report, British War Office announced today."[4]

In other damaging examples, INS copied AP errors directly. For example:

> On December 8, The Associated Press sent to its members the following despatch (sic):
> "Paris, December 8—1:45 p.m.
> "President Poincare has awarded a gold medal to Mrs. Harry Duryea of New York for her service during the last two years as head of the American Aid Committee for War Victims."

> The Paris Office of The Associated Press confused the names of [two women in the story]. The name should have been Mrs. Nina Duryea. The said Washington Herald (an INS paper) on the morning of December 9 published the following despatch:

> "Paris, December 8.
> "Mrs. Harry Duryea of New York was awarded a gold medal by President Poincare for her services in war relief work. Mrs. Duryea has been president of the American Aid Committee for two years. She returns to America tomorrow."[5]

Stone's testimony provided strong evidence of piracy. Other testimony was more specific about who took AP news, how it was done, and how AP came to know about it.

INS Cleveland bureau manager Fred Agnew was the key witness in the case for AP and provided the most damaging evidence against his former employer. In October 1916, Agnew asked for a raise from INS management but was denied.[6] Agnew grew fearful that he was losing clout with INS brass, who criticized him for poor coverage of a serious bridge disaster in Cleveland. Colleagues observed that Agnew became increasingly angry and upset over criticism of his performance.[7] Edward Campbell, an INS telegrapher, testified that:

> Agnew stated that if the International News Service gave him a "dirty deal" he would give them the self-same thing, and that he would get square with them. That on one occasion said Agnew, while still manager of the Cleveland office, stated that he hoped the International News Service would lose every client it had and that he was not going to do anything more for them. That said Agnew on many occasions repeated the above threat in different forms, stating that if the International News Service discharged or demoted him he would "do them all dirt."[8]

Another INS telegrapher, George T. Hattie, testified that Agnew was "particularly embittered" against INS and was prone to "fly into a rage at the slightest annoyance."[9]

On Nov. 17, 1916, INS demoted Agnew to telegrapher. Not long after, he made good on his threat and revealed to AP a secret arrangement by which INS received AP news from Benjamin Cushing, a telegraph operator at the *Cleveland News*, a member of both AP and INS.[10]

The record is not entirely clear how Agnew made the secret arrangement with Cushing known to the AP. Kent Cooper, traffic manager of the Associated Press, wrote in his autobiography that he was the "first to discover the theft of news in Cleveland" and exposed it to the publisher of the *Cleveland News*. He also collected "all the affidavits confessing the practice and had them notarized."[11]

The affidavits in the case reveal that Agnew was a former AP telegrapher in Ohio,[12] where Kent Cooper once worked. It is possible that the two men knew each other. When Agnew faced a career crisis with INS, it is conceivable that he may have contacted Cooper, who, with General Manager Melville Stone, was looking for a piracy case that would establish a property right in news. Agnew may have provided that opportunity.

In his affidavit, Agnew offered the most detailed examples of INS piracy by describing twelve AP stories that he said INS stole and transmitted to INS customers. Some of his testimony offered damaging proof of INS's direct or nearly direct theft of AP news. In other cases, it was unclear whether some AP stories were used as "tips" so that INS could independently verify and add to the information.

For example, Agnew explained an exchange between the Cleveland and New York offices of INS regarding Lloyd George, Great Britain's secretary of war, who was expected to resign his position and be appointed that nation's new prime minister by King George. Agnew testified:

On December 5th (1916) at 12:27 p.m. the following message was sent to D.R., the Cleveland office of International News Service, by the New York office.

"D.R. Has Lloyd George resigned war secretaryship?" B.F. N.Y. December 5, 12:27 p.m."

At 12:30 p.m. the following message was sent by the Cleveland office to the New York office of International News Service:

"Ansonia says he has written his resignation but has not been presented. Ward. December 5."

Ansonia was [a] code word used by the International News Service for The Associated Press.

At 12:48 p.m. on the same day the following bulletin lead was sent by the New York office of the International News Service over its New York-Chicago wire:

"Bulletin Lead.
"London, December 5.

"War Secretary Lloyd George was reported in political circles this afternoon to have prepared his resignation although, so far as could be learned, it had not been presented."[13]

While it is clear that INS monitored AP news in this exchange, it is less clear from this evidence alone that INS directly used that information in its own story. Between 12:30 and 12:48 p.m., it is possible that INS contacted other sources that led it to write its 12:48 bulletin. Nonetheless, it appeared that INS managers in New York were aware of the arrangement between the INS Cleveland office and Cushing.

More damaging evidence came in the form of phrases and mistakes made by AP that were then copied by INS. For instance, in an AP story sent to the *Cleveland News*, the AP made note of a ship named the "Narzal" that was missing off the coast of England. The news from AP was followed by a message from the INS Cleveland bureau to INS in New York that the "Neptune" was missing. Within seven minutes, the INS reported the Neptune missing on its wire. Not long after, the New York and Cleveland bureaus of INS had this exchange:

"D.R. are you sure English statement says 'Neptune,' N.Y."?

This was immediately followed by the following message:

"Does it show whether sea forces attacked last night, N.Y."

The following answer was sent immediately:

"Will know both questions in ten minutes. D.R."

At 12:55 p.m. (on November 28, 1916) the following message was sent by the Cleveland office of the International News Service to the New York Office:

"B.F. Narzal, not Neptune, attack on night of the 26th Ward."

This message was sent after the manager of the International News Service in Cleveland had obtained the information from someone in the employ of the Cleveland News.

At 12:55 p.m. the following correction was sent by the New York office of the International News Service:

"Correction.
"Editors. In London story of German naval raid make fourth sentence read "The British armed trawler Narval was reported missing not Neptune as sent. International News Service." (According to the testimony, the INS corrected the "Narzal" to the "Narval" after checking a British Maritime Register in New York.)[14]

In this exchange, INS not only monitored AP but took its news: INS repeated the wrongly named ship involved, engaged in a discussion on its message wire regarding the AP's error, and turned around that news within the same minute it received it, leaving little doubt that INS did not independently verify such information.

The distinction between stealing AP's news and using it as a "tip" for independent verification was subtle but important, and both agencies would attempt to define the difference in court. Assuming that the appearance of news in an AP member newspaper and on the AP wire constituted publication, INS, in theory, was free to follow the "tip" and pursue its own newsgathering on the story, if not also use the facts of the story. This, news organizations had done for some time leading up to the case. However, as AP would argue, taking the news — at any point in the publication process — and republishing it in similar form without independent verification was unfair because it exploited the resources of another.[15]

Benjamin Cushing's testimony was equally damaging to INS. Described by colleagues at the *Cleveland News* as an impatient man with a high-pitched voice that "carried a long distance,"[16] Cushing admitted in his affidavits to divulging AP news to INS. Cushing testified that he would leave his desk at the *Cleveland News*, find a private telephone booth or some remote part of the newsroom, and then would make his calls to INS.[17] Cushing said that at first, similar to his arrangement with the AP, he was simply hired by INS to be a "correspondent." He delivered local news for a fee that varied from "a small amount to forty dollars a month."[18] As time went on, however, Cushing was asked to include news from the AP wire. Cushing testified that Agnew "impressed upon him the importance of protecting INS on important AP news."[19] Cushing did not offer specific examples of the stories he shared with INS, and in their affidavits, INS news managers in New York and Cleveland either denied receiving information from Cushing[20] or claimed he was paid only for "tips."[21]

The record indicates that Cushing may have played both sides in his unique position as monitor of the INS and AP wires at the *Cleveland News*. Several affidavits from *Cleveland News* employees suggested that Cushing had a similar arrangement with the AP in which he shared INS news. E.A. Smiley, a former *Cleveland News* telegrapher, said that he sat near Cushing and that he and Cushing regularly offered INS news to the AP. Smiley testified:

> When an item of news came in on the International News
> Service report that was not contained in the Associated
> Press report, [Smiley] or Cushing would call up the
> Manager of the Associated Press, and say, for example:
>
> "Hearst says forty dead in New York shirt waist fire. What have you?"
>
> [Smiley] further says that he distinctly remembers that one day, when he was substituting for Cushing, after Cushing had quit for the day, the Cleveland News had prepared an advance to issue instantly an extra edition immediately upon the death of Pope Pius, who for some time had been very ill; that the Associated Press on this afternoon carried a flash, reading "Pope dead"; that on this information the Cleveland News issued and circulated an extra edition, announcing the death of the Pope; that at this time and for some time afterward, the International News Service carried bulletins declaring the Pope was sinking rapidly but insisting he was still alive. When the rival paper of the Cleveland News failed to issue an extra edition, announcing the Pope's death, the Associated Press was asked by [Smiley] whether it was positive that its "death" bulletin was absolutely correct. Some time after this conversation a similar conversation was held between [Smiley] and the Associated Press in course of which [Smiley] told the Associated Press in reply to a question "what does Hearst say?", that the International News Service insisted the Pope was still alive; that the Associated Press at that time said to [Smiley] "Hearst has good connections in Rome." As a matter of fact, the International News Service bulletin was

correct and Pope Pius did not die until early the next morning, Cleveland time.[22]

AP executive Roy Martin denied that AP carried news of the Pope prematurely.[23]

For his services to the AP, Smiley testified that he was paid $3 per week by Cushing and received $10 per week when Cushing was on vacation. Smiley and *Cleveland News* telegrapher Benjamin F. Field also testified that Cushing had regular access to *Cleveland News* proofs headed for publication, which contained INS news, and that he shared these regularly with the AP. Field testified:

> It was Cushing's custom to make frequent trips to the composing room to get the proofs just before the closing time of each edition, and after getting possession of the proofs he busied himself at his typewriter writing stories from the said proofs for the Associated Press. These stories were placed in the carrier and shot down the pneumatic tube by the said B.E. Cushing to the Associated Press offices.[24]

Field and two other Cleveland News telegraphers, Sam B. Anson and Karl Shimansky, also testified that Cushing would call up the AP, share INS news, and ask what AP had on the story.[25] In his testimony, Cushing denied ever sharing INS news with the AP.

In addition, other INS telegraphers and former AP telegraphers testified that AP took INS news at other locations. INS Syracuse bureau manager William G. Warnock testified that during coverage of a local trial, INS and AP telegraphers set up telegraph equipment near each other at a Syracuse courthouse. When news of the sinking of the Lusitania came in over the INS wire at the courthouse, the AP correspondent transcribed the news coming over the INS sounder and sent it to AP.[26] Henry Leary, who like many telegraphers, worked for AP, INS, and United Press at different points during his career, testified that while working for the AP, he was instructed to transmit "any and all news" that came into his possession and that "he never heard that his news was supposed to exclude news furnished by International News Service or any other agency."[27] AP telegraphers believed such actions would be credited to their record.[28]

Kent Cochran, a telegrapher for Western Union, described his duties as a transcriptionist for an INS report that the *Los Angeles*

Herald shared with the *San Francisco Call*, which was an AP member. Cochran and an AP telegrapher shared a room at the *Call*, and Cochran testified that the AP telegrapher routinely took INS items that came in over his sounder, although Cochran denied this to management of the *Call* because telegraphers "stand together," and he was afraid his colleague might lose his job. Cochran testified:

> In some of the instances referred to in this affidavit, the matter sent out by [the AP telegraphers at the Call], was more than a tip . . . and was such an extended report of the matter that the Associated Press could write the story and send it out over their wires from the tip itself, and without making any independent inquiry or ascertaining any additional facts.[29]

Edward Sartwell, an INS telegrapher and former AP and UP telegrapher, similarly testified that some INS "tips" were taken wholesale by the AP and that the practice was common to both AP and UP:

> Very frequently, these tips sent out were sufficiently complete as to the nature and character of the story and its point of origin to enable the central office of the association to whom the tip was sent to re-write the information, and then send it out over its own wires to its own customers, as its own bulletin, without making an independent investigation.[30]

Sartwell and former AP telegraphers William M. Baskervill, William Schwinger, and Fred Harvey also testified that it was common for AP to rewrite INS news published in INS member newspapers.[31] Harvey testified:

> When I was in charge of the Up-State wire of The Associated Press, I frequently took stories which had appeared in the New York Morning Sun, revised or re-wrote fifty or a hundred words of the first part of the story, commonly called the "lead" and pasted up the rest of the story to the revised "lead," and then transmitted the same on the wire to the up-state (New York) clients and customers of The Associated Press. The stories which I obtained and transmitted, as stated, were

substantially the stories which I took from the Sun, excepting for a change in the "lead," as described above.[32]

AP General Manager Melville Stone and other AP executives vehemently denied AP use of INS news, or, if such news was used, stated that such use was against AP policy.[33] AP bombarded the record with testimony from *Cleveland News* telegraphers and AP employees to discount these accounts.[34] Traffic Chief Kent Cooper said:

> Any story sent to the members of The Associated Press is based solely upon news obtained by these correspondents from original sources, and if no such information can be obtained, no story is sent out. This is the definite and invariable rule of The Associated Press, and any employee discovered violating it would be dismissed from the service. Such correspondents and representatives have not been authorized to use the news despatches (sic), either in whole or in part, before or after publication, of any rival or competing newsgathering association, or of any newspaper not represented by membership in The Associated Press, and so far as I know, The Associated Press has not done so. When any rumor or current report is received, The Associated Press investigates the subject through its own independent sources, and any despatches (sic) it sends out are based upon it own investigation and the product of it own enterprise and expense.[35]

AP managers familiar with the former AP employees who testified also denied the practice. Jackson S. Elliott, who was the supervisor for Edward Sartwell, denied that his bureau used INS news in AP stories either before or after INS newspapers printed it.[36]

Thus, the testimony in *INS* offered strong evidence of INS's piracy of AP news, but offered some evidence that AP similarly engaged in taking INS news and rewarding telegraphers who were aggressive gatherers of INS news. Many of the examples of pirated news offered by Stone and Agnew appeared to be outright theft, but in some cases, the news may have served more as "tips" that could be confirmed by other information, raising the question whether such a practice was illegal. The courts would address the difference between outright theft of news and the taking of "tips." Finally, the structure of the newsgathering system at the time, as described in the testimony, appeared to lend itself to the easy theft of news. During the course of their careers, telegraphers often worked for AP, UP, Western Union, and INS, getting to know how each organization operated and making it easier to steal another's news. At newspapers with both AP and INS, telegraphers for the paper were able to monitor both services and alert either service on breaking news. Furthermore, the wire services often placed their own local operations at the member paper or paid a member telegrapher to act as an agent. This also made it easier for wire services to have access to competitor news. With a desire to have the best news delivered quickly, member loyalty was not always assured. Indeed, the affidavits raise questions about why AP did not pursue part of its case against the AP member papers that failed to safeguard the AP report. These are some of the factual issues raised by close analysis of the testimony.

THE DISTRICT COURT

The District Court considered the three claims raised by AP General Manager Melville Stone in the AP's complaint and his affidavit. The AP requested an injunction to stop INS from:

1. Arranging with employees of members of the Associated Press to furnish its news to [INS] for a consideration before publication;
2. Inducing members to violate [AP's] by-laws and permit [INS] to obtain news of the Associated Press before publication; and
3. Copying news on bulletin boards and in early editions of [AP's] members and selling this news to [INS's] customers.[37]

Before ruling on the claims, Judge Augustus N. Hand reviewed the bylaws of the AP and the customs of the wire service agencies. Hand noted that both agencies had rules that prohibited members from sharing their reports and required members to share local news with the agency serving it. While there were many rules for members, the "rules" for the agencies were based on custom. Hand noted that the value of news to both wire services depended upon the accuracy and speed of the report. Because news was released at one moment in time, and papers across the country published at many different times, it was possible for a news agency to take advantage of the clock by stealing a competitor's news and delivering it westward — or in the case of news that was reported in the morning, steal a competitor's report and publish it in a competing afternoon edition ahead of the originating agency's report. Judge Hand observed:

> It is therefore undoubtedly a part of the successful operation of a country-wide news agency that rivals shall not be able to sell the news which its customers have published in the East to newspapers published several hours later in the West.[38]

With this opening observation, Hand set the tone for his opinion. His primary goal throughout would be to protect "the successful operation of a country-wide news agency." He chose not to question these agency rules or customs, particularly AP's bylaws that forbid its members from sharing local news with any other agency but AP.[39]

On the first claim, Judge Hand ruled in favor of the AP, convinced the record provided clear evidence that the Cleveland bureau of INS had arranged with Benjamin Cushing to furnish AP news before its publication. In his opinion, Hand mentioned some of the stories AP said had been taken, but he did not discuss them in depth. Instead, he said the affidavits, particularly those from INS management to the Cleveland bureau, demonstrated that it was "sufficient that the system existed and the acts were frequent and continuous."[40]

On the second claim, Judge Hand relied on the testimony of the AP repairmen who witnessed INS editors taking AP news at the *New York American*. While INS also denied these claims, Judge Hand noted that none of the INS editors who were charged with taking news at the *American* testified. This, he said, was "very significant," and therefore, the testimony of the AP repairmen "should prevail."[41] Thus, AP also won an injunction on the second claim.

Judge Hand then addressed INS's defense against these claims – that AP should be barred from "seeking the aid of a court of equity" because it similarly engaged in taking news from INS.[42] Known more commonly as the doctrine of "unclean hands," this principle specifies that a party "cannot seek equitable relief or assert an equitable defense if that party has violated an equitable principle, such as good faith."[43] While acknowledging that it appeared AP took some INS news, Judge

Hand characterized it as "limited to but a few sporadic instances at most"[44] and "very different from the systematic disclosure by Cushing to the defendant."[45] Judge Hand was critical that INS's testimony was not specific enough about AP's theft of INS news and seemed "to indicate that Cushing was seeking information for the *Cleveland News*, rather than imparting to the Associated Press any information he had received from the defendant."[46] In characterizing the testimony this way, Judge Hand seemed to ignore that AP was in a special position. As the complainant in the case, AP spent months analyzing specific news reports to include in its case before INS knew there would ever be a case. INS had only the recollections of those who testified on its behalf. It was clearly much easier for AP to track INS's transgressions than for INS, in hindsight, to dig up specific examples of AP's offenses. While INS's examples were less specific, there were nearly as many INS telegraphers who testified that AP took INS news as there were AP telegraphers who testified that INS took AP news. Above all, the testimony demonstrates the individual ambitions of the telegraphers to get paid, get credit, and move ahead, regardless for whom they worked.

While the first two claims involved INS theft that occurred *before* publication of the news in AP newspapers, the third claim involved "theft" by INS that took place *after* publication. In its final claim, the AP said INS took news from early editions of AP member newspapers — namely those on the East coast — and sold that news to INS's customers, particularly those on the West coast. Again, INS defended itself by alleging that AP did the same and that such news was in the public domain.

No AP bylaws governed the responsibilities of members after publication, and under common law copyright (which governed uncopyrighted, published news agency reports) a publication of this sort was generally considered to be a dedication to the public. While both sides argued that there were differences between published news they took from newspapers as a "tip" and news they simply took and redistributed, Judge Hand was unimpressed. He found the distinction "grotesque," calling it a matter of business policy rather than law.[47] He concluded:

> The real matter for consideration is whether news gathered and sold to a newspaper, which publishes it, can be used after

publication by a competing news agency, either as a tip for further investigation *or* as authentic news for immediate distribution before sufficient time has elapsed for the news to be published within the territory in which the gatherer is engaged in the general dissemination of news. This question is most novel and important.[48]

While Hand was convinced that INS had unfairly competed by obtaining AP news *before* publication, he wasn't as certain that taking AP news *after* publication constituted unfair competition. After all, when news is published, readers routinely share with each other what they have read. By ruling that INS unfairly competed with AP by republishing its news *after* publication, the court could, in effect, rule that no person could share what had been essentially dedicated to the public by the press. With no AP bylaw restrictions on the use of news after publication — indeed Hand admitted such a rule would be impractical — the court struggled to find protection for the newsgatherer that didn't, in some form, interfere with the rights of the public to the news. One solution Hand found was in defining publication as incomplete until its value, particularly as against a competitor, was recognized:

> The only way to afford full protection to the newsgatherer is to prevent the use of news by a rival, either in the form of tips or otherwise, for a sufficient time to enable the daily newspapers throughout the country to receive and publish the news. There is no real publication, or purpose to abandon to the public, until that time.[49]

In Judge Hand's view, publication, a principle of copyright law, had occurred when the value of news, a principle protected by unfair competition, had been exhausted. As he put it: "The question in any given case is whether abandonment to the public has been so complete that no further justifiable cause remains for protecting these business interests from competitive interference."[50]

This decidedly economic view of publication, which would strongly influence the Supreme Court's review of the case, did not address the question of the public's interest in publication and the dissemination of information. Hand makes only one reference to the issue:

Undoubtedly the public is legitimately interested in and benefited by the dissemination of news, and the dissemination, when once begun, should not be long delayed; but no adequate reason occurs to me for allowing a competitor to sell and disseminate the news obtained through the efforts of the gatherer until the ordinary customers of the gatherer, within the field in which it operates, have had sufficient time to receive and publish the news.[51]

Hand wrote that he was "personally satisfied" that a right existed to prevent INS from taking AP's news before AP saw the full benefit of its value, but he concluded that "my decision cannot be regarded as sufficiently free from doubt" to grant the injunction.[52] Thus, this last claim was left largely undecided.

On March 29, 1917, Judge Hand handed down his decision. He granted an injunction that prohibited INS from engaging any AP employee or AP member employee in "using or selling" any news produced by or gathered for AP. He also prohibited INS from inducing any AP member newspaper to violate its contract with AP. INS appealed to the Second Circuit Court of Appeals on the first two claims and disputed Judge Hand's interpretation of the facts in the case; AP appealed on the third claim, asking the Second Circuit to grant an injunction on the use of AP news by INS after publication.

THE SECOND CIRCUIT

The Second Circuit quickly dismissed the appeal on the first two claims. Without discussion, Judge Charles Merrill Hough was convinced that INS had taken AP's news before publication and that this was unfair competition. Hough was not persuaded that the AP had similarly taken INS's news. He spent the remainder of his decision addressing the third claim: whether it was legal for INS to use published AP news in total and/or as tips.

On appeal, INS argued that the information it took from published sources were facts that could not be owned. If such facts were property, INS argued, ownership was lost at the moment of publication. AP argued that the news was more than just facts, and as such, there was a property right in news. AP also argued that such a property right belonged to AP and its member newspapers and did not cease upon one member's publication of that news. Finally, AP said the principles of publication under copyright law were inapplicable to news.[53]

Judge Hough addressed three issues raised by these arguments: (1) whether news stories were facts, and therefore incapable of protection; (2) whether there was a property right in news; and (3) if there was a property right in news, what was the duration of that property right. Finally, Judge Hough addressed whether the laws of unfair competition could be applied in the case.

On the first issue, Judge Hough concluded that news stories may contain facts, but they were more than just facts. Facts were not news, Hough wrote, "unless they have that indefinable quality of interest, which attracts public attention."[54] Did that make news a "literary" work, qualifying for copyright protection? Hough concluded that news was also not "literary," and therefore, copyright principles did not apply. He wrote:

> It still remains true that plaintiff's property in news is not literary at all, that it is not capable of copyright, and that "publication" as that word is used in the long line of decisions regarding literary rights, has no determinative bearing on the case. . . . The word is legally very old, and of no one certain meaning. . . . We discover no magic in the word "publication" which takes away or terminates the rights of others[55]

Judge Hough concluded that despite the lack of a "literary" quality in news, news organizations had a property right in the news they published. Hough wrote that such a right arose from the "exchangeable value" of news.[56] News required "labor and expense in acquisition, transmission, and dissemination," making the exposure of news a loss in commercial value. Any loss in commercial value was a lost property right.[57]

Finally, Judge Hough addressed the duration of such a right. Relying on the ticker cases as precedent, Hough concluded that a property right in news should last "until the reasonable reward of each member is received, and that means (with due allowance for the earth's rotation) until plaintiff's most Western member has enjoyed his reward, which is, not to have his local competitor supplied in time for competition with what he has paid for."[58] "Surely," he wrote, "This is a modest limit of rights."[59]

In addressing the difference between the attainment of "tips" and the actual appropriation of news from published sources, Hough sought to prohibit wholesale appropriation, not the practice of "tips." He saw "no difficulty" discriminating between the two:

> One who, on hearing a rumor or assertion, investigates and verifies it, whether with much or little effort, acquires knowledge by processes of his own; the result is his. In all the relations of life, most of what most of us say we know is but the result of verifying "tips," given, consciously or unconsciously, by those in our environment.[60]

Thus, the court said that AP's purpose for providing the news was to benefit from its own labor, that this was a property right, and that AP should be permitted to benefit for as long as the news had value.[61] Furthermore, Judge Hough had little trouble applying principles of unfair competition to the case, despite the fact that it was a new form: "Equity, however, is not stayed because a name does not fit, or one is not at hand to accurately describe a wrong of a kind necessarily infrequent."[62] He remanded the case to the district court to write the injunction on the third claim.

In his dissent, Judge Henry Galbraith Ward of the Second Circuit Court of Appeals refused to accept the concept of news as property. He argued that the news gatherer does not create the news, nor does he invent, compose, or manufacture anything that would deserve property protection under the rules of unfair competition. He criticized the Second Circuit's dismissal of established law on the definition of publication. Once news saw the light of day, he wrote:

> Everything in the nature of a confidence about the communication has ceased. That the rotation of the earth is slower than the electric current is a physical fact the [AP] must reckon with in doing its business.[63]

THE SUPREME COURT

INS appealed to the U.S. Supreme Court, which ruled on the case in December of 1918, about a year and a half after the Second Circuit decision. The Supreme Court addressed only the third issue in the case: whether INS's appropriation of AP news after publication constituted unfair competition or whether the publication of AP news was a dedication of uncopyrighted material to the public.

The AP presented five primary arguments to the Supreme Court: (1) News is a commodity and therefore, is property. This, the AP argued, had been suggested in a number of cases leading up to *INS*;[64] (2) The AP's property right in news lasted for as long as the news had value and did not expire simply because AP members published their news;[65] (3) The AP was entitled to relief by injunction under the rules of unfair competition;[66] and (4) The AP did not have "unclean hands." The AP argued that INS had failed to prove that AP did.[67]

INS presented four main arguments: (1) Even if AP had a property right in the facts of news, that right was lost at publication;[68] (2) There were no elements of unfair competition in the case;[69] (3) The AP had similarly taken news from INS and was not entitled to seek equity with "unclean hands";[70] and (4) The appeals court decision, which barred INS from using AP news and the news of its members for a limited time after publication, would create "a most intolerable monopoly."[71]

The Court considered these issues by addressing three questions:[72]

1. Was there a property right in news?
2. If there was a property right in news, did it survive first publication?
3. Did INS's actions constitute unfair competition in trade?

A Property Right in News

The universe of uncopyrighted works in 1918 was much larger than it is today. While the 1909 Copyright Act protected books, maps, and charts, it left dozens of works, like news, unprotected.[73] Thus, when courts at the time looked to address the question of whether an uncopyrighted work should be protected as property, they often looked at the nature of the work itself and compared it to works that were protected.

Defining what news was in *INS* in 1918 was at the root of identifying whether there was a property right worth protecting. Was news like a chapter in a book, in the sense that it possessed a literary quality? Or was it just a set of facts, a discovery of pre-existing knowledge, not created in any way by its author? If news was literary, then it might be protected by copyright. If the news was a collection of facts, then such information would be free to use at any point.

While INS and AP attempted to separate the discussion of protection for news articles from protection for the facts of news, this distinction was often lost in the case briefs. The AP clearly defined news as "the communication of information of events contemporaneously with their happening."[74] To avoid the publication rules of common law copyright, which would have allowed the reuse of AP news, it insisted that news had no literary qualities whatsoever:

> News has no resemblance of any kind to literary property except the accidents that, like trade-marks, it is expressed in words, and in print and on paper. There is no imaginative or intellectual quality in its production, except the imagination and intellect which go into the organization for its collection and distribution. Indeed its character as news disappears when invention or imagination is introduced into its substance, and it then becomes what is known as a "fake."[75]

As an example of the non-literary quality of news, the AP wrote that the item, "The Austrian Emperor died today," was identical to "The death of the Austrian Emperor occurred today."[76] The real value of these sentences was not in their literary quality, but in knowing that the facts that the emperor had died today. In this way, AP argued, news was different than a book or a work of art because news had little "permanency."[77]

Furthermore, the AP argued that intellectual property law in general was "wholly inapplicable to news" because such rights were awarded to authors or inventors who showed a "peculiar creative skill."[78] News, the AP said, was different, and everyone had equal opportunity to seek it out:

> [The] source is not locked in the brain of the producer, but is the event to which all persons have equal access. A right in the owner of a certain report of this event to prevent an appropriation by others of his report in no sense deprives the public of the benefit of knowledge of the event. Any other person can make a similar report. . . .[79]

Instead, the AP claimed its property right in news was based on the news as a "Service,"[80] a commodity[81] in which the raw material was the event and the product was the message. As a service, it was not different from the railroad or the telegraph: It moved a product from one point to another. As such, the AP argued it was property deserving of protection from appropriation.[82]

In presenting news strictly as a commodity, the AP drew comparisons to the sale of stock quotations and sales information.[83] AP cited *Board of Trade v. Christie Grain & Stock Co.*[84] to support the proposition that news stories, like stock quotations, were commodities worthy of trade protection. Other cases cited by AP included *Board of Trade v. Tucker*[85] and *National Telegraph News Co. v. Western Union Tel. Co.*[86]

INS did not see how news could be controlled as property. INS described news as the "Genie of the Arabian fable": Once the bottle that contained news was uncorked, it "pervaded the entire atmosphere and could not be bottled up again."[87] It also contended that news had literary qualities, despite the impracticalities of registering every dispatch under copyright. INS argued that by characterizing news as a commodity, the AP devalued the work of great authors and inventors:

> Is it possible that one who learns of a railway accident or of the death of a crowned head, or of a convulsion of nature in the Caribbean Sea, has a property right in this information which is superior to the right of . . . "Huckleberry Finn" or "Evangeline," of "Joseph Vance" or "Lorna Doone," or of the telegraph, the telephone, the phonograph or the submarine? The obvious difficulty in finding apt language in our ordinary vocabulary to point out the distinction does not create it.[88]

INS also compared news to a trade secret, that once divulged was no longer protected. It argued that in taking news from the AP members, it did not break some "seal of secrecy. Whatever information [INS] obtained it secured in common with others — openly, publicly and notoriously."[89]

In characterizing news, both parties cursorily addressed the public interest aspect. In its brief, the AP challenged INS's notion that news "was an automatic stream filling a reservoir to which the public interest would give everybody free access."[90] AP argued that the collection process was part and parcel of the distribution and that the right to protect news extended to both. Furthermore, the AP argued that the public interest would be hurt when INS took news from AP: "[T]he public does not get the benefit of news collected by two independent associations. Its interests will be better served by the efficient administration of both associations required by fair competition between them."[91]

The AP argued that its membership structure — in which AP provided news in return for member news contributions to the AP — brought a unique public benefit that should be protected. Each member, the AP argued, "had an equal interest in the news gathered at the expense of all,"[92] and thus, the suit against INS was not just a battle of two competitive wire services, but a struggle against the soul of the cooperative itself. This argument pitted INS not just against AP, but also against 950 member newspapers whose purpose was to cooperate. In its description of the cooperative, the AP suggested that its operation was driven less by profit and more by the collective good:

> If such a co-operative organization is effectively administered, and protected in its rights, obviously its service to its members must be cheaper than that of any profit making news agency, because it makes no profit and because of its large membership, which not only divide the burden but also supply it [the member] without substantial cost with their own local news.[93]

The AP argued that its members did not intend to abandon the benefit of their membership in AP when they published and allow competitors to pirate such news.

INS argued that AP news served only its members, to the detriment of the public. With bylaws that gave AP members exclusive control over who could gain entry to the cooperative and that prohibited an AP member from sharing its local news with any other outlets, the AP would be assured of "absolute domination"[94] if also given a limited property right in news. INS argued: "*Reductio ad absurdum* could not go to further lengths. This would fasten upon the country a most dangerous and intolerable monopoly. . . ."[95]

In an attempt to move away from the strict characterization of news as a commodity, INS focused on the benefits news brought to the public:

The purchaser of a newspaper containing [news] has the undoubted right to communicate the intelligence which it embodies to anybody, either by handing over the newspaper to be read or by oral statement of its contents, or by telephoning or telegraphing them. He has the absolute right to read the despatches [sic] found in the newspaper to whomsoever he chooses, whether it be the worshippers in a church or to an audience in a public hall, or to the attendants at a public meeting, however numerous they may be. . . . The news which [the newspaper] contains of necessity becomes the possession of the purchaser of the paper on which it is printed.[96]

In deciding whether there was a property right in news, the Supreme Court ruled that news had a "dual character." It was information — what it called the "news element" — as well as a work of literary writing.[97] The Court concluded that news stories, as a whole, could be copyrighted. But it was unlikely, the Court wrote, that the copyright clause was "intended to confer upon one who might happen to be the first to report a historic event the exclusive right for any period to spread the knowledge of it."[98] Thus, the facts of news were not protected by copyright. By this reasoning, the Court might have concluded that there was no property right in the "news element."

Instead, the Court agreed with AP and wrote that the case rested on a question of property under unfair competition in business, not on the question of property under principles of copyright.[99] The news was a product, and the commercial value of the product constituted a business:

What we are concerned with is the business of making [news] known to the world, in which both parties to the present suit are engaged. That business consists in maintaining a prompt, sure, steady, and reliable service designed to place the daily events of the world at the breakfast table of the millions at a price that, while of trifling moment to each reader, is sufficient in the aggregate to afford compensation for the cost of gathering and distributing it, with the added profit so necessary as an incentive to effective action in the commercial world.[100]

Because this was an unfair competition action, the Court said, the issue was not the rights of each party against the public, as in copyright, but their rights against each other. So the Court ruled that against the public, there was no property interest in news, but against each other, a *quasi property right* existed. This was because both parties labored to produce news and seek a profit.[101]

The Duration of a Property Right in News

To strengthen its case that news was property, the AP argued that the value of the AP news "service" was not only in its "adequacy, reliability and cheapness," but was most importantly in its speed or "exclusiveness."[102] AP described this as the news report's "firstness;" that is, in being the first to bring information to the attention of a reader.[103] The AP admitted that this quality of "firstness" was relative to the individual: The article one reader reads at 6 a.m. and that another reader reads at 8 a.m. represent two individual "firsts." But for the purposes of the case, the AP argued that the only "firstness" that mattered was that relative to the AP member newspaper. By declaring a right to that "firstness," AP said it was merely looking to recoup its labor and investment:

> We are not asking any exclusive right to merely communicate to the world the happening of events. We are not asking even that our own recital of events, as we gather them from day to day over the world, be regarded as exclusive for any extended period of time. . . . What we ask is simply that this quality of firstness in news, that gives it as a service its whole commercial value to the member newspaper, be recognized as ours, to the extent that it is the product of our labor, skill and expenditure; and that it be recognized as ours for the period that, as applied to the community served by a newspaper, rather than to the individual, measures its quality of firstness to the community as a whole, rather than to the earliest rising individual.[104]

Interestingly, the AP argued that without the element of "firstness," there could be no limited property right in news:

If conditions of the world were such that every happening anywhere became automatically known to everybody everywhere, there could hardly be any property value in news; but as the world actually is, a great organization of vigilance, investigation, transmission and distribution is necessary to connect the fact with those who wish to know it. The organization, composed of capital and labor, is what creates the business commodity of news.[105]

INS questioned how a property right in news could be exclusive for a limited time and then suddenly, at some "undefined period its value as news has diminished or vanished."[106] While not stating it directly, INS's argument was based on the public's interest in news rather than the commercial interest:

A property right is not dependent upon its commercial value. If it is only worth a farthing, it still is property. To the man in the Blue Ridge or the Ozark Mountains, or in the Adirondack Forest or the Everglades, or in Alaska, news gathered today may continue to be news six months hence. It would seem, therefore, logically to follow from the [AP's] reasoning, that no publication, however general, can destroy the property of the collector of news in the information that he has gathered.[107]

INS ridiculed AP's insistence that its property right was to the "precommunicatedness"[108] of news. "The invention of a sesquipedalian and unpronounceable symbol can only mystify," INS wrote. "It does not explain."[109]

The Supreme Court wrote that the difference in *INS*, compared to previous cases, was that *published* news could now "easily outstrip the rotation of the earth,"[110] resulting in opportunities for piracy across time zones. In other words, when a member of the public took published AP news on the East Coast and wired his friend on the West Coast to relay the information to him, AP had no property interest or right to prevent that exchange, namely because the individual had no commercial interest. But when that person was a competitor, AP had a right to protect its investment in the gathering of news. Thus, the Court established a *limited or quasi property right* against a competitor.

INS's Actions and the Extent of Protections

If news was property, what was the nature and extent of the protection that was owed to the gatherer of news during that period in which the news had its greatest value? Without the benefit of copyright law or the misrepresentation that characterized typical unfair competition cases at that time, the AP appealed to the Court's broader sense of equity and fairness. Simply put, the AP argued that the Court should not stand by and allow INS to take AP news from — or "free ride" on — East Coast editions and send that news to the West Coast. Without the benefit of precedent, though, the more difficult question was "why not?" In helping the Court to reach its rule of law, the AP appealed to the Court's sense of duty against the "parasitic" activity that threatened to kill AP's business:

> [I]s there public policy in permitting one to steal what another has created? Does public policy take no heed that if the parasite is given immunity to live, the thing on which it feeds may die — for unremunerative service cannot survive — and that with the death of the thing on which it feeds, it also will die. Is there in the whole history of industry — of the rivalries of men to minister to the comfort and the happiness of other men — a case in which the public welfare has been subserved, or been believed to have been subserved, by giving encouragement to the vampire?[111]

INS first argued that its actions were part of custom, not law, and were not, therefore, subject to action by the courts.

> [It] has long been a well known and practically universal custom for publishers of newspapers . . . to obtain and read editions of newspapers published by others . . . and to obtain various items of news . . . and to rewrite such items of news . . . and to publish them, sometimes with and sometimes without additional verification and without revealing the original source from which such news items were obtained.[112]

Secondly, INS insisted that AP had showed no specific injury:

[W]here is the injuria to be found? What principle of law has been violated? What property right has been infringed, when the petitioner has only taken that which it was the right of anybody and everybody to take who had access to the newspaper or to the bulletin board . . . ?[113]

Furthermore, INS argued there was no precedent in unfair competition upon which the Court could base a right to what AP had described as the "firstness" or "precommunicatedness" of news. Unfair competition cases, up until that time, granted relief to plaintiffs in cases in which the defendant claimed the plaintiff's product as his own in commerce. In taking AP's news, INS made no misrepresentations in the sale of the news; it did not claim it had AP news. It simply took the news as its own. INS argued that the news, after publication, was not property that could be owned. AP argued news was property that needed protection for as long as the news had value.

Because the Court declared a property right in news, it wasn't difficult for the Court to award it property protections. The Court was clear: INS attempted to "reap where it has not sown,"[114] which the Court ruled was a form of unfair competition. Furthermore, the Court said such "reaping" would harm AP. The Court wrote that INS's actions "would render publication profitless, or so little profitable as in effect to cut off the service by rendering the cost prohibitive in comparison to the return."[115] Thus, the Court created a new tort of "misappropriation" by concluding:

> Stripped of all disguises, the process amounts to an unauthorized interference with the normal operation of complainant's legitimate business precisely at the point where the profit is to be reaped, in order to divert a material portion of the profit from those who have earned it to those who have not; with special advantage to defendant in the competition because of the fact that it is not burdened with any part of the expense of gathering the news. The transaction speaks for itself and a court of equity ought not to hesitate long in characterizing it as unfair competition in business.[116]

The Court warned that this conclusion did not give AP the right to monopolize the news, but simply gave it protection against a competitor for the short time necessary to "reap the fruits" of its effort and investment. The Court declined to say how long such a right would last.

The Court agreed with the lower courts that AP had not similarly engaged in taking news from INS, which would have prevented it from seeking a remedy against INS. It acknowledged that both parties appeared to take "tips," but that this was different than INS's wholesale and repeated piracy of AP news in which stories were printed verbatim and never independently verified. However, the Court seemed to recognize that the "tips" practice was widespread and could include piracy or lead to it. The Court wrote: "[I]n the present state of the pleadings and proofs we need go no further than to hold" that AP did not have "unclean hands."[117]

DISCUSSION

While the Court stressed that its ruling was based on principles of unfair competition, its discussion of publication and abandonment was evidence of the struggle the Court faced in reconciling the rules of copyright with principles of unfair competition. Copyright law alone would have provided the Court with two equally unsuitable options. Had the Court ruled for INS and held that news was not property, the door to rampant piracy would have been opened. Had the Court held that the facts of news were copyrightable, it would have created a powerful monopoly. Thus, a limited, quasi property right against a competitor under unfair competition law allowed the Court to achieve an equitable result without rewriting copyright law. But questions remained about the duration of such a right and the standards courts would follow to know whether "tips" had been independently verified by competitors and therefore, were not unfair. In addition, some factual questions remained about whether AP engaged in similar piratical practices.

That the Court was most "concerned with the *business* of making news known to the world" and the "unauthorized interference with the normal operation of complainant's *legitimate business*" was not, through a historical lens, surprising. The courts' response to Progressive Era policy, discussed in Chapter Two, made it more likely that the Supreme Court would look to protect the AP's large and reputable business. This gave AP the chance to argue that its business was due special, new protection. The *INS* Court's development of a limited property right in news stemmed from that Progressive Era influence and the Court's earlier decision that businesses had due process rights.

Although the Court did not spell out a specific test for hot news in *INS*, it did recognize several key elements of this new unfair competition claim: That the right was the result (1) of AP's significant labor and investment; (2) the great value of its news for the short period after it was published; (3) INS's "reaping where it had not sown" by free-riding on AP's investment in the news; (4) the competition between AP and INS; and (5) the harm INS would cause to AP's business by such actions. The discussion of these elements would be critical in future cases.

THE DISSENT

Justice Louis Brandeis's dissent in *INS* argued that it was not the Court's job to expand the notion of property and the protections for it: Only the legislature could accomplish this. Brandeis pointed out that Congress had, in the 1880s, considered whether news should receive protection after publication and rejected the idea.[118] Brandeis wrote that the legislature was better positioned than the courts to consider the "facts and possibilities"[119] of such protection, such as the length of a property right in news and the standards by which news piracy would be measured. Furthermore, the legislature might seek alternatives to an injunction, such as damages, much as "courts of equity ordinarily refuse (perhaps in the interest of free speech) to restrain actionable libels."[120]

In discouraging the Court from creating a property right in news, Brandeis also was concerned about the public's interest in the dissemination of news. He wrote that because news was a public "report of recent occurrences," it was dangerous to ascribe to it notions of property:

> An essential element of individual property is the legal right to exclude others from enjoying it. If the property is private, the right of exclusion may be absolute; if the property is affected with a public interest, the right of exclusion is qualified. But the fact that a product of the mind has cost its producer money and labor, and has a value for which others are willing to pay,

is not sufficient to ensure to it this legal attribute of property. The general rule of law is, that the noblest of human productions — knowledge, truths ascertained, conceptions, and ideas — become, after voluntary communication to others, free as the air to common use.[121]

Furthermore, Brandeis suggested that business competition, by its nature, is often unfair and wrote that the law has protected those who "follow a pioneer" into a market seeking "profits due largely to the labor and expense of the first adventurer. The law sanctions, indeed encourages, the pursuit."[122] Because INS took AP news from published papers, it was well within the bounds of fair competition, Brandeis argued.

RESPONSE TO THE DECISION

Wire service historian Victor Rosewater wrote that the AP was overjoyed by the Court's decision in *INS v. AP*: "The sense of supreme satisfaction over the outcome could not be concealed by the jubilant Associated Press."[123] In the wake of the decision, The Associated Press stepped up its antipiracy efforts, according to Rosewater, by passing new bylaws that punished members for "omission and commission endangering the integrity of the report."[124] The AP first required that every member newspaper print the following warning:

> The Associated Press is exclusively entitled to the use for republication of all news dispatches credited to it, or not otherwise credited, in this paper, and also the local news published herein. All rights of reproduction of special dispatches herein are also reserved.[125]

In addition, the AP devised new restrictions that dictated where AP's wire machines could be placed relative to competitive services within newspaper buildings. It also wrote new restrictions for members who posted their news on public bulletin boards and tried to regulate premature publication of AP news in competing morning and afternoon papers.[126] It passed a resolution condemning piratical practices by Hearst-owned papers that were members of the AP. As radio grew in importance, Rosewater wrote, the AP also considered new rules regarding member use of AP news on member-owned radio stations.[127]

Finally, the AP also moved to prevent criticism of the cooperative or any comments "hurtful to the character and repute of the service."[128]

Response to the decision also showed that some understood the ruling in *INS* would be open to debate in future cases. *Editor & Publisher* reported that the decision was "destined in time to affect all newspapers, as well as news-gathering organizations" and that "newspapers large and small will henceforth invoke the protection of the Supreme Court's decision against rivals" who steal their news.[129] It wrote that the biggest mystery for publishers was exactly how long the property right would last and whether the state legislatures would soon incorporate the new ruling in tort law so that punitive damages would be awarded.[130]

An examination of eight law review articles at the time of the decision revealed support for the outcome, but some concern over the lack of clarity in the Court's definition of the quasi-property right. The *University of Pennsylvania Law Review* called the Court's decision one of "greatest importance to newspaper publishers throughout the country" but said the case "leaves us somewhat in the dark as to the exact status of collected news as property."[131] *Harvard Law Review* generally acknowledged the need for greater legal protections for news and said that *INS v. AP* helped to elucidate some of the growing principles of unfair competition law at the time.[132] *Virginia Law Register* praised the decision as "wise,"[133] and *Columbia Law Review* said that the Court did "not reach too far" with such a ruling.[134] The *Yale Law Journal* agreed:

> When one notices that the protection asked for, if given, is for a very limited time —only so long as the statements of fact have commercial value as news — one can hardly share the fears expressed by (Justice Brandeis) that the rule established by the majority will result in any serious interference with the acquisition by the public of information as to the happenings of the world. On the contrary, it seems to the present writer that the protection given the news gatherer by the decision will in the long run have the effect of stimulating the gathering and publication of news. Indeed it is difficult to see how, without it, a great and efficient newsgathering organization could be maintained, in view of the enormous expense necessarily involved.[135]

The *Illinois Law Review* was the only publication to criticize the ruling. While it agreed with the result in the case, it argued that the rule developed by the Court was too broad. The article said the case should have rested on the question of whether there existed a true property right in news, not on an issue of unfair competition between competitors:

> To award an injunction in such a case is logically to adopt the broad legal rule that no one shall compete with another by a substantial appropriation of his ideas. The consequence of such a rule need hardly be stated. . . . Such a rule has the appearance of at least moral soundness in a system of individualistic ethics, but it will not admit of too close inspection either in morals or in law, for to act upon it, would be destructive of all progress.[136]

SUMMARY OF FINDINGS AND CONCLUSION

For the first time, the highly competitive but customary battles between news agencies were presented to the U.S. Supreme Court as a legal question of unfair business practice. The testimony in *INS* presented strong evidence of INS's piracy of AP news, but raised questions about whether AP similarly engaged in taking INS news and rewarding telegraphers who were aggressive news gatherers. The structure of the newsgathering system at the time, as described in the testimony, appeared to lend itself to the easy theft of news. Telegraphers, often looking to personally profit, jumped from wire service to wire service, making it easier to know how to steal the other's news.

The record revealed that INS took not only the facts of news, but also the expression of the news from AP. But with news dispatches left uncopyrighted at the time, this use of the expression was largely ignored. Without the benefit of modern copyright law – which protects news from the moment it is "fixed" – the case centered on principles of common law copyright and unfair competition, with AP's argument for unfair competition winning judicial approval. Today, the theft of wire service news is addressed under both copyright law and principles of unfair competition.

The arguments and decisions in *INS* revealed three issues for the courts: (1) whether there was a property right in news; (2) if such a right existed, whether there was a limit to the length of that right; and

(3) whether INS's actions constituted unfair competition. The U.S. Supreme Court was ultimately persuaded by AP's argument that news was a commodity, and therefore, was property. For the first time the U.S. Supreme Court recognized published news and information as a valuable business commodity deserving of the law's protections. As such, news deserved protection for as long as it had value. The Court also ruled that published news wasn't necessarily free to use by competitors; INS's actions represented a form of unfair competition. The Court awarded a new hot news right of "misappropriation" in which news and information gatherers were given a property right in the facts of news for a limited period after publication. The establishment of this new right followed logically from the Progressive Era's influence on the courts. The courts sought to protect such businesses, and new torts served that need.

Although the Court did not explicitly label the elements of a misappropriation claim, it addressed some of the boundaries of the new tort. The Court said that the new misappropriation tort was a result of: (1) the AP's significant labor and investment in the news; (2) the great value of its news for the short period after it was published; (3) INS's "reaping where it had not sown" by free-riding on AP's investment in the news; (4) the competition between AP and INS; and (5) the harm INS would cause to AP's business by such actions.

While the Court's decision would make clear that news could be protected, the doctrine was far from fully developed: Did any other kinds of works, in addition to news, deserve similar protection? How long did the protection of hot news last? How were the elements of a hot news claim to be applied in similar cases? With these unanswered questions and the evidence presented in the legal record, the foundation for the hot news doctrine appeared tentative at best. Yet, the technology of telegraphy made these battles more intense. Without the benefit of modern copyright law, the AP – and INS, too – arguably needed the courts to intervene. That news could be stolen more regularly, more routinely and more efficiently changed the nature of what was once a customary practice to "borrow dispatches" into an all-out free-for-all in which the real beneficiaries were the individual telegraphers who used their expertise for personal gain.

CHAPTER 4
Interpreting *INS v. AP*

While the Supreme Court in *INS* clearly warned courts that they should "not long hesitate" to find for a news business whose product is misappropriated, the Court left few instructions regarding the application of the new doctrine or its scope. The Court indicated that the new misappropriation tort was a result of: (1) the AP's significant labor and investment in the news (the labor and investment element); (2) the great value of its news for the short period after it was published (the time element); (3) INS's "reaping where it had not sown" by free-riding on AP's investment in the news (the free-riding element); (4) the competition between AP and INS (the competition element); and (5) the harm INS would cause to AP's business by such actions (the harm element). But the Court did not specifically outline these elements as a formal legal test or specify whether all – or just some – of these elements constituted a successful misappropriation claim. It did not address whether the new tort applied to other products besides news. Furthermore, the Court did not outline the duration of hot news protection or the nature of the competition; that is, it was not clear just how long "hot news" remained "hot" or just how much harm constituted a hot news violation. For more than 80 years, courts grappled with these issues, interpreting and analyzing the Supreme Court's decision in *INS*, a struggle that continues today.

This chapter analyzes three eras of misappropriation law, between 1918 and 1997.[1] These three eras were determined by changes in copyright law and in technology, both of which significantly affected interpretation of the doctrine. Each era demonstrated some variation in judicial interpretation of the doctrine and the elements needed to raise and successfully argue a claim of hot news.

THE ADVENT OF RADIO AND THE EXPANSION OF MISAPPROPRIATION (1920s – 1960s)

Most judges in decisions immediately following *INS* were reluctant to engage in application of the misappropriation doctrine to new factual situations. During the 1920s, only two of six decisions favored a finding of misappropriation.[2] In *National Telephone Directory Co. v. Dawson Mfg. Co.*,[3] a state appeals court argued that unfair competition law had "been greatly expanded in its scope to encompass the schemes and inventions of the modern genius bent upon reaping where he has not sown."[4] In the case, National Telephone sued Dawson Manufacturing for producing "false" telephone book covers and backs with advertising that obscured the advertising found on the true covers of the telephone books produced by National Telephone. In the spirit of *INS*, the court ruled that such actions were within the scope of unfair competition law:

> The petition discloses that the defendants purpose to pass off their own advertising medium as the advertising medium of the plaintiff, not merely by simulating the plaintiff's medium, but by actually tacking their own medium upon that of the plaintiff. By this unfair means the defendants purpose to place their advertising business in competition with that of the plaintiff. A more flagrant case of unfair competition is nowhere disclosed by the books. In fact, the scheme is more than unfair competition; it amounts to an actual appropriation of the plaintiff's property by the defendants to their own business purposes. A court of equity ought not to hesitate long to interpose its protection against a scheme of this character.[5]

This ruling relied on just two elements mentioned by the Supreme Court in *INS*: the elements of free-riding and competition between the plaintiff and defendant.

But in most cases during the 1920s, courts ruled against a finding of misappropriation because the product at issue had little value,[6] minimal competition,[7] or its use by the defendant failed to harm the plaintiff.[8] In these cases, the courts applied some *INS* elements, although courts did not examine them all.

Judge Learned Hand of the U.S. Court of Appeals for the Second Circuit went further than most in limiting the doctrine; he was particularly critical of applying *INS* to other cases. In *Cheney Bros. v. Doris Silk Corporation*,[9] Hand denied the misappropriation claim of the plaintiff, a manufacturer of silks, who sued the Doris Silk Corp., which had copied one of the plaintiff's popular designs. At the time, copyright law did not protect fabric designs. Nonetheless, Judge Hand refused to extend the reasoning in *INS* to the case:

> Although [INS] concerned another subject-matter — printed news dispatches — we agree that, if it meant to lay down a general doctrine, it would cover this case; at least, the language of the majority opinion goes so far. We do not believe that it did. While it is of course true that law ordinarily speaks in general terms, there are cases where the occasion is at once the justification for, and the limit of, what is decided. This appears to us such an instance; we think that no more was covered than situations substantially similar to those then at bar. The difficulties of understanding it otherwise are insuperable.[10]

Judge Hand said the primary difficulty with expanding *INS* to other cases was that it would conflict with Congress' century-old role as author of the nation's copyright and patent laws. In Judge Hand's mind, the rights granted by misappropriation duplicated the rights legislated by Congress. Judge Hand was ahead of his time; such a conflict would become more apparent as other courts applied *INS* more liberally.

The monumental growth of radio changed how *INS* was interpreted. In twenty-five misappropriation decisions from 1930 through 1959, sixteen involved the piracy of radio signals or the piracy of sound recordings or live radio performances.[11] Plaintiffs in thirteen of those sixteen decisions were successful making a claim of misappropriation.[12]

These misappropriation cases typically involved the reading of printed news from a newspaper on air, the rebroadcast or recording of live radio performances, and the reuse of live radio descriptions of sporting events, such as baseball games.

The Broadcast of Printed News

The cases most closely connected to *INS* were those in which news organizations sued radio operations for reading news off their printed pages. In *Associated Press v. KVOS, Inc.*,[13] the AP sued KVOS, a radio station in Bellingham, Washington, for obtaining copies of AP member newspapers in the area and misappropriating those news reports by reading them on the air. Following Judge Hand's lead on the interpretation of *INS*, the district court ruled that *INS* should be read narrowly. The court said there was no absolute property right in published news stemming from *INS*, and there was no *direct* competition between the AP and KVOS, as required by *INS*: "The mere fact that the defendant radio station competes for business profit with complainant's member newspapers in the advertising field does not make of the defendant and such newspapers competitors for business profits in the dissemination of news."[14] The court was also convinced there was no direct competition because KVOS delivered the news reports to its listeners "gratuitously and without profit."[15] Furthermore, the court said it should not interfere with the new medium of radio and the benefits it brought the public:

> Another very important phase of this case is that disclosing the everlasting conflict between private enterprise and public interest. The case occasions restatement of the principle that improved instrumentalities for the advancement of social progress and public convenience, including agencies for improved free speech and free press, must not be discarded for the sake of private enterprise, unless such hindrance of the public interest be required by positive law or clear contract. . . [I]t is in this situation for Congress alone to abridge the public interest in favor of complainant's private enterprise.[16]

The Ninth Circuit overturned the district court's decision by ruling that newspapers and radio sought the same advertiser income, making them competitors, and that KVOS's free-riding damaged AP member newspapers by depriving them of advertising income. The court acknowledged that since *INS*, radio had a "great business created in circulating advertising along with news and other features to attract its audiences to the advertising."[17] The speed of radio could easily attract readers of newspapers to the radio news, persuading the public not to "purchase and read the advertising or the news of papers upon which the piracy is committed, because, to some, the pirated news is stale by the time the newspapers are received and, as to others, the pirated matter is certain to be received by them, without paying for it. . . ."[18] Furthermore, the court ruled that the public interest wasn't in allowing KVOS to take such news but was in "protecting the business of news gathering and disseminating agencies against the impairment of their efficiency."[19]

The U.S. Supreme Court overturned the Ninth Circuit's decision.[20] The Court ruled that The Associated Press had failed to show that the case was within the district court's jurisdiction because AP failed to prove that it was actually harmed. The Court wrote:

> The allegation of possible damage to [AP] is wholly inadequate, because the asserted danger of loss of members is a mere conclusion unsupported by even a suggestion that withdrawal has been threatened by any newspaper, and no intimation is given of the character or extent of the damage they would suffer by such withdrawal.[21]

The Court admitted that the same question of jurisdiction had not been raised in *INS*, though it "lurked."[22] The Court refused to speculate about what might have happened in *INS* had the issue of actual harm been raised.

KVOS illustrates how slightly different interpretations of the elements of misappropriation led (and continue to lead) to vastly different results, even within the same case. While both the district and appeals courts considered the extent of competition between newspapers and the new medium of radio, the district court in *KVOS* concluded there was no "direct" competition: Radio and newspapers were different media, operating on entirely different business models. Newspapers were bought; radio was acquired freely. The Ninth Circuit, by comparison, concluded that while radio and newspapers ran different businesses, both similarly competed for advertising support and that by free- riding on the printed news reports, KVOS harmed the AP and its members. Finding that there was competition, the appeals court noted the time advantage gained by KVOS over the AP paper. News broadcast immediately by KVOS made the same printed news that much less valuable. Thus, the definition of the competition between the litigating parties was different depending on the court's approach. Finally, the Supreme Court threw out the case for lack of jurisdiction, ruling that the AP had failed to show it had been damaged. The Court criticized the complaint for "asserting danger" without showing the "character and extent of the damage."[23] The Court said harm must be shown, but the *INS* elements failed to say how. Thus, throughout *KVOS*, *INS* failed to provide clear guidance on the specific elements involved in a misappropriation case, particularly the elements of competition and harm. The *KVOS* case served as a harbinger of more confusion to come.

The Broadcast of Performances and Recordings

The recording of radio performances for phonographic records and the unlicensed use of phonographic records by radio programmers boosted the misappropriation doctrine and its elements from a limited property right for news gatherers to a stronger right extending to any content of a pecuniary nature. This expansion of the misappropriation doctrine was a clear response to the gaps in copyright law, which did not address the new technology of radio. Where Congress did not act, equity courts extended misappropriation to cover new technologies:

> Equity, since its inception, has been a flexible tribunal extending its arm of protection to persons affected by new conditions. The machine age has changed our mode of living and has created new problems in the relations of human beings one to another, and the law, while ever slow to change, is ever ready to protect, and it must keep pace with changing conditions either by its growth or extension along legislative lines, or by its flexibility in equity. No statutory protection exists for such a complainant, no copyright can be obtained by him, and no civil or criminal redress at law can give adequate relief.[24]

After courts extended the reach of misappropriation in cases involving radio and recording technology, the doctrine was claimed more frequently in an attempt to protect other subject matter of the period that lacked copyright protection. Some claims were successful.[25] Others were not.[26] Only Judge Learned Hand would continue to warn against extending the scope of *INS*. In *RCA Mfg. Co. v. Whiteman*,[27] the RCA record label sued Paul Whiteman, an orchestra conductor with an RCA contract, for attempting to prohibit the radio broadcast of his recordings with RCA. Judge Hand ruled that neither RCA nor Whiteman had rights in the recordings because Congress had not granted such rights. The courts, he warned, should stay out of the business of creating law:

> We cannot know how Congress would solve this issue; we can guess — and our guess is that it would refuse relief as we are refusing it — but if our guess were the opposite, we should have no right to enforce it. If the talents of conductors or orchestras are denied that compensation which is necessary to evoke their efforts because they get too little for phonographic records, we have no means of knowing it. . . .[28]

In decisions awarding a misappropriation right, courts recognized some *INS* elements but ignored others that didn't apply well. In *Waring v. WDAS Broadcasting Station, Inc.*,[29] Waring, an orchestra conductor, sued WDAS to prohibit it from broadcasting his recordings made under contract with RCA. An appeals court in *Waring*, as in *KVOS*, ruled that Waring and WDAS competed for the same advertising dollars and the same audience, and that such competition was harmful to Waring:

> It probably must become increasingly difficult for [Waring] to demand and obtain $13,500 for a single performance over the radio if innumerable reiterations of their renditions can be furnished at a cost of seventy-five cents [the cost of a recording].[30]

Here, competition was defined in terms of advertising revenue and listenership, as well as the ability to command income for future performances. Competition was not defined in terms of the businesses in the lawsuit (one was a musician, the other a radio station) or their similarity to the businesses in *INS*.

In *Uproar Co. v. National Broadcasting*,[31] a court found that a publishing company misappropriated the "goodwill" and "cheapened the value" created in an NBC radio program by selling a pamphlet promoting the show's host and his routine. While the court acknowledged that the publisher and the network radio operation were not competitors, it said that the publisher was "seeking to take unfair advantage of the popularity of widely advertised programs, the proprietary interests in which belong exclusively to [NBC.]"[32] Citing *INS*, it claimed courts had frequently ruled that such behavior was unfair competition, despite the lack of competition.[33]

In *Metropolitan Opera Association v. Wagner-Nichols Recorder Corp.*,[34] a New York state court radically expanded the scope of *INS* by declaring that direct competition was not a necessary element to a finding of misappropriation. In that case, the Metropolitan Opera sued Wagner-Nichols for recording radio broadcast performances of the opera and selling them as phonographic records.[35] The court cited a number of New York decisions that indicated the scope of misappropriation had been expanded to include a new tort of "commercial immorality":

> The modern view as to the law of unfair competition does not rest solely on the ground of direct competitive injury, but on the broader principle that property rights of commercial value are to be and will be protected from any form of unfair invasion or infringement and from any form of commercial immorality, and a court of equity will penetrate and restrain every guise resorted to by the wrongdoer. The courts have thus recognized that in the complex pattern of modern business relationships, persons in theoretically non-competitive fields may, by unethical business practices, inflict as severe and reprehensible injuries upon others as can direct competitors.[36]

Metropolitan Opera would open the floodgates to future misappropriation actions based on ethical violations in business. Plaintiffs needed only to demonstrate that they had been harmed by the defendant's effort "to profit from the labor, skill, expenditures, name and reputation" of the plaintiff.[37] Thus, the element of labor and investment and the element of free-riding were essentially all that were needed to prove commercial immorality. Because most competitors have benefited at some point from each other's work in a particular field, raising a misappropriation/commercial immorality claim was often an easy task.

Thus, these radio cases helped to broaden the scope of the doctrine. Recording businesses were more likely to raise a successful misappropriation claim whether or not they met all the *INS* elements. The element of competition remained open to judicial interpretation (*Waring*), and the element of labor and investment and the element of free-riding took precedence as courts considered claims of commercial immorality (*Uproar, Metropolitan Opera*). The element of time was not considered, and the element of harm was defined only in general free-riding terms, and not in terms of actual harm to the plaintiff.

The Broadcast of Sports Events

The unique character of sports events—live, unscripted action made available to the public by private organizations— combined with the new medium of radio to bring sports to many more fans. But the nature of such events on radio also created many more opportunities for others to use or pirate parts of the broadcast left unprotected by copyright. Such actions infuriated private sports organizations and their owners who financed and ran such events. Most courts were sympathetic to such misappropriation actions and in their decisions, found it easy to apply elements of misappropriation that found defendants liable.

In one of the earliest sports radio cases, *Twentieth Century Sporting Club, Inc. v. Transradio Press Service*,[38] the plaintiffs, who included NBC Radio, obtained the exclusive rights to broadcast a 1937 boxing match between Joe Louis and Thomas Farr at Yankee Stadium. On the night of the fight, Transradio Press, planned to provide "up-to-the minute descriptions" by "obtaining tips" from the NBC radio broadcast and "authenticate them by independent investigation by newsgathering representatives of defendants located at vantage points outside the stadium but within view of the bout."[39] Finding for the plaintiff, the court wrote that NBC and Transradio were competitors and that Transradio was poised to "derive profits from the exhibition without having expended any time, labor, and money for the presentation of such exhibition."[40] The court ruled that any rebroadcasting of the plaintiff's account would "fall within the prohibitions laid down by the United States Supreme Court in *International News Service v. Associated Press*."[41]

A year later in *Pittsburgh Athletic Co. v. KQV Broadcasting Co.*,[42] the owners of the Pittsburgh Pirates baseball team sought to restrain Pittsburgh radio station KQV from broadcasting play-by-play descriptions of Pirates games. KQV obtained live reports of the games by stationing reporters at vantage points above the walls of Forbes

Field, where the Pirates played. Pirates owners claimed the KQV reports harmed their relationship with local NBC radio affiliates that had paid considerable fees to carry Pirates' broadcasts. Following *INS*, *KVOS*, and *Transradio*, a U.S. district court ruled that the Pirates had a property right in the accounts and descriptions of its games, that KQV's actions were a "direct and irreparable interference with, and appropriation of, the plaintiffs' normal and legitimate business," and that the station deprived the Pirates of their labor and investment in the games.[43]

Both cases emphasized the element of labor and investment and the element of free-riding. In particular, the courts emphasized the proprietary nature of the contracts with NBC and the ability of the private sports organizations to negotiate assignment of their property rights in the description of the games. Neither case addressed the value of the reports in distributing minute-by-minute descriptions. In other words, the misappropriation element of time was not addressed.

These cases were different from *INS* in at least one other important respect. While the International News Service could have clearly gone out and covered war news on its own instead of taking such news from AP, the defendants in these cases were not able to gather such information because they were interested in "private events," and access was restricted. This made the plaintiffs' misappropriation rights that much more powerful; courts were more likely to punish accused pirates in these cases than not.

For example, the court in *National Exhibition Company v. Fass*[44] followed the *Transradio* and *Pittsburgh Athletic Co.* courts. In that case, the plaintiffs operated the New York Giants baseball team and sued the defendant, an independent sports reporter, for sending play-by-play descriptions of broadcast Giants games over Teletype. Fass claimed that such accounts were "news in the public domain," but the court ruled that Fass' actions greatly diminished the plaintiff's rights to accounts of the game and caused "great and irreparable loss, injury, and damage."[45] The court called the games "original and unique performances of highly skilled performers which are of great interest to the public and have commercial value to [the Giants] as the creator and exhibitor of the games and as licensor of rights to prepare and to radio broadcast and telecast descriptions and pictures of its games."[46] But unlike *Transradio* and *Pittsburgh Athletic Co.*, the court in this case considered the time element. It said that the commercial value of the broadcast accounts lasted for 24 hours after the completion of the game or "in unusually important or exciting games, such commercial value extends for years."[47]

In some cases, defendants attempted to draw a distinction between pirating the transmission as a whole and taking the transmission of the game and recreating the play-by-play action. In *Mutual Broadcasting System, Inc. v. Muzak Corporation*,[48] the plaintiff had exclusive rights to broadcast the 1941 World Series Games. Rather than create its own broadcast as the defendants did in *Transradio* and *Pittsburgh Athletic Co.*, or send accounts by teletype as Fass did in *National Exhibition Company*, the Muzak Corporation took Mutual's radio signal, broadcast it to its radio listeners, and claimed there was no misappropriation because it used Mutual's pure signal without "elimination, addition or alteration."[49] The court did not buy the difference. Citing *INS* and *KVOS*, it ruled that the Muzak Corporation had similarly invaded the plaintiff's right to control its accounts and descriptions of the game and its "large sums of money and laborious effort."[50]

The only sports broadcast decision to reject a finding of misappropriation during this time was *Loeb v. Turner*.[51] In that case, Howard Loeb, who owned KRIZ radio in Phoenix, sued A.L. Turner, who owned KLIF radio in Dallas, for recreating broadcast accounts of stock car auto races held in Phoenix. KLIF stationed outside the racecar track a reporter who listened to the KRIZ accounts and recreated the race for Dallas listeners. KRIZ, which had an exclusive arrangement to broadcast the races, claimed its broadcasts had been misappropriated. The court did not agree and ruled that KLIF was well within its rights to listen to the KRIZ broadcast and "inform his fellow agent in Dallas of the bare facts in abbreviated form." The court wrote:

> The actual happenings of each day, including sporting events, become part of the facts of history immediately upon their happening. News of them cannot be copyrighted; nor, so far as the public is concerned, can the news itself become the subject of a property right belonging exclusively to any person. To hold otherwise would be to contravene our constitutional guaranty of freedom of speech and freedom of press.[52]

The court also noted that there was no competition between the two stations due to the distance between them.

Throughout the sports radio cases of this period, the element of labor and investment and the element of free-riding were most often cited as key to a finding of misappropriation. While the elements of time and competition were sometimes mentioned, greater emphasis was placed on the ethics of the defendant's actions and his free-riding on the plaintiff's exclusive contracts. As with the broadcast performance and sound recording cases, the sports broadcasts lacked the protection of copyright, and misappropriation became the tool by which plaintiffs could seek redress. Unlike the sound recording or newspaper cases, however, the sports broadcast cases involved awarding the exclusive rights to accounts of the games to various broadcast outlets. This boosted the value of these events and made a finding of misappropriation much more likely.

Thus, during the first post-*INS* period, the misappropriation or "hot news" doctrine served two important roles. First, it plugged gaps in copyright law, which did not yet address the development and growth of radio and award additional rights to creators whose works were broadcasted. Secondly, by plugging the gaps, it brought attention to copyright law, which led to the introduction of some forms of licensing and later, the copyright protection of recorded broadcasts.[53]

While lower courts claimed to follow *INS*, the elements of the doctrine during this period were left unclear enough by the Supreme Court for lower courts to interpret them more broadly or ignore some elements altogether. Overall, the element of labor and investment and the element of free-riding were significantly emphasized during this time and were expanded to include notions of "commercial immorality." The element of time was not often addressed. The element of competition was, on the whole, interpreted more broadly to include competition for the same advertising dollars rather than direct competition between the plaintiff and defendants' businesses. Finally, the element of harm was often linked to the degree of free-riding and the element of labor and investment; few courts, with exception of the Supreme Court in *KVOS*, required concrete evidence of the harm suffered.

Overall, the elements of misappropriation were molded to fit the need: the new technology of radio made piracy easier and the legislature had yet to catch up to the needs of those producing content for radio. Thus, the courts were asked to intervene. The acute struggles in radio did catch Congress' attention, but it took more than 40 years for Congress to rewrite the Copyright Act to address some of the unique challenges posed by radio and other new technologies, including television and cable.

REWRITING COPYRIGHT LAW AND QUESTIONS ABOUT MISAPPROPRIATION (1960s – 1976)

Since the 1920s, Congress attempted to rewrite copyright law as authors and composers who created works using new technologies demanded rights that the 1909 Copyright Act did not provide.[54] Efforts to revise copyright law began with proposals to abolish notice and registration and a movement by the motion picture industry to abolish ASCAP, the American Society of Composers, Authors and Publishers, the organization that helped musicians receive licensing fees for the broadcast of their music on the radio.[55] From the mid-1920s through the late 1940s, authors, librarians, musicians, motion picture producers, and others lobbied Congress to reform copyright and consider their interests. None was successful with Congress, and when the Second World War began, interest in copyright reform petered out.[56] After the War, copyright "remained frozen in the form it had taken" after the 1909 Act. Professor Jessica Litman described the chaos in copyright that emerged after the War:

> Where the copyright statute failed to accommodate the realities faced by affected industries, the industries devised expedients, exploited loopholes, and negotiated agreements that superseded statutory provisions. The broadcast industry formed its own performing rights society to compete with ASCAP. . . . Live or videotaped television programs, radio programs, and phonograph records were deemed uncopyrightable. . . . The motion picture industry established an ASCAP-like operation to deal with unauthorized exhibition of films. . . . New technological uses waited in the wings. Cable television, xerographic photocopying, and digital computers were all invented in the 1940s. It was difficult to figure out what provisions of the copyright law would apply to the new technologies and what effects the technologies would have on the copyright law.[57]

In 1956, Congress appointed a special committee of experts to look into the conflicts. It took six years for the experts to write their report and another five years of conferences to produce a bill that addressed the recommendations.[58] Congress itself took another eleven years to debate the bill, which finally passed as the 1976 Copyright Act.[59]

In addition to changes in the federal statute, copyright and unfair competition law also underwent significant changes in the courts. Three major Supreme Court rulings affected copyright and unfair competition during this period, and subsequently affected the growth and application of misappropriation. In *Erie Railroad Co. v. Tompkins*,[60] the U.S. Supreme Court ended federal common law. The Court ruled that only states could write common law. In *Erie*, the Court grappled with the proliferation of diversity of citizenship actions that arose as a way for litigating parties to escape the confines of state law. At the time, federal courts were free to exercise independent judgment and were not required to follow the laws of the state in which the case arose. Justice Louis Brandeis in *Erie* ruled that this was wrong:

> Except in matters governed by the Federal Constitution or by acts of Congress, the law to be applied in any case is the law of the state. And whether the law of the state shall be declared by its Legislature in a statute or by its highest court in a decision is not a matter of federal concern. There is no federal common law.[61]

Erie threw many common law doctrines of federal courts, including the Supreme Court, into question. After *Erie*, state courts were forced to reexamine federal common law, and since *Erie*, the misappropriation doctrine, as articulated by the Supreme Court in *INS v. AP*, has been reexamined. Thus, though it began as federal common law, the misappropriation doctrine is now state common law and has been officially accepted by fourteen states.[62]

The other major Supreme Court cases of this period to affect interpretation of the misappropriation doctrine were *Sears Roebuck & Co. v. Stiffel Co.*[63] and *Compco Corp. v. Daybright Lighting, Inc.*,[64] otherwise known as the *Sears/Compco* decisions. In *Sears*, Sears manufactured a pole lamp that copied an unpatentable lamp made by Stiffel, and Sears sold its lamp at a lower price. The lower courts found Sears guilty of unfair competition, but the U.S. Supreme Court held that state courts could not grant patent-like protection for items that under the federal patent law were not patentable. In *Compco*, Compco manufactured a fluorescent lighting fixture that was identical to one made by Day-Brite. Like Stiffel, Day-Brite's fixture was not patentable under federal law. The Court ruled that Compco could not recover damages from Day-Brite. In both cases, the Court said the states' unfair competition laws conflicted with federal patent law. The Court wrote:

> To allow a State by use of its law of unfair competition to prevent the copying of an article which represents too slight an advance to be patented would be to permit the State to block off from the public something which federal law has said belongs to the public. The result would be that ... States could allow perpetual protection to articles too lacking in novelty to merit any patent at all under federal constitutional standards.[65]

The *Sears/Compco* decisions threw the constitutionality of state unfair competition law into question. Did states have any right to create intellectual property or unfair competition law after these decisions, or was any work not protected by federal law automatically part of the public domain? Did *Sears/Compco* nullify the misappropriation doctrine? It would take another ten years before the Court would answer that question in *Goldstein v. California*[66] and another twelve years before Congress would directly address the issue in the 1976 Copyright Act. In the meantime, courts grappled with interpreting *Sears/Compco*, the role of state unfair competition law, and the advent of new technologies, most especially the introduction of cable television and recording by tape.[67]

The Cable Television Cases

Cable television emerged in the late 1950s as a means to bring over-the-air television programming to remote areas that could not receive broadcast antenna signals. Cable operators set up large microwave antennas that picked up the broadcast signals and then transferred those signals into coaxial cable and delivered them to homes that were connected by wire. Early on, cable operators set up their antennas to capture over-the-air signals without permission of local broadcasters or network affiliates, leading to several misappropriation cases in the early 1960s.

The first reported cable misappropriation case was *Intermountain Broadcasting v. Idaho Microwave, Inc.*[68] The plaintiffs, who ran KSL-TV and KUTV in Salt Lake City, arranged with KLIX-TV in Twin Falls, Idaho, about 200 miles away, to pick up broadcasts of both stations for rebroadcast in the Twin Falls area. The defendant, Cable Vision, captured the KLIX-TV signal by antenna and sent that station's programming to its customers linked by cable wire. Plaintiffs KSL-TV and KUTV sued Cable Vision for picking up their signals without consent. Without copyright protection or any other protection for their broadcast signals, the plaintiffs pursued a misappropriation claim against Cable Vision. Because INS took and rewrote portions of AP's news and did steal AP's reports in their entirety, Cable Vision argued the signal it took was *copied* in whole and was not "recreated," and thus, was not *misappropriated* in any way.

The court in *Intermountain* ruled that between the Salt Lake television stations and Cable Vision there was no "solid base" to a misappropriation claim. Following *Erie*, the court in the case said Idaho law had embraced an expanded view of unfair competition to include misappropriation, but hesitated to extend *INS* to the facts in the case. The court said the plaintiffs were not competitors. They did not engage "in the same kind of business" and operated "in different ways for different purposes."[69] Furthermore, the court said Cable Vision's actions did not cause damage to the Salt Lake stations; Cable Vision did not interfere with the plaintiff's profit. Lastly, in one of the few cases prior to *NBA v. Motorola* to note that INS hurt AP by publishing AP news in advance of the AP's own distribution, the court said no time factor was involved in the current case: "Defendants' microwave and cable relay plaintiffs' broadcasts to reception sets for appearance thereon, not only in the same manner, but at the same time as was intended by plaintiffs themselves."[70] The court also accepted Cable Vision's argument that copying an uncopyrightable cablecast in its entirety was not misappropriation.

A year later, the broadcasters in the Salt Lake-Twin Falls area challenged that conclusion. In *Cable Vision, Inc. v. KUTV Inc.*,[71] the defendant, KUTV, which owned KLIX-TV in Twin Falls, counterclaimed that it had rights to the first run of network programs in the Twin Falls area and that Cable Vision misappropriated those rights by taking its signal. This time, the court ruled in favor of the broadcast station. The court said the case was comparable to *INS* in that the defendant and plaintiff were competitors and the cable antenna reaped the broadcast station's profit and its investment in network programming.[72] There was no specific discussion about the degree of harm inflicted or any time element. The emphasized elements in this case were KUTV's labor and investment and Cable Vision's free-riding. Without the benefit of either copyright protection or some FCC rule regulating cable's use of a broadcast signal, the court was easily compelled to award some protection to the broadcaster.

The Ninth Circuit vacated the decision of the district court shortly after the U.S. Supreme Court had ruled in the *Sears/Compco* cases.[73] The Ninth Circuit concluded that that *Sears/Compco* precluded a misappropriation claim in the case. The court said KUTV could not use its programming contract with the networks to "bootstrap into existence rights from subject matter which at their source lie in the public domain."[74] Following the spirit of *Sears/Compco*, the court said it was up to Congress to decide what rights should or should not be awarded.[75]

In the final cable misappropriation case of this period, *Herald Publishing Co. v. Florida Antennavision, Inc.*,[76] Herald Publishing, which owned broadcast facilities in Panama City, Florida, sued cable provider Florida Antennavision for picking up its broadcast signal and sending it to Antennavision subscribers. The court did not consider *Sears/Compco* in its decision. It ruled that there was no misappropriation because there was no competition between Herald Publishing and Antennavision. The court wrote that Antennavision "merely passes on to its subscribers the television programs it receives on its antenna from the air waves which are in the public domain and available for anyone with a sufficiently equipped antenna to receive and enjoy."[77]

Thus, courts in the misappropriation cable cases of this period were, on the whole, reluctant to extend misappropriation rights to broadcasters whose signal had been picked up by cable operators. Courts in these cases used other elements in addition to the element of labor and investment and the element of free-riding to thwart misappropriation claims, particularly the elements of time and competition to dismiss misappropriation claims. The Supreme Court was eventually forced to consider the problem of cable retransmission of broadcasts in two cases that pitted programmers who owned copyrights in the shows they produced against cable operators. In *United Artists v. Fortnightly*[78] and *Teleprompter Corporation v. CBS*,[79] the Supreme Court found that cable operators did not infringe on programmers' copyrights because they did not "perform" their works, but rather, they passively received and transmitted them. Congress then stepped in and addressed broadcast industry concerns in the 1976 Copyright Act. The Act overturned the Supreme Court decisions by giving copyright protection to broadcast transmissions, but the Act also ensured that cable operators could obtain reasonably priced cable licenses.[80] In this way, misappropriation indirectly helped to serve as fuel for changes in copyright law.

The Tape Recording Cases

The advent of tape recording technology forced both the courts and the legislatures to attempt to resolve some of the struggles over application of the misappropriation doctrine and the extent to which courts could award intellectual property rights not defined by Congress. Between 1969 and 1975, thirteen "tape piracy" decisions related to the misappropriation doctrine were handed down, including one case, *Goldstein v. California*, that was decided by the U.S. Supreme Court. Of those thirteen decisions, ten favored a finding of misappropriation or supported state laws against tape piracy;[81] three did not.[82] The tape piracy cases contributed to one of the most active and expansive periods for use of the misappropriation doctrine, and like the cable cases, resulted in changes to the law.

The typical tape piracy case involved a record company whose phonographic recordings had been transferred onto magnetic tape and sold more cheaply than the record. Although piracy of recordings had been around for some time — the industry had lobbied for protections as early as 1906 — the introduction of the "relatively inexpensive and efficient tape recorder" made pirating records easier than ever.[83] It was estimated that in 1969 alone, tape pirates sold $100 million in unauthorized tape recordings.[84]

The courts were more sympathetic to the recording industry's war against the tape pirates than they were to the broadcasters' crusade against cable companies. Without the protection of copyright, sound recordings were left vulnerable to independent operators looking to profit from popular recordings using tape technology. As in the cable cases, *Sears/Compco* compounded the problem. Courts in the tape piracy cases struggled with whether the misappropriation doctrine was still viable after *Sears/Compco*. If *Sears/Compco* had abolished state causes of action like misappropriation, it would be very difficult for the recording industry to battle the tape pirates, short of some legislative action. As it turned out, both the judicial and legislative branches came to the recording industry's rescue.

First, courts quickly found ways around *Sears/Compco*. Courts looking to protect the recording industry saw a distinction between "copying" or "recreation" and wholesale "appropriation." The distinction was hair-splitting and akin to the difference between imitating the essence of a work and copying the work verbatim. *Sears/Compco*, these courts argued, forbid only state law that restricted copying, not the wholesale "appropriation" of works in their entirety. Thus, such state misappropriation claims involving wholesale "appropriation" could withstand the *Sears/Compco*.

In the tape piracy decisions, courts favoring a finding of misappropriation argued that defendants were "appropriating" sound recordings —taking such works without adaptation and not merely "copying" them. This reasoning allowed courts to steer clear of federal law conflicts. Among the tape piracy cases to articulate this view of *Sears/Compco* was *Liberty v. Eastern Tape*,[85] a North Carolina case in which the defendants were accused of pirating the recordings of bands such as "Sugarloaf" and "Canned Heat." The court said:

> Defendants here are not copying a design or concept. They have not obtained the same artist to record the same song in an identical manner. This type of "copying" would presumably be protected by the decisions of Sears and Compco. Conduct of that sort, however, is a far cry from appropriating, for use in competition with the plaintiff, the very product which plaintiff produced with its own resources.[86]

Similar reasoning dismissing *Sears/Compco* was articulated in *Capitol Records v. Spies*,[87] *Capitol Records v. Erickson*,[88] *CBS v. Custom Recording Company*,[89] and *Tape Industries Association of America v. Younger*.[90] In that last case, the court wrote:

> Plaintiffs in the instant case do not imitate the product of the record companies. They actually take and appropriate the product itself — the sounds recorded on the albums — and

commercially exploit the product. Sears and Compco would cover and immunize the plaintiffs [the Tape Industries, in this case] here only if they had copied and imitated the product — that is, if they had listened to the sounds performed and embodied on the records and then had expended the necessary sums to copy and imitate the sounds on their own tapes.[91]

Only two decisions in the study, *International Tape Manufacturers Ass'n v. Gerstein*[92] and *CBS v. Melody Recordings*,[93] rejected this reasoning. In *CBS*, the court wrote:

> While some courts, as indicated, have found a distinction between the copying of an unpatented design and the exact duplication of a recorded musical composition, I find such distinction to be conceptually meaningless. There is absolutely no difference in the end result when Sears makes a mold from a lamp pole designed and produced at great expense by Stiffel or when a so-called "pirate" makes an exact duplicate of a recording produced at great expense by CBS. Although the means may differ, the end result is exactly the same.[94]

In these cases, the courts saw *Sears/Compco* as controlling and found that tape misappropriation claims were invalid because they conflicted with federal law as interpreted by the Supreme Court.

The legislatures responded. In Florida and California, state laws were passed protecting the recording industry from tape piracy. A 1971 Florida statute prohibited the knowing and willful transfer of "any sounds recorded on a phonograph record, disc, wire, tape, film or other article on which sounds are recorded, with the intent to sell or cause to be sold for profit, such article on which sounds are so transferred."[95] The California statute was similarly worded.[96] The Florida statute was struck down in *Tape Industries* in light of the Supreme Court's ruling in *Sears/Compco*, but the California statute against tape piracy was upheld by the Appellate Department of the Superior Court of California. The defendants in that case appealed to the U.S. Supreme Court. In *Goldstein v. California*,[97] the Court ruled 5-4 to uphold the California statute. The Court said that the statute did not violate federal copyright law because the states were permitted to draft laws in areas in which it was clear that Congress had not acted. In discussing the application of *Sears/Compco* to *Goldstein*, the Court drew a distinction between the way Congress drafted patent laws (at issue in *Sears/Compco*) and the way it had drafted copyright laws related to sound recordings:

> The standards established for granting federal patent protection to machines thus indicated not only which articles in this particular category Congress wished to protect, but which configurations it wished to remain free. The application of state law in these cases [Sears/Compco] to prevent the copying of articles which did not meet the requirements for federal protection disturbed the careful balance which Congress had drawn. . . . *No comparable conflict between state law and federal law arises in the case of recordings of musical performances*. In regard to this category of "Writings," Congress has drawn no balance; rather, it has left the area unattended, and no reason exists why the State should not be free to act (emphasis added).[98]

Thus, *Goldstein* resolved the question of whether the misappropriation doctrine had been abolished by *Sears/Compco*. The answer: It had not.

The U.S. Congress also responded to the growth of tape piracy. In 1971, Congress passed an amendment to copyright law, awarding copyright protections to sound recordings. The law became effective for records made after Feb. 15, 1972. Thus, after 1972, two copyrights in music existed: the composer owned one copyright, which covered the making, distribution, or public performance of the song. The second copyright covered the recording, which was owned by the music publisher, and covered the distribution of that particular recording.[99]

Thus, the misappropriation cases of this period encouraged legislation that protected record publishers, because of some of the uncertainties surrounding the doctrine after *Sears/Compco*. In the courts, the focus during this period was more on the doctrine's continued viability, rather than on its specific elements, although throughout this period, courts most often cited the doctrine's elements of labor and investment, free-riding, harm, and competition. Not surprisingly, the element of time sensitivity was least mentioned. There was virtually no time sensitivity connected with the piracy of sound recordings.

Interestingly, the only tape piracy case in the study to address the time element was *Mercury Record v. Economic Consultants*.[100] In that case, the court acknowledged the *INS* time element; that is, the *INS* Court had awarded a limited property right in published news for the short period in which the news had value. But the *Mercury* court said the practical result of this ruling was that AP maintained a much longer right in the news. Indeed, the *INS* court never defined exactly when the value was lost. Thus, the *Mercury* court wrote that a similar injunction against tape pirates "need only be maintained until the commercial value of the recording to the plaintiffs is reduced to substantially zero."[101] Here, the issue was not the time sensitivity of sound recordings, but the commercial value of the appropriated recordings over time.

Finally, the U.S. Supreme Court's decision in *Goldstein* put fears to rest that misappropriation had been abolished. The doctrine survived and continued to encourage legislation that expanded copyright law. But questions about its specific elements would resurface and problems with interpretations of *INS* would still linger.

Other Cases of the Period

Other misappropriation cases of this period ranged from the taking of ads to the pirating of comic strips, with the doctrine of commercial immorality still followed by some courts.[102] News piracy cases involving misappropriation were still prevalent at this time, although not as prevalent as the theft of sound recordings and cable signals. Therefore, it is difficult to draw any broad conclusions about the evolution of the *INS* elements in these cases.

One of the most cited news piracy cases of this period was *Pottstown Daily News v. Pottstown Broadcasting*.[103] The facts in this case were similar to those in *Associated Press* v. *KVOS*. The *Pottstown Mercury* newspaper sued WPAZ, a local radio station, for reading newspaper stories on the air. The Pennsylvania Supreme Court upheld the paper's misappropriation claim. The court said the paper and radio station were competitors by virtue of their similar advertisers, and the court "jealously protected" any attempts to stifle competition:

> [N]o court can fail to take note of the fact that newspapers, radio and television stations compete with each other for advertising which has become a giant in our economy. In fact,

the presentation of news and entertainment has become almost a subsidiary function of newspapers, radio and television stations. Advertising is the life-blood of newspapers, radio and television and the presentation of news by all three media is a service designed to attract advertisers.[104]

This decision helped to solidify the notion that newspapers and broadcasters were competitors in the context of a misappropriation case involving the use of printed news on the radio.

Another noteworthy decision of this period, *Independent News v. Williams*,[105] raised some interesting questions about those who are contractually involved in a piracy scheme, as the *Cleveland News* was in *INS*. In *INS*, the AP had a contract with the *Cleveland News* that prohibited it from sharing news from competitors like INS. But the *INS* decisions did not focus on the *Cleveland News'* liability in contributing to the piracy; the focus, instead, was on the actions of *INS* and its employee who paid a *Cleveland News* employee to hand over AP news. In *Independent News*, a second-hand periodical dealer purchased old coverless comics from a waste dealer who acquired the comics from a wholesaler that had an agreement with the publisher to destroy the comics. The waste dealer was unaware of the agreement. The second-hand periodical dealer, Harry Williams, sold the coverless comics from Independent News, the publisher, at a reduced price. Independent News sued Williams for misappropriation. The district court ruled that there was no misappropriation because Williams purchased his copies from the waste dealer; he did not pirate them.[106] Furthermore, the court said the sale of return copies of comics had been going on for twenty years, and it was not the court's function "to invade the free enterprise system unless the law *clearly* directs."[107]

On appeal to the Third Circuit, the court affirmed the district court's decision, writing that Independent News had failed to enforce its contractual provision with the wholesaler, and therefore, Williams was free to purchase the books from the waste dealer. However, unlike *INS*, the defendant in *Independent* did not aid in the breach of contract between the plaintiffs and their wholesalers. Despite some factual differences, the comparison of *INS* to *Independent* raises questions about the extent to which the plaintiff is responsible for control of his news or publications and the extent to which he is responsible for contracts he initiates prohibiting reuse of his product. At the very least, a plaintiff who knows its contracted parties have failed to live up to their agreement to protect the plaintiff's content can pursue a contract claim against that party.

NEW LAW, NEW TECHNOLOGIES, AND NARROWING MISAPPROPRIATION (1976 – 1996)

In 1976, Congress passed a new federal copyright law that became effective in 1978. The new law attempted to do what the 1909 Copyright Act did not, which was to more effectively award protections to developing technologies. Rather than protect only categories of works, the new law protected any "original work fixed in a tangible medium of expression."[108] Furthermore, the new law no longer required registration for a work to receive copyright protection; original works were protected from the moment they were fixed. Facts, processes, and systems were explicitly ineligible for protection.[109] It was thought the Act's new language would make it simpler for new technologies to receive the protections of copyright:

> Under the [Act] it makes no difference what the form, manner, or medium of fixation may be — whether it is words, numbers, notes, sounds, pictures, or any other graphic or symbolic indicia, whether embodied in a physical object in written, printed, photographic, sculptural, punched, magnetic, or any other stable form, and whether it is capable of perception directly or by means of any machine or device "now known or later developed."[110]

Thus, Congress attempted to introduce in statute some of what the common law doctrine of misappropriation had for 58 years tried to provide — a means by which creators could claim property rights in works that didn't fit the traditional boundaries of copyright. Some scholars, however, have argued that the 1976 Copyright Act did not resolve this problem. Professor Jessica Litman has argued that the act was actually more specific than it should have been, catered to special interests more than it should have, and resulted in many more amendments and exceptions.[111]

Within the new Copyright Act, Congress addressed concerns regarding state versus federal protection of various works by summarizing in statute form the combined principles of *Sears/Compco* and *Goldstein*. In section 301 of the Act, the "preemption" section, Congress prohibited the states from enacting "legal or equitable rights that are equivalent to any of the exclusive rights within the general scope of copyright. . . and come within the subject matter of copyright."[112] Simply stated, no state law can substitute rights that the law of federal copyright already addresses. Thus, states are permitted to act in areas where Congress has not acted, but interpreting what these areas are has not proven easy for courts.

In misappropriation decisions since 1976, the first issue addressed by courts under preemption has been whether such claims come within the "subject matter" and "general scope" of the laws of copyright. If the claims do, they are preempted, and the courts will not normally consider the merits of the misappropriation/hot news claim. If the claims fail to come within the subject matter or general scope of copyright, the claims will stand, and courts will consider the merits of the claims.

The congressional record on preemption demonstrated that lawmakers believed in the survival of limited state misappropriation claims in the spirit of *INS*. A House Report in 1976 stated:

> Misappropriation is not necessarily synonymous with copyright infringement, and thus a cause of action labeled as misappropriation is not preempted if it is in fact based neither on a right within the general scope of copyright . . . nor on a right equivalent thereto. For example, state law should have the flexibility to afford a remedy (under traditional principles of equity) against a consistent pattern of unauthorized appropriation by a competitor of the facts (i.e., not the literary expression) constituting "hot" news, whether in the traditional mold of International News Service v. Associated Press (citation omitted) or in the newer form of data updates from scientific, business, or financial data bases.[113]

Although it appeared Congress intended for *INS*-type claims to survive preemption, the focus on preemption in misappropriation cases after 1976 made for substantially fewer successful misappropriation claims overall. In 40 misappropriation decisions examined from 1976 to 1996, only eleven decisions favored a finding of misappropriation.[114] Preemption was a significant deterrent, whether it was addressed directly or not. Thus, the scope of misappropriation narrowed after passage of the 1976 Copyright Act and the introduction of the preemption section.

The range of subject matter addressed in misappropriation cases between 1976 and 1996 varied greatly, but the most interesting new application of misappropriation was in cases that involved the piracy of large factual computer databases and stock listings. Courts in these cases struggled to reconcile the need to protect the investment in these works with the legal requirement that facts and data be left open to reuse. Furthermore, courts during this period began to demand greater similarity between the facts of these new cases and the facts in *INS* and the elements the Court cited in *INS* for misappropriation. The doctrine of commercial immorality, an expansion of the misappropriation doctrine, became increasingly less accepted. Thus, the courts began to reverse the expansion of misappropriation that they had begun in the 1930s.

Stocks, Databases, and the "Extra Element"

One of the most fundamental principles reinforced in the new copyright law was the idea that facts, ideas, systems, and processes were ineligible for copyright protection.[115] As computer technology improved during the 1980s and 1990s, it was soon apparent that machines could provide complex, commercially valuable tools and databases to customers using such unprotectible facts and data. Businessmen, scientists, retailers and others all benefited from the computer's ability to take large quantities of information and compile them in useful ways. But these same groups struggled with how to provide such valuable products profitably if the components of such products were ineligible for protection and could be freely reused or pirated.

During the 1980s, computerized stock listings, in particular, made the piracy of stock listings easier than ever. As a result, stock listings reemerged as a source of misappropriation battles, much as they were a source of contention prior to *INS* in the "ticker cases." A number of courts sought to protect such data from being misappropriated, but no clear consensus emerged on a rationale for it.

In *Standard & Poor's Corp. v. Commodity Exchange*,[116] the Commodity Exchange or "Comex" sought a license to use Standard &

Poor's 500 Index, a measure of the performance of 500 common stocks. When Standard & Poor's chose to license a Comex competitor instead, Comex decided to create its own S&P 500 Index called the "Comex 500 Index," which essentially duplicated the S&P 500. Standard & Poor's sued Comex for misappropriation, among other claims. The Second Circuit concluded that though the data were unprotected by copyright, Standard & Poor's expended significant labor and expense in producing the index, that it competed with Comex, and that trading volume would be adversely affected by the Comex index.[117] In ruling for the plaintiffs, the court did not consider the *INS* element of time in its decision.

Similar protections were awarded in *Board of Trade v. Dow Jones & Co.*[118] In that case, Dow Jones rejected a proposal from the Board of Trade (BOT) to use the Dow Jones Industrial Average to construct an index for new futures contracts. The Board of Trade proceeded anyway and planned to use the Dow Jones Industrial Average to formulate the Board of Trade Stock Market Index. An Illinois appeals court ruled that although the two parties were not direct competitors and the Board of Trade had planned to invest its own time and labor into its new index, the new index was not different from the Dow Jones Industrial Average and represented a misappropriation of Dow Jones' property right.[119] On appeal, the BOT argued that competition and harm —two traditionally necessary elements for misappropriation — were not present in the case. The court ruled that although the BOT's index might cause Dow Jones to lose prospective licensing revenue, such reasoning was "correct" but "circular."[120] Instead, the court introduced its own "public interest" element and ruled that whatever harm awarding a property right to Dow Jones might cause was overshadowed by the "infinite number of stock market indexes which could be devised" if the BOT was prohibited from using Dow Jones property:

> We conclude that the possibility of any detriment to the public which might result from our holding that [Dow Jones'] indexes and average may not be used without its consent in the manner proposed by [the BOT] are outweighed by the resultant encouragement to develop new indexes specifically designed for the purpose of hedging against the "systematic" risk present in the stock market.[121]

In contrast, a U.S. district court in *Financial Information v. Moody's Investors Service*[122] ruled that Financial Information, Inc. (FII) had failed to show competition or harm in its case against Moody's, which it accused of commercial immorality by pirating its municipal and corporate bond reporting service. On appeal, the Second Circuit went one step further and ruled that copyright law preempted the claim.[123] The claim, the court ruled, was equivalent to the exclusive rights provided by the copyright.[124] In its decision, the court began a gradual retreat from the doctrine of commercial immorality, ruling that such a claim did not survive preemption. The Second Circuit also began to limit application of *INS* by reintroducing the importance of the *INS* time element. The court ruled that the bond data from Financial Information was not "hot" and therefore was not misappropriation:

> FII proved neither the quantity of copying nor the immediacy of distribution necessary to sustain a "hot" news claim. Because of lead times, to the extent that Moody's did copy from FII, the information it published would have been at least ten days old. The "hot" news doctrine is concerned with the copying and publication of information gathered by another before he has been able to utilize his competitive edge. We hold that FII failed to prove such a claim here.[125]

The decision represented a significant retreat from the expansion of the misappropriation doctrine, and the element of time in *INS* distinguished this decision from past decisions of the Second Circuit.

In a 9-0 decision in 1991, the U.S. Supreme Court indirectly weighed in on the viability of the misappropriation doctrine. In *Feist v. Rural Telephone*,[126] the Court ruled that originality was a constitutional requirement for copyrighted works and that facts must left open to reuse.[127] Feist specialized in the publication of large, regional phone directories. When it decided to produce a directory for northwest Kansas, it approached eleven telephone companies, including Rural, to buy their white page listings. All agreed to license their listings to Feist except for Rural. Without Rural's listings, Feist's new directory would be incomplete. So, Feist proceeded to publish nearly 5,000 of Rural's listings without permission. Rural sued for copyright infringement. While the case most directly dealt with copyright law, it affected misappropriation cases because it reinforced the notion that individual facts or data — in this case, Feist's individual listings — could not be owned. The Court, in ruling for Feist, said:

> This is because facts do not owe their origin to an act of authorship. The distinction is one between creation and discovery: The first person to find and report a particular fact has not created the fact; he or she has merely discovered its existence. . . . The same is true of all facts — scientific, historical, biographical, and news of the day. "They may not be copyrighted and are part of the public domain available to every person."[128]

The Court did not address the viability of the misappropriation doctrine as an alternate means of protecting the listings. It mentioned that *INS* reinforced the notion that "news matter" could not be copyrighted, but it chose not to explore the relationship between the *INS* Court's doctrine of misappropriation and the new ruling in *Feist*. Justice Sandra Day O'Connor wrote about *INS* doctrine in a footnote: "The Court ultimately rendered judgment for Associated Press on non-copyright grounds that are not relevant here."[129]

Thus, *Feist* stood for either one of two interpretations in the context of misappropriation cases. One interpretation was that the Court did not abolish the doctrine of misappropriation when it might have, so it was still a viable tort. The other interpretation was that *Feist* reinforced the notion that fact-based works have no or very thin protection; thus, any application of the misappropriation doctrine must be used sparingly. Indeed, *Feist* seems to have influenced the latter trend, and most decisions against a misappropriation claim cite *Feist* to remind creators that fact-based works receive thin, if any, protection.

The combination of *Feist* and copyright preemption presented a new and formidable hurdle for misappropriation claims. But the doctrine would survive with the introduction of new technologies and the ease with which facts and information could be easily pirated using these new technologies. While courts were extremely careful to work within the boundaries of *Feist* and preemption, the sentiment was that some property protection must remain for the producers of complex, largely factual computer databases and products. Misappropriation would serve that end.

For a misappropriation claim to withstand preemption, courts began to require an "extra element." The phrase originated with Professor Melville Nimmer in his treatise on copyright law. Nimmer wrote:

> [A] right which is "equivalent to copyright" is one which is infringed by the mere act of reproduction, performance, distribution or display, . . . will in itself infringe the state created right, then such right is preempted. But if other elements are required, in addition to or instead of, the acts of reproduction, performance, distribution or display, in order to constitute a state created cause of action, then the right does not lie "within the general scope of copyright," and there is no preemption.[130]

Not surprisingly, defining an "extra element" was (and is) largely open to judicial interpretation. But since the 1980s, courts have ruled that state law contracts, some state unfair competition statutes, and breaches of trust have met the extra element test, allowing various state claims to survive preemption.[131] For misappropriation claims, the key question became what, if any, aspects of the doctrine exemplified an extra element that allowed such claims to survive preemption.

Commercial immorality, courts increasingly decided, was not an "extra element" that allowed a misappropriation claim to stand. Although in 1982 the Second Circuit still supported use of commercial immorality, by 1985, the U.S. District Court for the Southern District of New York was deciding it was too broadly constructed to survive preemption. In *Mayer v. Josiah Wedgwood & Sons, Ltd.*,[132] Sandra Mayer, an artist who created snowflake designs for Christmas ornaments, sued Wedgwood, maker of the famous brand china. Mayer claimed that Wedgwood misappropriated a snowflake design she presented to Wedgwood that it rejected. In response to Mayer's argument that Wedgwood's actions were commercially immoral and therefore survived preemption, the court wrote:

> [I]t is hard to see how [commercial immorality] is an extra element. In this case, the alleged misappropriation of Mayer's talent and effort is by the reproduction of the product of her time, talent, effort, i.e. the snowflake design. That is precisely the type of misconduct the copyright laws are designed to

guard against. To call such conduct immoral adds nothing. "Commercial immorality" appears to be merely a judgmental label attached to odious business conduct, not an extra element.[133]

The same court ruled similarly a year later in *Universal City Studios v. The T-Shirt Gallery*.[134] In that case, a T-shirt business was accused of misappropriating aspects of the television program *Miami Vice* for use on T-shirts. The court ruled the claim was preempted because the TV program came within the subject matter and scope of copyright. The court said "commercial immorality" was not an extra element that allowed the claim to withstand preemption: "To hold otherwise would allow the state to provide a cause of action for the same conduct which may be protected under federal copyright laws, merely because the state deems the conduct 'unfair' or 'immoral.'"[135]

In contrast, courts have found that rights created by contract are "extra elements" that do survive preemption.[136] For example, in *ProCD v. Zeidenberg*,[137] the Seventh Circuit ruled that a shrinkwrap agreement prohibiting the reuse of more than 95 million residential and commercial listings survived preemption. ProCD sued Matthew Zeidenberg for taking its listings and redistributing them on the Internet. In the case, the court ruled that copyright law "is a right against the world" and contracts "affect only their parties" and do not create "exclusive rights."[138] Therefore, contracts do not come within the general scope of copyright and are an extra element that survives preemption.

Thus, in cases involving stock listings and factual databases, courts have devised ways to entertain misappropriation claims despite limitations imposed by the preemption section of copyright law and the Supreme Court's decision in *Feist*. The introduction of the "extra element" enabled such claims to withstand preemption; but defining and understanding the nature of such "extra elements" has not been simple. In addition, courts in these cases demonstrated continued variation in their application of the traditional elements of a misappropriation claim. The element of labor and investment and the element of free-riding remained important, although courts began to raise more questions about the elements of time and competition. The Second Circuit began a gradual retreat from the more expansive notions of "commercial immorality," ruling in *Financial Information* that the time element in the hot news doctrine was more important than precedent had indicated.

News and Sports Information

Decisions involving the misappropriation of news and sports information during this period are interestingly few and far between. These decisions, too, indicated a gradual retreat from the more expansive interpretations of the doctrine. In *Gannett v. Rock Valley Community Press*,[139] the *Rockford Register Star*, a Gannett-owned newspaper, sued the owner of several free weekly "shoppers" in the Rockford, Illinois, area for misappropriating "news matter" from the *Register Star*. Gannett argued that the news was "sufficiently hot" and therefore was an "extra element" that survived preemption. A U.S. district court ruled that the claim was preempted. The court distinguished the case from *INS* by writing:

> [T]he driving force in the International News opinion was the need to provide an equitable remedy to protect one news agency's quasi-property interest in factual news from unauthorized use by a competitor where no alternative remedy was available. Such is not the case here where plaintiff has as potential remedies at the very least copyright claims and Lanham Act claims, if not a claim under the Deceptive Trade Practices Act.[140]

Furthermore, the court said Rock Valley did nothing to interfere with Gannett's right to publish timely, fresh news because the evidence showed that Rock Valley used the news matter *after* Gannett had published it. In a footnote, the court said that Gannett did not offer evidence that readers would turn away from its publication in favor of the weekly shoppers.[141]

In *NFL v. Governor of the State of Delaware*[142] and *USGA v. St. Andrews Systems*,[143] courts denied claims for the misappropriation of sports information because such actions painted "too broad a brush."[144] In *NFL*, the state of Delaware announced a plan to create a lottery based on NFL scores. The NFL objected to a "forced association with gambling" and sued for misappropriation. A U.S. district court denied the NFL's claim for failing to show harm despite a public survey conducted by the NFL that showed that its reputation would be hurt.[145]

The court said gambling on NFL games had existed for many years and "that this fact of common public knowledge has not injured plaintiff or their reputation."[146]

In *USGA*, the United States Golf Association sued to enjoin St. Andrews Systems from misappropriating its handicap formula that "allows golfers of different skill levels to compete with each other an equal basis."[147] St. Andrews Systems argued that the claim was preempted and that the formula was functional and in the public domain. In ruling against misappropriation, the Third Circuit said there were limits to *INS*, namely that INS and AP were *direct* competitors in the *same* market of newspaper customers, and INS's piracy of AP news reduced the incentive for AP to gather news. But had INS used AP news to publish news about war correspondents, for instance, the court said the market for news would have been different and the incentive would not have been reduced:

> Indirect competition of this sort – use of information in competition with the creator outside of its primary market – falls outside the scope of the misappropriation doctrine, since the public interest in free access outweighs the public interest in providing an additional incentive to the creator or gatherer of information.[148]

The court ruled that the competition between the USGA and St. Andrews Systems was indirect. The USGA was in the business of promoting golf and its position as golf's governing body and was not in the business of selling handicaps to golfers. The court concluded that protecting the handicapping formula under misappropriation would effectively give the USGA a national monopoly on the golf handicapping business. This, it refused to do.

Thus, the cases of this era, while limiting application of misappropriation, also raised several important new questions about how far the limitations extended. The element of labor and investment and the element of free-riding remained important, but courts began to question the element of competition. Did parties in a misappropriation lawsuit need to be competitors, direct competitors, or direct competitors within the same market? In *Dow Jones*, the court found direct competition wasn't required. In *Standard & Poor's*, the court identified competition, but not direct competition. In *USGA*, the court insisted on direct competition in the "primary market." Furthermore, *Gannett* raised questions about the time element: How important is the time element in *INS*, or better yet, how hot is hot? In *Gannett*, the court ruled that publication of pirated news matter days after the plaintiff's publication was not a hot news violation. Finally, the extent of the harm element was raised in *NFL*. How much evidence is required to show harm? These questions about the doctrine emerged despite a gradual retreat from more expansive interpretations of it.

SUMMARY OF FINDINGS AND CONCLUSION

The U.S. Supreme Court in *INS* left few guidelines regarding application of the misappropriation doctrine, and in three eras of decisions following INS, the courts demonstrated widely varying approaches to using the doctrine. In the first era immediately following *INS*, courts initially emphasized all or nearly all of the elements of misappropriation articulated in *INS* and limited application of the doctrine to cases that were factually similar to *INS*. But that soon changed with the growth of radio. Courts struggling to find protections for creators whose content was exploited by radio stations expanded the hot news doctrine by placing greater emphasis on the doctrine's element of labor and investment and the element of free-riding. Combined, these elements contributed to include notions of "commercial immorality," which some courts defined as acceptable within the scope of *INS*. The element of competition was interpreted more broadly to include competition for the same ad dollar and not just competition within similar businesses. The element of time was not often addressed, and the element of harm was attached to the degree of free-riding. Overall, interpretation of the doctrine favored plaintiffs looking to punish radio stations.

By the 1960s, the courts and Congress began to question the extent to which the states could define intellectual property law. The cases of this period are marked by questions about the expansion of misappropriation and whether the tort conflicted with federal law. The Supreme Court's decision in *Sears/Compco* led many courts to decide that the doctrine was no longer viable. But emerging technologies such as cable television and tape recording made piracy easier than ever and compelled courts to find ways around *Sears/Compco*. These courts sought and found protections for creators whose works were not yet protected by copyright under statute. Congress finally responded with new protections for new technologies in the 1970s and passed the 1976 Copyright Act. While the focus during this period was on the doctrine's survival rather than on its elements, courts most often cited the elements of labor and investment, free-riding, harm, and competition.

After passage of the new Copyright Act and the introduction of statutory preemption, the use of common law protections was reduced, and the last era examined in this chapter demonstrated that courts began to limit application of the hot news doctrine. The element of labor and investment and the element of free-riding remained important, but courts increasingly began to rely on the other elements to thwart the doctrine's success. Courts began to question the scope of the competition element, the need for the time element, and the need for showing actual harm.

By the mid-1990s, the doctrine of misappropriation had survived but had been arguably narrowed. There was little consensus regarding which of the original *INS* elements were crucial to a successful misappropriation claim. While the elements of free- riding and labor and investment were often easily defined, the elements of time, competition, and evidence of harm were less clear. Did the element of time in misappropriation claims refer to the timeliness or time sensitivity of the work or the timing of the publication? Did the element of competition require direct competition or not, and how was that defined? These questions remained as the federal courts in New York prepared to hear *NBA v. Motorola*, a case that would attempt to address remaining uncertainties regarding application of the doctrine.

CHAPTER 5

NBA v. Motorola and the New Boundaries of Hot News

The birth of mobile and online communication in the 1990s raised new questions about the applicability of the *INS* doctrine of misappropriation in the digital age. Like the advent of radio, the dawn of commercial digital, wireless, and Internet technologies opened up many new business opportunities for the creation and dissemination of information and entertainment. But like the height of radio, this new period saw and continues to see numerous and easy opportunities for the pirating of intellectual property. Again, interest in the hot news doctrine surfaced as these technologies dominated and producers of fact-based digital works looked for protections not found under copyright.

The doctrine of misappropriation received renewed attention in the 1990s as some businesses looked to profit from new media by using or "repurposing"[1] data and information that remained unprotected by copyright law. Companies and institutions that produced large quantities of facts and information argued that the increased threat of new media piracy meant more protections were needed for fact-based works. While many of these organizations continue to lobby Congress for specific statutory protections for data and information,[2] the common law doctrine of misappropriation is arguably still an option for these groups. The key question, however, is whether a decades-old doctrine that offers a limited property right in news is appropriate for cases involving the appropriation of facts and data using these new technologies.

Although the U.S. Supreme Court has yet to address this question, *NBA v. Motorola*,[3] a Second Circuit case involving the use of uncopyrightable real-time NBA game scores, attempted to provide some answers. In the case, the National Basketball Association filed a hot news claim against Motorola for misappropriating up-to-the-minute scores and information about its professional basketball games and transmitting them to Motorola's "SportsTrax" pager customers. A U.S. district court[4] found Motorola liable for misappropriation, but the Second Circuit reversed. Like the decision in *INS*, the decision in *NBA* was influenced by several factors: the histories of both organizations and the state of business competition and technology development; the unique facts of the dispute as reflected by the case record; and the development of law since *INS*.

CORPORATE HISTORIES

The NBA and Motorola couldn't have been more different as companies when their dispute brought them before a federal district court in 1996 and before the U.S. Court of Appeals for the Second Circuit in 1997. At the time of the lawsuit, Motorola was a veteran, 68-year-old family-run business that had grown into a multibillion-dollar technology company with hundreds of thousands of employees worldwide. The NBA, by comparison, was an association of basketball team owners. The league, which began in 1946, was for most of its history a marginal national sports organization, marred by player-owner disputes and drug problems until it merged with the American Basketball Association in 1976.

Motorola

Paul V. Galvin founded Motorola in Chicago, Illinois, in 1928. First known as the Galvin Manufacturing Association, Motorola's first product was a "battery eliminator" that allowed listeners to plug their radios into a household current rather than use a battery. The success of the "eliminator" paved the company's entrance into the car radio market. Under the brand "Motorola," a combination of the words "motor" and "victrola," the company designed "the first practical and affordable" car radio, essentially living up to its brand name and putting "sound in motion."[5] From there, business exploded. Motorola grew to design, manufacture, and sell two-way radios for law enforcement, new home radios, and televisions. By 1950, the company grew to more than 9,000 employees, with net earnings of more than $12 million.[6]

Motorola began its research into semiconductors in the 1950s.[7] Motorola used its semiconductors to build more advanced car and two-way radios, but in the 1970s, the company leveraged this knowledge to build Motorola's business in microprocessors, the circuits that control the operation of computers, for cars and computers.

By this time, Paul Galvin's son, Robert W. Galvin, had taken over the reins of the company. Facing increased competition from overseas, particularly Japan, the younger Galvin expanded into international markets and began to move the company away from consumer electronics. The company was now 36,000 employees strong with net annual earnings of more than $25 million.[8] Robert Galvin moved Motorola into high technology development for commercial, industrial, and government clients. One analyst noted:

> What must be appreciated is that Galvin did this proactively. There was no crisis at Motorola; the company and the industry appeared to be in good shape. Galvin did something highly unusual for an American executive – he anticipated the need for future change even though the company was not in imminent trouble.[9]

Furthermore, Robert Galvin instituted new management strategies and training designed to give the company's fleet of engineers room for experimentation and innovation and a chance for Motorola to exceed investor expectations.

Galvin's managers introduced and trademarked the concept of "Six Sigma," a business buzz phrase that represents a commitment to quality with the fewest number of errors. Six Sigma is based on the statistical term that reduces error so that six standard deviations lie between the mean and the nearest specification limit; in simplest terms, this means producing a product with no more than 3.4 defects per million parts or close to 99 percent production success.[10] Defects were defined in terms of the product, but also in terms of the process for production. Under Six Sigma, managers at Motorola looked to eliminate bureaucratization and time wasted in development. Business scholars John E. Walsh Jr. and William Coon wrote of this philosophy:

Galvin decided, in effect, to "bet the company" and make Motorola number one in semiconductors and retain the top spot in two-way communications over the next ten years. The overhaul at Motorola involved putting in place a mix of high-growth businesses, decentralizing the company allowing each division substantial autonomy while building up internal controls, establishing a long-term New Enterprises operation, introducing new personnel programs, and committing employees to very high quality – the formal goal was zero defects.[11]

Galvin's strategy to refocus Motorola's core businesses and invigorate development with the introduction of aggressive management strategies paid off handsomely. By the early 1980s, Motorola had more than 71,000 employees and net annual earnings of more than $186 million,[12] allowing the company to develop and invest in new wireless communications, including cellular phones and pager systems. In 1988, the U.S. Commerce Department awarded Motorola the first Malcolm Baldrige National Quality Award, recognizing Motorola's outstanding business track record and pursuit of quality. The award made Motorola a textbook case study of American corporate success.

Motorola entered the 1990s with more than 100,000 employees and nearly $500 million in net annual earnings.[13] But Motorola's fortunes began to change after Robert Galvin stepped down in 1990. Several upper management changes in the early '90s to replace Galvin eventually led to the appointment of Christopher Galvin, Robert Galvin's son, to chief executive officer in 1997. But the appointment left concerns that the junior Galvin was "too green" and a "lightweight" because he didn't have an engineering degree.[14] Motorola's continued investment in pager and analog cellular technology missed the mark. Its competitors in the mid-1990s jumped on the digital bandwagon and developed digital phones and other digital wireless products.[15] Motorola's biggest customers, such as Ameritech and Bell Atlantic, turned from the veteran developer and signed contracts with more digitally-minded competitors. Motorola found itself scrambling to catch up when the NBA initiated its 1996 lawsuit against the company for the use of its sports scores in a pager system called SportsTrax. A 1998 *Businessweek* article lamented Motorola's losses:

Now, the go-go growth company of a few years ago is barely inching along. Revenue growth, which soared an average 27% a year between 1993 and 1995, has slowed to 5% in the past two years, to $29.8 billion in 1997. Profits have tumbled, too. . . . Says Steven Goldman, a professor at Lehigh University who has done consulting work for Motorola: "It's hard to imagine that six or seven years ago Motorola was one of the most admired companies in the world. Now, you talk about Nokia and Ericsson and how they're eating Motorola's lunch."[16]

Motorola's history and management are instructive in a reading of *NBA* for several reasons. As a company of tens of thousands of engineers, Motorola's pursuit of innovative wireless technologies was nearly unmatched for six decades, creating a corporate culture of successful risk takers accustomed to dominating the market and creating successful new products. Combined with Motorola's Six-Sigma management style – which emphasized the reduction of errors in production and in the time needed to produce new products – Motorola's modus operandi was perfection on the first try and quickly, no matter the obstacles. This kind of rush for success may account, in part, for Motorola's decision to use the NBA's scores without NBA permission in its new pager product. In addition, Motorola's emphasis on decentralized management to accomplish its development goals, while no doubt helpful to a culture of creative engineers, also contributed to an atmosphere that was "too smug, too engineering driven, and too focused on internal rivalries."[17] Combined with multiple management changes just prior to the NBA lawsuit and its loss of business to more digitally-minded competitors, it is not surprising that Motorola took the NBA scores without permission and appeared willing to face the risk of NBA retaliation.

The National Basketball Association

The history and financial success of the NBA, until recent times, has been much less impressive and certainly marked by more ups and downs than Motorola's. The modern-day National Basketball Association began in 1946 as the Basketball Association of America (BAA) with Maurice Podoloff, a Russian-born, Yale-educated lawyer, as its first president. Eleven teams from around the United States paid a

$10,000 fee to join the BAA.[18] But the early league suffered significant financial losses in part because of player salary competition with a rival organization known as the National Basketball League (NBL).[19] Podoloff recognized that the future of a profitable BAA rested in a merger with the NBL, and in 1949, he orchestrated a deal in which six teams from the NBL merged with the BAA to become the National Basketball Association (NBA). Seventeen teams, however, were more than the league could sustain financially, and by the 1954-55 season, the NBA consisted of only eight teams.[20]

Since Dr. James Naismith invented the game in 1891 in Springfield, Massachusetts, as an indoor alternative to soccer and football during the cold New England winters, basketball has always had a following. But for much of its history, basketball failed to command the national spotlight as baseball had done. While some writers have attributed that failure to the early sport's changing rules and slow and occasionally rough play, basketball also suffered from frequent changes in team structure, management, and ownership.[21] Not until the eight teams of the 1954-55 season did basketball – as a national sport – gain stability.[22] Since that time, no NBA franchise has folded, and the league has grown.[23] However, stability was only one part of the equation in building a profitable league. The early NBA struggled desperately to make money.

With the growth of televised sports during the 1960s and early 1970s, the NBA's second president, Walter Kennedy, oversaw expansion of the NBA to eighteen teams and offered hope for profitability. Under his leadership, NBA franchises increased in value from $200,000 each to nearly $4 million by 1970.[24] In 1964, Kennedy was successful in negotiating an ABC network television contract totaling $650,000 for NBA Sunday afternoon games.[25] While ratings climbed, advertisers were still unhappy with the results. NBA owners blamed ABC for not doing enough to promote the sport.[26] In 1973, the NBA changed broadcast partners and awarded the rights to its games to CBS. CBS paid NBA teams $535,000 each annually. But ratings on CBS were also poor. Sports communication scholar John Fortunato wrote:

> The NBA was suffering from a poor perception of the game itself. The perceptions of the NBA included being a league that was drug-infested, featured too many African-American

players, was boring until the last two minutes of the game, and only featured one-on-one play. This poor perception and its status in comparison to other available sports programming to which CBS had broadcast rights dictated the poor exposure the NBA was receiving. . . . Ed Desser, president of NBA Television, says that the NBA "literally was shoe-horned in between other things and it wasn't the centerpiece. It wasn't a focal point, and they (the networks) didn't put resources into it."[27]

The NBA also faced pressures from new competitors and from the players themselves. In 1966, the American Basketball Association was formed to compete with the NBA, and "consumer demand, fate, and high-flying money players" combined to make the ABA a formidable threat.[28] Featuring such stars as Julius Erving, George Gervin, and Artis Gilmore, the ABA game attracted fans with its fast pace and continuous scoring.[29] By the early 1970s, the ABA had helped to drive up player salaries in both leagues. Players, teams, and both leagues sued each other over contracts with players who attempted to jump from one league to the other. With lawsuits flying and profitability for both leagues still in doubt, the NBA and ABA began merger talks in 1970. The two sides had reached a tentative agreement for a 1971 merger when the players, represented by Oscar Robertson, Bill Bradley, John Havlicek, and others, filed a federal class action suit on behalf of all players in both leagues.[30]

The players charged both leagues with restraining competition by using the college draft and contracts that gave teams the right to "reserve" a player once his contract expired.[31] A federal district court in May 1970 preliminarily enjoined the NBA-ABA merger, although the court left room for the two sides to seek special antitrust exemptions from Congress.[32] The battle stretched out for more than five years, preventing the merger. The court ultimately ruled in favor of the players. It found that the NBA was subject to antitrust laws and that the merger was a restraint of trade. But the court left some room in the decision, acknowledging that "some degree of economic cooperation . . . . . . may well be essential for the survival of ostensibly competitive professional sports leagues."[33]

Both sides reached a settlement in 1976. At the same time, the NBA's third president, Larry O'Brien, now known as "NBA commissioner," used "considerable political savvy" to acquire the ABA's four strongest franchises and receive congressional approval for the deal.[34] Still, the NBA lagged behind other major league sports. The health of the league in the 1980s was in doubt, leading some to label that period "the dark days" of the NBA.[35] Teams were losing money, rumors of team mergers flourished, and the NBA Finals were televised by tape delay.

With the help of a young lawyer named David Stern, O'Brien orchestrated a landmark collective bargaining agreement in 1983 after NBA players threatened to strike. The agreement, which included an "anti-drug program hailed as the most far-reaching and innovative in professional sports" and introduced a salary cap for players, ultimately set the stage for the growth of the league in the late 1980s and early 1990s.[36] Stern, a lawyer who had been involved in the NBA's legal battles as early as 1966, joined the NBA as general counsel in 1978 and became commissioner in 1984 after O'Brien retired. With the collective bargaining agreement in place, Stern began to change the drug-infested image of the league and engineered the development of NBA Properties and NBA Entertainment, divisions that marketed the league, its teams, and its players on everything from T-Shirts and retrospective videos to major television contracts with both the networks and cable. Helped by the popularity of new stars such as Magic Johnson, Larry Bird, and Michael Jordan, the sale of NBA licensed products grew from $10 million in 1981 to $2.8 billion in 1994.[37] By 1997, the NBA's television contracts totaled $2.64 billion.[38]

What had begun as a fledgling group of basketball teams had emerged into a sports marketing powerhouse. With David Stern at the helm, the NBA jealously guarded its gains and did not shy away from legal action in instances that threatened the league's control of its television broadcasting and cable rights. In 1991, Chicago superstation WGN[39] sued the NBA for restraint of trade when the league's board of governors decided to limit the number of game broadcasts that local teams could sell to local cable stations.[40] WGN, which broadcast about 25 Chicago Bulls games under old league rules, was told new rules allowed it to retransmit just 20 games. The NBA was concerned that WGN's games, which featured superstar Michael Jordan, would hurt other teams around the country and would trump the league's own cable deal with Turner Sports, which cablecasted other NBA games on cable station TNT. The lawsuit stretched out for six years, resulting in a compromise between the NBA and WGN in which WGN was permitted to televise as many games as it wanted to Chicago-area viewers but only 15 to cable TV viewers in other parts of the country.[41]

The league has been equally protective of its trademarks since Stern took over. The NBA has repeatedly gone after makers of merchandise who are not licensed to use the league or team logos, and has carefully guarded its trademarks to terms such as "dream team" and "three-peat."[42]

The history and leadership of the NBA are useful in understanding the league's battle against Motorola in *NBA v. Motorola*.[43] Unlike Motorola, the NBA came from humble, insolvent beginnings, with more than three decades of constant change in structure and leadership, plus a host of player and team legal battles that threatened the league's stability. Once the dust had settled in the 1980s, the league was able to begin protecting what it had built, particularly its most valuable assets: the league's broadcast and cable television intellectual property rights and the rights to the use of its name in commerce. Unlike the creative, decentralized engineering culture of Motorola, the culture of the new NBA was tightly managed and was based on leveraging and protecting these assets at any cost. After all, the NBA had fought long and hard to achieve its 1990s successes and was prepared to defend its gains. As David Stern once commented after he criticized the producer of a telecasted NBA game: "[N]obody was going to care about the NBA as much as we care about ourselves. And so we were fiercely protective to the point of combativeness. That's why I wouldn't hesitate to call an executive producer and complain about the way he'd presented a certain game on TV."[44] Therefore, it is not surprising that the NBA aggressively pursued its case against the use of its sports scores on Motorola pagers. The NBA viewed the use of its scores as a threat to the very soul of the NBA, its new media pursuits, and most directly to its broadcast and cable contracts on which the newfound successes of the league had been built.

THE FACTS

In 1994, the NBA learned of a professional baseball pager system developed by Motorola called SportsTrax, in which Major League Baseball scores and other baseball game statistics were routinely updated.[45] Motorola was licensed by Major League Baseball to provide that product. The original complaint in *NBA* stated that Motorola contacted the NBA about making a similar product for professional basketball. But Douglas Kirk, director of NBA New Media, later testified that he had seen the baseball product written about in *The New York Times* and had asked one of his employees to call Motorola and arrange a meeting about the technology.[46]

Kirk and the NBA were interested for several reasons. First, like many companies at the time, the NBA had begun a new media initiative to explore how the NBA could make money using new technologies such as the Internet, CD-ROM, and proprietary online services such as America Online.[47] Second, the NBA was in the process of revamping its statistics technology and moving toward a system called GameStats, which would provide the NBA, its teams, the media, and other licensed distributors with a more advanced and updated statistical system for processing and accessing statistics on the games. The new system also promised new revenue sources from those who craved basketball statistics. Kirk described the benefit of this system in a company memo:

> [T]he centralization of statistics from each arena on a real time basis will provide a means by which users can access and download stats for manipulation and analysis. Here, the true NBA junkie can create his/her own customized set of statistics that are unavailable anywhere else. For example . . . users will be able to analyze how a specific team or player shoots from 18 ft. on the left side of the court – either contested or alone! Key strength of this application is that these stats are unique to the NBA and officially sanctioned.[48]

The very early phases of instituting GameStats had begun when Motorola and the NBA began their discussions regarding SportsTrax. The NBA's software had been installed around the league. But the process of creating a "real-time" networked statistics database at all 29 NBA teams that worked in conjunction with arena clocks and scoreboards had not been completed.[49] "Real-time" statistics implied scores and game information delivered shortly after their execution by players. But throughout the testimony in the case, no consensus emerged as to how quick "real-time" was versus "live" scores, "delayed" scores or any variation in between. With this new technology, questions began to emerge within the NBA about how quickly such data should be reported. If reported too quickly, did such information run the risk of trumping lucrative television contracts and angering broadcast and cable partners? As one witness described the problem generally:

> [W]hen you kind of cut through it, no one has ever decided what the rules are. We often wondered if the electronic delay, if you will, of the time it would take for data to go through a system, was enough to appease those who were concerned that we were doing things live. But we – but no one has – there is no rule book, if you will, and so we were never really able to conclude what was appropriate and what wasn't for sure.[50]

This part of the record foresaw some of the problems the NBA faced in making a hot news claim. The time element of the hot news doctrine gave a limited property right in information after publication. One question for the courts in this case was whether scores qualified for protection, and if so, for how long were they protected.

The NBA had instituted strict rules in 1993 regarding the frequency with which scores could be updated by the media and other interested parties. One reason such rules were needed, the league said, was because the score changes in basketball more frequently than in other professional sports, making the value of updated scores that much greater and any product or service that promoted the scores a threat to televised NBA games. The new policy prohibited accredited media from transmitting "scores and/or other game information out of an NBA arena (by telephone or by any other means) more than three times during each quarter and once during each of the two quarter breaks."[51] Those who violated the policy would lose their media credentials. While the policy was distributed to those media that covered NBA games, the NBA signed a formal agreement on the policy with SportsTicker,[52] a media organization devoted to selling sports statistics to publishers and that describes itself as the "world's leading real-time sports news and information service."[53]

By negotiating such an agreement with SportsTicker, the league was apparently very concerned that a service solely dedicated to sports statistics understood the rules. As a private organization, the league clearly considered the scores of its games private property. Any use of the scores beyond these rules was a violation of the league's right to its property. As Edwin Desser, president of NBA Television and New Media Ventures, complained about Motorola in his deposition:

> They are getting the advantage of utilizing our property without having paid for the creation of that property; and they are taking from us the opportunity to provide that product or service on an exclusive basis by virtue of going off and doing it on their own.[54]

> [W]e create the events and we create the statistics about the events, and to the extent that those are ownable, and that extent I think is a legal matter, we own them.[55]

The NBA made it clear to Motorola during its meetings about SportsTrax that Motorola would have to license a stats feed from the NBA to create such a product.[56] But with GameStats in development, the NBA was not yet able to provide Motorola with the kind of statistical data it needed to develop a SportsTrax for basketball. It hoped to deliver such a service by the 1995-96 NBA season. But Motorola was unwilling to wait that long. Motorola SportsTrax president Michael Marrs testified that he decided to move on the pager without an agreement with the NBA because the NBA reneged on sharing market research costs and because of the "tremendous pressure" he was under. Those pressures arose, according to Marrs, because of a *USA Today* article publicizing the baseball SportsTrax.[57] By March 1995, Motorola decided to develop a SportsTrax for basketball with or without the NBA but did not tell the NBA of its decision. Quoting a Motorola document presented during discovery, NBA President Edwin Desser said Motorola made its decision

> without any regard to the legal aspects of such a step. . . . [Motorola] came to meetings and wrote letters about its various plans and desires and even about attendance at focus groups, but there was no letter or written communication about this key decision, notwithstanding the clear understanding by Motorola from the very beginning that "the NBA takes a strong stance on the dissemination of game information. At present they only allow the game in progress score to be sent out and only every two minutes." (Exhibit 28).[58]

In January of 1996, Motorola launched its SportsTrax for basketball. The new product regularly updated the score, quarter, ball possession, time remaining, and fouls of games occurring all around the NBA.[59] The user's guide stated that such information was delivered within two minutes of the on-court activity.[60] Sometimes, information was delivered even more frequently, particularly toward the end of games.[61] The NBA found out about the product's launch after an NBA executive spotted an ad for the product in an in-flight magazine. The NBA sent a cease and desist letter to Motorola and not long after filed the lawsuit. The NBA later learned that Motorola had also made arrangements with several NBA teams to sell the basketball SportsTrax in arena stores.[62]

At the same time the NBA was meeting with Motorola, it was also meeting with a company called Sports Team Analysis and Tracking Systems, Inc., known as "Stats." Stats was interested in becoming the NBA's official statistician. Like SportsTicker, Stats collected statistical information on professional sports games and provided statistics to Motorola for its other SportsTrax products. Aware that the NBA was developing GameStats, Stats made several presentations to the NBA in 1994 and 1995, demonstrating how Stats could "manipulate the data stream collected by the NBA and find customers who would make commercial use of the data."[63] Stats also proposed to the NBA that it be allowed to use NBA logos and marks on its products. According to the NBA's Ed Desser, there was "mutual interest" in a relationship, but Stats "didn't particularly like" the NBA's view that "distribution of statistics on a real time basis constitutes a broadcast," which could jeopardize NBA deals with NBC and TNT.[64] In return for producing the NBA's new statistical products, Stats proposed paying royalties to the NBA.

In the midst of these talks and apparently unbeknownst to the NBA, Stats joined Motorola in development of the basketball SportsTrax. Stats provided Motorola with updated scores by hiring freelancers who watched NBA games on television and reported various statistics to Motorola.[65] Stats and Motorola launched the basketball SportsTrax in January of 1996, much to the NBA's surprise. Stats also provided real-time NBA statistics on its America Online site, updating scores every 15 seconds to a minute – faster than scores delivered on SportsTrax.[66] The case record reflects the NBA's shock upon learning of the Stats/Motorola partnership; it also reflects debate about how much the NBA knew about the relationship between Stats and Motorola prior to its conversations with either company. Stats claimed the NBA was aware of its collaboration with Motorola on the SportsTrax for baseball; the NBA denied knowing. Desser recalled his phone conversation with Stats' president John Dewan after the NBA found out:

> I said something to the effect of, "John, I can't believe that you guys went off and did this after all the time that we've spent pursuing doing a deal. I'm just shocked." . . . I think he said, "I'm sorry that you feel that way, and we'd still like to make a deal."[67]

From the record, it appears that Stats and Motorola were indeed aware of the NBA's strong position on use of its scores and that legal action might be one consequence if SportsTrax was developed without the league. In a memo, one Stats employee worried that the NBA might find out he was arranging for freelancers to watch NBA telecasts and report the scores:

> Anyway, I hope this doesn't blow the cover off what we're trying to do – i.e., I hope the league doesn't find out and try to stop us. . . . Other than that, I'm trying to keep them in the dark.[68]

From the record, it also appears that Motorola and Stats thought their introduction of the basketball SportsTrax might induce the NBA to speed up its plans and sign up with both companies. It did not. Instead, the NBA filed its suit in federal court against Stats, Motorola, and America Online on March 5, 1996. Thus, the case facts reveal both companies' interest in aggressively pursuing new media products. The facts also reflect the NBA's commitment to tight control over redistribution of its game statistics and Motorola's attempts to aggressively pursue new wireless pager products. And it foreshadowed debate regarding the degree to which the NBA could claim ownership of its scores after publication.

THE LEGAL CLAIMS AND ARGUMENTS

The NBA's initial complaint accused Motorola and Stats of (1) infringing the NBA's copyright in its game broadcasts and in its games;

(2) violating New York unfair competition law, specifically the "hot news doctrine"; (3) violating the NBA's trademark under the Lanham Act; and (4) violating the Communications Act of 1934.[69] On the first claim, the district court ruled that Motorola had not infringed on the NBA's copyright in the broadcast of the game. The district court also ruled that there was no violation of either trademark law or the Communications Act of 1934. On the hot news claim, the district court entertained three issues addressed by both parties: whether NBA's hot news claim was preempted; whether *INS* applied to the case; and whether the NBA's pursuit of an injunction violated the First Amendment.

Preemption

The first argument was whether federal copyright law preempted the NBA's hot news claim. Federal copyright law stipulates that state claims that come within the rights defined by copyright law and within the subject matter of copyright are preempted.[70] The purpose of preemption in copyright law was to clear up confusion between state-created intellectual property rights and federal intellectual property rights, giving emphasis to federal rights because the Constitution gave Congress the power to create intellectual property law.[71]

The NBA argued that its claim survived preemption under copyright law. The NBA concluded that its *games and scores* fell outside the subject matter of copyright (i.e. – they were uncopyrightable material) because Congress did not specifically grant protection for games and scores in the 1976 Copyright Act. The league also argued that the rights it claimed were not equivalent to rights under copyright because its claim contained the "extra element" of hot news.[72] Furthermore, the league said that its claim was not preempted by copyright law because the congressional record showed that Congress intended for narrow hot news claims to survive preemption and that the Supreme Court accepted that view.[73]

Stats and Motorola argued that the NBA's hot news claim was preempted because both organizations took the scores for SportsTrax from *copyrighted telecasts* of NBA games.[74] The telecasts fell within the subject matter and scope of rights under copyright and thus, they argued, the claim was preempted.

The arguments point out that the preemption analyses in hot news cases like *NBA* are distressingly tortuous. The preemption analysis in hot news cases requires courts to characterize two critical issues: the kind of the material produced by the plaintiff and how deeply the plaintiff's rights extend in that material. Courts had to consider whether Stats and Motorola took uncopyrightable statistics from the copyrighted telecast or from the game as reflected by the telecast, leaving some possible common law protection. As one leading text on copyright law has commented, preemption can be "exceedingly difficult to apply" in these kinds of cases:

> What approach should be taken with respect to subject matter that the Act has specifically excluded from protection [such as news matter or sports scores]: should it be treated the same as subject matter that is simply omitted from statutory consideration, or should the express exclusion of certain categories of works be read as placing them irretrievably in the public domain?[75]

Application of *INS*

The second argument revolved around the applicability of *INS* and its progeny to the case. The NBA claimed that Motorola misappropriated its game scores and information in the same way INS stole news and information from the AP in *INS*. The league argued that it met each of the elements necessary for a "hot news" claim under *INS*, and that New York law had repeatedly protected sports game broadcasts from piracy.[76] By contrast, Motorola and Stats argued that *INS* did not apply because there was no direct competition between Motorola or Stats and the NBA, making a claim of hot news "fatal."[77] The two defendants also argued that New York courts had interpreted *INS* narrowly. Not surprisingly, the arguments on both sides were somewhat overstated.

In its brief, the NBA outlined what it called "four critical findings" in *INS* that constituted a hot news claim. The league characterized these findings as follows:

(i) The AP generated its news bulletins "at the cost of enterprise, organization, skill, labor, and money" and therefore had a proprietary right in their dissemination;

(ii) The information gathered by AP had significant commercial value, particularly during the period "while it is fresh";

(iii) INS systematically took the news accounts generated by AP for its own commercial purposes, without engaging in efforts or incurring costs similar to those of AP; and
(iv) AP and INS were in competition with one another with respect to the information in question.[78]

This characterization of *INS* was accurate with two important exceptions. While the Court ruled that AP had a right to the news it generated using its "skill, labor, and money," the Court made clear that such a right was limited for a short period after publication. The NBA characterization of the doctrine mentions that the Court emphasized the commercial value of fresh information, but the NBA's description fails to articulate the important limitation on this property right. Indeed, this is a critical part of the NBA case because as one deposed executive in the case admitted, it was difficult to know when the greatest commercial value of game information had expired.[79]

In addition, the NBA mentioned the element of competition necessary for a misappropriation claim, but added that the competition in *INS* was "with respect to the information in question." The league said that the SportsTrax pager "clearly competed" with the NBA's television and radio licenses, as well as its efforts to sell real-time game information to "emerging media."[80] As the NBA put it, "this case is solely about commercial competition."[81] But Motorola and Stats argued that the *INS* Court required *direct* competition for a hot news claim and that the NBA had failed to show it suffered any harm. Motorola and Stats argued both direct competition and harm were necessary to a successful hot news claim. Attorneys for STATS wrote:

Unlike INS and AP, the NBA and STATS are not "in the keenest competition"; in fact, they do not compete at all. Statistics about sports events is STATS's "stock in trade," while the NBA's primary business is staging and promoting basketball games. The NBA's business of staging basketball games is not affected when, after the exciting action of a basketball play is broadcast to and witnessed by millions, SportsTrax reports the dry fact of the current game score. Moreover, unlike STATS, the NBA has never made any income from the sales of scores or statistics of in-progress games. Indeed, the NBA presented no credible evidence of indirect competition; there was no testimony from NBA broadcast licensees or survey evidence from consumers indicating that periodic updates of game scores diminish the audience for NBA game broadcasts or lessen the value of broadcast rights.[82]

The reality is that the *INS* Court was not particularly clear on the issue of "direct" competition or competition "with respect to the information in question," although it did generally characterize the AP and INS as competitors.[83] The Court did not distinguish direct from indirect competition. Like the timing element, the element of competition was not left fully defined by the Court, and would, as a result, be a question for the courts in *NBA*.

Furthermore, in applying these "findings" about *INS* to its own misappropriation claim, the NBA argued that the live game action of league games was its most commercially valuable asset. Approximately 80 percent of the league's revenues were derived from live games.[84] Thus, as a reflection of those games, the real-time scores were very valuable property. The NBA said that Stats and Motorola took these scores without contributing to the creation of this information and without expending any time, labor, or money in the production of the games or telecasts. Motorola and Stats argued that unlike INS, which took AP news directly from the AP wire, Motorola and Stats invested time, labor, and money using a network of stringers to gather NBA scores from NBA telecasts.[85] Motorola and Stats argued that these scores, though gathered from copyrighted telecasts, were unprotected by copyright and freely available in the public domain. These arguments reflected several unresolved issues for the courts: whether the NBA had a limited property right in the scores; whether the labor involved in obtaining such scores was enough to give Stats and Motorola some right to what they used; and whether it mattered if the scores were characterized as elements of the copyrighted telecast or elements of the uncopyrightable game.

The First Amendment

The last major argument in the case was whether a misappropriation claim involving the reporting of facts, such as scores, implicated the First Amendment. Stats and Motorola argued that since *INS* was decided, First Amendment case law supported the "gathering and reporting of truthful facts of interest to the public," putting the reporting of sports scores "squarely within the protection of the First Amendment."[86] The NBA argued that its misappropriation claim did not threaten the First Amendment, because the key issue was the defendants' threat to the NBA's legitimate business and property interests and not some scheme to restrict the free flow of facts.[87]

The NBA contended that Motorola and Stats could not "wrap themselves in the mantle of First Amendment newsgatherers."[88] The league argued that its pursuit of an injunction against Motorola and Stats under New York's unfair competition law was not an unconstitutional prior restraint[89] and that New York's hot news doctrine did not target specific kinds of news or information and was, therefore, "content neutral."[90] The NBA insisted that Stats and Motorola could not claim the First Amendment because the league's interest in restricting the use of game scores was "entirely commercial." The league also argued that Stats and Motorola lacked a First Amendment interest because information on NBA games was freely available through many other media. Finally, the NBA said that the defendants' First Amendment arguments had no precedent:

> Wherever the First Amendment line may rest, defendants' systematic and continuous taking of detailed real-time NBA games information for their own commercial profits crosses that line. This result is all the more obvious because . . . defendants are not even members of the news media. On these facts, an injunction preventing defendants from violating New York's law of unfair competition poses no threat whatever to freedom of speech under the First Amendment.[91]

Stats and Motorola presented three primary First Amendment arguments. First, the defendants argued that the First Amendment equally protected gatherers of newsworthy and factual entertainment information and traditional newsgatherers. Attorneys for Motorola wrote:

> [T]he distinction the NBA makes between news reporting by the so-called media and defendants' supposedly entertaining commercial enterprise is, under the law, not a line that the District Court or the NBA is entitled to draw. The First Amendment guarantee of free speech is not limited to the "press," but extends to all speakers, including corporations

that make a profit. . . . The Supreme Court has long recognized that the First Amendment applies to media which entertain.[92]

Secondly, Stats and Motorola argued that an injunction restricting the use of NBA scores would not be content neutral and, thus, would violate the First Amendment. Stats lawyers wrote:

> An order dictating that defendants may not report the news until it is no longer fresh is no incidental restraint on speech; it strikes at the very essence of news reporting, which is the timely reporting of facts of interest to the public. The First Amendment allows reporters to be reporters, not involuntary historians.[93]

Finally, Stats cited *Zacchini v. Howard*,[94] a 1977 Supreme Court case, as precedent that not all state common law claims survive First Amendment scrutiny. In *Zacchini*, the plaintiff conducted a human cannonball act, which was shown on a local TV news program. The plaintiff sued the TV station for misappropriation of his right of publicity. The Supreme Court ruled for the plaintiff and held that by filming the plaintiff's "entire act," the defendant had violated the plaintiff's right of publicity in a manner not protected by the First Amendment. Despite the appearance that such a case might support the NBA's argument, Stats argued that the Court's emphasis on the misappropriation of the "entire act" in *Zacchini* meant that Stats' use of sports scores in *NBA* did not constitute misappropriation because it did not take the entire NBA game. Stats also wrote that the *Zacchini* Court "cautioned against the extension of [its] holding to pure reporting of facts."[95]

The defendants' First Amendment arguments presented interesting new concerns for the study of hot news doctrine in a modern context. First Amendment law has grown considerably stronger since 1918, when *INS* was decided, and so, it is only natural that First Amendment arguments relative to proprietary rights under the hot news doctrine received greater attention than they did when the Supreme Court decided *INS*. Such First Amendment arguments are compelling but are new and untested. First Amendment law offers Stats and Motorola the same free speech protections as traditional media. But free speech is not absolute, and First Amendment law tolerates time, place, and manner restrictions on speech, provided such restrictions serve a substantial government interest. Thus, an injunction prohibiting Stats and Motorola from reporting sports scores for a limited time, until the commercial value of such information was exhausted, might fall well within these boundaries, particularly since the information is reported through other outlets.[96] Ultimately, the question may be whether the issuance of an injunction to protect a business's limited property right in information under the hot news doctrine serves some greater governmental interest than having such information flow freely and in a timely manner.

THE DECISIONS

In September of 1996, the U.S. District Court of the Southern District of New York ruled on both the findings of fact in *NBA* and the merits of the main arguments presented by the NBA, Stats, and Motorola. The district court's decision was appealed to the U.S. Court of Appeals for the Second Circuit, which in 1997 ruled on two of the three misappropriation arguments presented in the case.

The District Court

On the question of whether the misappropriation claim was preempted by federal copyright law, the U.S. district court concluded that the NBA's claim was only "partially preempted" and allowed the claim to stand. Under copyright law, preemption occurs when both the subject matter of the claim and the nature of the rights claimed by the plaintiff fall within the scope of copyright. The court ruled that the nature of the rights claimed by the NBA were essentially the same rights guaranteed by copyright; that is, the rights to reproduction, distribution and display.[97] But in terms of the claim's subject matter, the court ruled that the NBA's claim was only partially preempted by copyright. The court said this part of the claim was preempted to the extent that "it relies on misappropriation of property rights in the [copyrighted] broadcasts of NBA games," but was not preempted to the extent that the claim related to the NBA games themselves, which were not protected by copyright.[98] Therefore, the court said, the NBA's misappropriation claim was not preempted.

In ruling on the misappropriation claim, the court found that Stats and Motorola misappropriated the NBA's real-time scores, taking "the tremendous commercial value of NBA games, a value which would not exist but for years of NBA's effort and investment in cultivating a high level of public interest in NBA games."[99] Finding that the defendants "reaped where they had not sown" – a reference to *INS* – the court said that the defendants had taken "the NBA's most valuable property – the excitement of an NBA game in progress"[100] and "its most valuable asset – real-time game information."[101] The court highlighted four of five key *INS* elements, including free-riding by the defendants, the value of the timeliness in the NBA's games scores, and the NBA's labor and investment in its games. It also concluded that the defendants' SportsTrax pager competed with the NBA's own efforts to market its scores to other providers and launch its own real-time pager service, but the court did not characterize the extent of the harm, saying only that the NBA's ability to profit was "adversely affected."[102]

Furthermore, the court spent seven pages reviewing the development of misappropriation in New York and the doctrine's "broad and flexible" nature, which in New York included any form of "commercial immorality."[103] The court's decision to grant an injunction based on the NBA's hot news claim was based on a wide-ranging combination of some of the elements constituting a specific hot news claim under *INS* with a more generalized attack on the defendants' immoral conduct, under the reasoning of some of New York's commercial immorality cases.

On the final question – whether the First Amendment was implicated in the NBA's hot news case against the defendants – the court was unconvinced. Citing a Supreme Court decision that concluded some injunctions have only incidental effects on speech and don't rise to the level of a prior restraint, the court said the NBA's request for an injunction against Stats and Motorola was one such example. In *Madsen v. Women's Health Center*,[104] the Supreme Court ruled that an injunction was not an unconstitutional prior restraint if it was content neutral and did not permanently bar expression. The *NBA* district court similarly ruled that the NBA's misappropriation claim was content neutral and that the defendants were not "totally thwarted" in their efforts to report NBA scores.[105] The court suggested that the defendants need only compensate the NBA for such information to be able to report it.[106]

The Second Circuit

On appeal, the Second Circuit considered only whether the defendants' actions constituted a hot news violation and whether the NBA's claim was preempted. The court did not address the parties' First Amendment arguments, writing that its decision on the first two questions meant it "need not address" the defendants' First Amendment arguments.[107]

On the preemption question, the Second Circuit first concluded that the NBA's claim came within the subject matter of copyright because the broadcasts of the game were copyrighted.[108] The court said that because copyrighted works often contain portions that are copyrightable (in this case, the broadcasts) and portions that are not (in this case, the NBA games), the claim also came within the subject matter of copyright and therefore, would be preempted under this part of the analysis. The Second Circuit rejected the district court's "partial preemption" analysis, which allowed the NBA's hot news claim to survive preemption because only the broadcasts of the games were copyrightable and the games themselves were not. The court wrote:

> [A]doption of a partial preemption doctrine — preemption of claims based on misappropriation of broadcasts but no preemption of claims based on misappropriation of underlying facts — would expand significantly the reach of state law claims and render the preemption intended by Congress unworkable . . . . Partial preemption turns that intent on its head by allowing state law to vest exclusive rights in material that Congress intended to be in the pubic domain and to make unlawful conduct that Congress intended to allow.[109]

The court then turned to the nature of the rights asserted in the NBA's claim. First, the court concluded that the 1976 Copyright Act preempted the commercial immorality doctrine under New York misappropriation law; thus, the cases cited by the NBA were no longer good law. The court wrote:

> Such concepts [such as commercial immorality] are virtually synonymous for wrongful copying and are in no meaningful fashion distinguishable from infringement of copyright. The broad misappropriation doctrine relied upon by the district court is, therefore, the equivalent of exclusive rights in copyright law.[110]

Courts have recognized that "certain forms of commercial misappropriation otherwise within [this] requirement will survive preemption if an 'extra element' test is met."[111] What constitutes an "extra element" has been the subject of considerable debate by courts.[112] The Second Circuit ruled that because the NBA's claim was a "narrow" hot news claim and contained such "extra elements," the nature of the rights in the claim did not come within the general scope of copyright law. Therefore, the claim survived preemption. The court identified five specific "extra elements" within the NBA's claim that allowed it to stand. These were:

(i) a plaintiff generates or gathers information at a cost;
(ii) the information is time-sensitive;
(iii) a defendant's use of the information constitutes free-riding on the plaintiff's efforts;
(iv) the defendant is in direct competition with a product or service offered by the plaintiffs; and
(v) the ability of other parties to free-ride on the efforts of the plaintiff or others would so reduce the incentive to produce the product or services that its existence or quality would be substantially threatened.[113]

Of these, the court said the NBA's claim withstood preemption because of the time-sensitive value of factual information, the free-riding by a defendant, and the threat to the very existence of the product or service provided by the plaintiff.[114]

However, in applying this test to the facts in the case, the court concluded that Motorola did not engage in misappropriation based on these extra elements. The court ruled that there was no direct competition between the SportsTrax pager and the NBA's primary business: The production of its games and the live descriptions of those games.[115] The court said the NBA's production of scores and statistics about its games constituted another NBA product (called Gamestats), but the court ruled the defendants did not free ride on that system because the defendants expended their own resources in collecting "purely factual information" from NBA games.[116] If the defendants had taken such information from Gamestats directly, the court said that would be free-riding. Furthermore, the court ruled that the NBA had not shown any damage to any of its products based on the defendants' actions.[117]

Thus, for the first time, a court laid out a definitive series of five elements required for a hot news claim and severely limited use of the claim. The *NBA* test was a clearer articulation of the hot news elements first defined by the *INS* Court,[118] and for the first time, made those elements mandatory. Although the decision articulated the doctrine in more concrete terms, the newly defined elements also raised new questions: If *direct* competition was required, what standards would courts use to determine what was direct competition? If the harm done by the defendant had to be *substantial* for a hot news claim to stand, exactly what evidence was required to demonstrate a such harm? The Second Circuit also did not shed light on either the length of the limited hot news right or how "hot" the time-sensitive information needed to be to qualify for protection. Finally, by refusing to address the parties' First Amendment arguments in the case, the question of reusing factual information produced by private interests remained unresolved.

The practical outcome of the case did not reflect the legal significance of the *NBA* decision. Motorola's SportsTrax was not a successful product. The NBA was ultimately able to introduce its own pager products that were far more sophisticated and successful than SportsTrax, despite its loss in the case against Motorola.

HOT NEWS AFTER *NBA*

Because *NBA* so significantly narrowed application of the hot news doctrine, the questions raised by Second Circuit's five-part hot news test in *NBA* have surfaced in a relatively few cases since 1997. Only six cases have specifically addressed hot news claims and the five-part test.[119] Of these, only five resulted in published decisions. Although six cases provide a limited basis for review of the hot news doctrine after *NBA*, they do form the beginnings of a new judicial approach to the 84-year-old doctrine and are worthy of study.

Application of the Five-Part NBA Test

Courts evaluating hot news claims after *NBA* did not consider the *NBA* test in its entirety. In *Fred Wehrenberg Circuit of Theatres v. Moviefone*,[120] a district court ruled that a telephone movie listing service did not misappropriate movie listings from a theater operator in the St. Louis area. Moviefone, the telephone listing service, claimed that its use of the owner's information did not "substantially threaten" the theater owner's business. Wehrenberg, the theater chain owner, claimed its own listing service was in direct competition with Moviefone's service. The court listed the five parts of the NBA test for hot news but only applied the fifth part of the test; that is, whether the plaintiff's actions "would so reduce the incentive to produce the product or service that its existence or quality would be substantially threatened."[121] In examining only this element, the court said it was "unnecessary to evaluate the other four elements because plaintiff has failed to establish the last one."[122]

Indeed, in *McKevitt v. Pallasch*,[123] the Seventh Circuit ruled that the fifth part of the *NBA* test is the most important part: "The meat is in (v) with (i) through (iv) identifying the conditions in which the criterion stated in (v) is likely to be satisfied."[124] In that case, Michael McKevitt faced prosecution in Ireland for membership in a banned organization and for directing terrorism. McKevitt sought tape recordings of a key witness filmed by a group of journalists for his defense. The journalists claimed reporter's privilege and misappropriation of their reports. Regarding the latter claim, the Seventh Circuit ruled that McKevitt had "no commercial motive in 'stealing' the defendant reporters' work product."[125] In examining the fifth element of the *NBA* test, the court said, "No showing has been made, or would be plausible that the reporters will have to abandon the … biography if the information contained in the recordings of their interviews with him is made public."[126]

In *Pollstar v. Gigmania*,[127] the plaintiff, creator of a Web site with time sensitive concert information, sued Gigmania, a similar Web site, for taking its concert information and posting it on the Gigmania site. Pollstar argued its case using the *NBA* test, alleging that it produced information about the concert industry that was time sensitive; that Gigmania used such information in direct competition with Pollstar; that Gigmania free rode on its costly efforts, which if continued would reduce Pollstar's incentive to produce; and that Pollstar had been "irreparably damaged" by Gigmania's actions.[128]

The court ruled Gigmania was a free-rider (the third element) and threatened the existence of Pollstar by taking its concert listings (the fifth element), but admitted that it was not clear whether such information was sufficiently time-sensitive (the second element). Nonetheless, the court allowed the claim to proceed.

In *Morris Communications Corp. v. PGA Tour, Inc.*,[129] a district court initially upheld a hot news counterclaim raised by the PGA, which defended itself against an antitrust action filed by Morris Communications, a media company. The PGA prohibited Morris from publishing real-time golf scores obtained from a media center at PGA events. The PGA argued for a limited property right in its data; Morris claimed the PGA scores were no different from the NBA's scores and that both existed in the public domain. In its initial ruling, the court focused on the third part of the hot news test (whether the plaintiff's conduct constituted free-riding) and the fifth part (the extent of the harm), without a full discussion of the other parts of the test. Indeed, the court lamented the lack of "a complete factual record"[130] to determine the extent to which Morris was free-riding and the effect on the PGA's business.[131] The court later found the hot news claim was inapplicable because unlike Motorola in *NBA*, Morris got its real time PGA statistics directly from the PGA and not from a broadcast that then put those scores in the public domain.[132] On appeal, the Eleventh Circuit upheld the lower court's ruling, saying the case was not about "copyright law, the Constitution, the First Amendment, or freedom of the press in news reporting," but rather was about the possibility that the PGA violated antitrust law by prohibiting Morris to reuse the scores.[133] The court ultimately ruled that the PGA did not violate antitrust law.

In *Scholastic, Inc. v. Stouffer*,[134] Scholastic and J.K. Rowling, author of the Harry Potter series, sought a declaratory judgment against Stouffer, the author of several books based on a set of characters called "Muggles," which were created by Stouffer before the Potter series in the 1980s. Because "Muggles" similarly appear in Rowling's books, the plaintiffs sought a declaratory judgment that they had not violated Stouffer's copyright or trademark. The district court rejected Stouffer's attempt to fashion a hot news counterclaim that the plaintiffs had misappropriated her work. The court rejected the claim on the basis of the first, second and fifth elements of the *NBA* test. The court summarized these three parts of the *NBA* test in one sentence and concluded "the instant case ambiguously falls outside these factual parameters."[135]

The Free-Riding Element

Of the five parts of the *NBA* test in these cases, the two that received the most consideration by courts after *NBA* were the third element (free-riding) and the fifth element (the effect of the free-riding on the content provider's business). Despite the perception that free-riding is easily identified (the defendant either "reaped" where he shouldn't have or he didn't), the issue can be complicated by mitigating circumstances, such as reduced or obstructed access to information. If access to information is denied to all competitors except one, the potential for anticompetitive behavior may be a more important consideration for courts than a hot news claim.

In *INS*, the majority did not consider that INS had been shut out of covering war news by European nations, giving AP a virtual monopoly on war news for U.S. readers. Although INS had been restricted by European nations and not by the AP, Justice Louis Brandeis warned of the consequences to INS, as well as to the free flow of information during wartime:

> The facts of this case admonish us of the danger involved in recognizing such a property right in news, without imposing upon news-gatherers corresponding obligations. . . . The closing to the International News Service of these channels for foreign news (if they were closed) was due not to unwillingness on its part to pay the cost of collecting news, but to the prohibitions imposed by foreign governments upon its securing news from their respective countries and from using cable or telegraph lines running therefrom. . . . The prohibition of the foreign governments might as well have been extended to the channels through which news was supplied to the more than a thousand other daily papers in the United States not served by the Associated Press; and a large part of their readers may be so located that they can not procure prompt access to papers served by the Associated Press.[136]

This issue was more directly addressed in *PGA*. Unlike the access Motorola had to NBA telecasts in *NBA*,[137] Morris was prohibited by the PGA from sending its own reporters with cell phones to gather real-time "hole-by-hole" statistics, giving the PGA what Morris argued was an illegal monopoly. Morris claimed that the PGA unfairly used that monopoly power "to stifle competition in the separate market for syndicated real-time golf scores."[138] Its primary claim was based on the essential facilities doctrine in antitrust law, which provides that "a monopolist must provide reasonable access to that facility if it is reasonable to do so."[139] A defendant in such an action need only show that the denial of access is for a "legitimate business reason" to overcome the claim.[140] The PGA claimed its access rules for private PGA events protected its legitimate property right interests. In ruling to allow the misappropriation claim to stand but making clear that the antitrust issue was far from settled, the district court in *PGA* was initially hesitant to rule on the force of antitrust law relative to the PGA's misappropriation claim.[141] The court eventually ruled that the PGA did not violate antitrust law because it had valid business reasons for protecting its scores. With this determination, the court threw out the hot news claim. It distinguished Morris' case from Motorola's case by arguing that Morris looked to take its scores directly from the PGA whereas Motorola invested in its own "reporters" to get NBA scores off television broadcasts at which point the scores then entered the public domain.[142] The Eleventh Circuit upheld this determination.[143] The collision between antitrust and intellectual property law is not a new problem, but the new *NBA* rules regarding free ridership and competition have the potential to exacerbate the conflict.

The free-riding element after *NBA* was equally problematic in *Washington Post v. Total News*,[144] the first hot news case to arise after *NBA*. It was settled out of court in 1997. *The Washington Post* and several other news organizations sued Total News, a Web site that compiled news from around the Internet by framing it.[145] By framing *Washington Post* news and the news of others, Total News essentially redisplayed that content within a smaller window, surrounding it with Total News advertising. The *Post* and its co-plaintiffs claimed that the Total News Web site "openly free-rides on Plaintiffs' efforts by simply lifting Plaintiffs' content wholesale and selling advertising based on proximity to that content."[146] But it was arguable whether the wholesale display of the plaintiff's content would have survived the subject matter requirement under preemption, because the copy and the screen display were protected by copyright. However, if the court had proceeded with the claim and decided this case on just the elements of free-riding and the threat to the plaintiff's business, the court's analysis would need to rest on more than simply the lifting of content and the ads sold. In other words, the issue of free-riding in a hot news claim may be inseparable from the other factors, particularly time sensitivity and the issues of direct competition between news Web sites and newspapers. Courts may need to weigh some factors together and receive substantial evidence of others.

The Threat Element

Finally, the fifth element of the *NBA* test — the reduction of incentives to produce and the threat to the existence or quality of the service or product — leaves enormous wiggle room for courts looking to make the necessary comparisons. In *PGA*, the district court initially suggested that the issue was whether Morris' use of real-time PGA scores was a threat to the PGA's own scores service, not to the PGA as a whole.[147] By contrast, the court in *Moviefone* compared Moviefone's use of the theater listings to the theater owner's "core" business, and not to the owner's listing service. By comparing the Moviefone listings to the plaintiff's entire theater business, the plaintiff had little chance to win his claim:

> The Court agrees with defendant that plaintiff here has failed to establish the last element of the "hot news" exception. . . . The core of plaintiff's business and the source of the majority of its profits is not the publication of movie schedules, even though plaintiff contends it receives some revenue in exchange for its movie schedules. The core of plaintiff's business is exhibiting movies and the profit it makes from ticket and concession sales. If defendant continues to display plaintiff's movie show time on its web site or offers plaintiff's schedules to its listeners over its phone system, defendant's actions will not reduce plaintiff's incentive to generate movie schedules or publicize them to the point that the existence or quality would be threatened, even assuming defendant incorrectly recites the information.[148]

The court in *NBA* provided little guidance on the interpretation of this part of the test, but acknowledged in a footnote that historically "some authorities have labeled this element as requiring direct competition between the defendant and the plaintiff in the *primary market*."[149] Indeed, the court may have been reluctant to settle this issue in its new test. Furthermore, the *Moviefone* court reinterpreted the fifth element of the NBA test as something beyond just a "substantial threat": "For a claim of misappropriation of 'hot news' to succeed, defendant's actions must make plaintiff *virtually cease to participate* in the business in question."[150]

Here, the evidence of the threat in *Moviefone* is limited, other than a passing argument that the owner's movie theaters will likely survive the taking of listings. The district court in *PGA* was initially far more circumspect and unwilling to make such a business judgment about the future,[151] which is what this fifth element of the test essentially requires: Just how bad would business get for the plaintiff if the court let this action continue? Just what constitutes a "substantial threat?" These determinations present two dangers for courts. First, they involve courts in the evaluation of business decisions, which courts are ill-equipped to consider. Second, they require courts to make predictions about the future of such businesses, which most courts work hard to avoid.[152]

Throughout the evolution of this aspect of hot news, the concern over the threat to business has been inconsistently defined. In *INS*, the Court expressed concern that INS's behavior would "render publication profitless" or "so little profitable as in effect *to cut off the service* by rendering the cost prohibitive in comparison with the return."[153] That evolved in *NBA* to the reduction of incentives "to produce the product or service that its existence or quality would be *substantially threatened.*"[154] And now in *Moviefone*, the actions must make the plaintiff *"virtually cease to participate"* in the business in question.[155] If anything can be said about the risk to the plaintiff in a hot news claim, it is that the threat must be real. But just how serious the threat must be is not at all clear.

Thus, while there have been few hot news claims after *NBA*, the evidence they offer indicates several issues for future courts to consider. First, the elements of the *NBA* test have not been applied in total, a fact that may offer courts flexibility but may leave the future of hot news in debate. Secondly, the free-ridership requirement, which attempts to set boundaries on competition, is likely to continue on its collision course with antitrust law and is in need of a definition that can account for situations in which access to information is limited. And because free-riding is about copying, the question of preemption will also linger. Finally, the threat to the plaintiff needs specificity: Is the threat to the competing product or to the core business? How serious must the threat be, and how much and what kind of substantive evidence must the plaintiff produce? Can the future threat be known?

These are just some of the key questions that will affect the viability of hot news claims in the future.

SUMMARY OF FINDINGS AND CONCLUSION

This chapter demonstrated how the hot news doctrine was notably narrowed by and after *NBA*. The doctrine changed because of new technology and the aggressive push to introduce fact-based new media products. It also changed because courts were cautious about copyright law's dedication to keeping facts freely available and copyright law's preemption section, which routinely challenged the viability of the hot news doctrine.

The histories of the NBA and Motorola contributed to the outcome in *NBA*. Both companies shared a relentless drive to develop new revenue using new technologies. For the NBA, that meant protecting its most important intellectual property asset -- the game and all its elements. For Motorola, that meant developing new products quickly and efficiently, whatever the costs. When Motorola decided to take the NBA's game scores without permission and develop a new pager that delivered such information in "real-time," it was not surprising that the NBA responded by claiming a "hot news" right in its scores and taking Motorola to court.

NBA v. Motorola represented the first time that a court better defined the boundaries of the hot news doctrine. Motorola's use of NBA game scores without permission from the league brought into focus some of the key issues courts had been struggling with since the introduction of the doctrine in *INS* in 1918 -- including whether *INS* was restricted to its facts, how conflicting precedent since *INS* should be interpreted, whether changes in copyright law (especially the introduction of preemption) affected application of the doctrine, and whether the growth of First Amendment law since 1918 affected the constitutionality of the doctrine.

The U.S. Circuit Court of Appeals for the Second Circuit addressed some, but not all, of these issues. It narrowed use of the doctrine in the case by articulating five elements necessary for a successful hot news claim:

(i) a plaintiff generates or gathers information at a cost;
(ii) the information is time-sensitive;

(iii) a defendant's use of the information constitutes free-riding on the plaintiff's efforts;
(iv) the defendant is in direct competition with a product or service offered by the plaintiffs; and
(v) the ability of other parties to free-ride on the efforts of the plaintiff or others would so reduce the incentive to produce the product or services that its existence or quality would be substantially threatened.[156]

The *NBA* test was a clearer articulation of the hot news elements first defined by the *INS* court,[157] and for the first time, made those elements mandatory.

But in cases after *NBA*, the new elements raised more questions. Just how direct must the competition be for a successful claim, and must the defendant and plaintiff be in the same business (as INS and AP were)? Courts after *NBA* were divided. Furthermore, what constituted "substantial" harm, and what evidence was required to prove this element? *NBA* was not clear on this, and courts following NBA were also unsure. Finally, if the material must be time-sensitive, what qualified as time-sensitive? Are scores delivered every two minutes more "hot" than those delivered every three minutes? And were movie and concert listings hot enough to be "time-sensitive?"

The hot news doctrine remains viable after *INS*, but its narrowed application in *NBA* and subsequent interpretations of the *NBA* test would indicate its use is limited. That courts are reluctant to reject the doctrine entirely, however, is telling, and its history offers good reasons for not rejecting it entirely.

CHAPTER 6
Conclusion

The hot news doctrine has existed for more than 80 years. It has been used by many news organizations and other creators whose works – or portions of works – have been left unprotected by copyright law. Though the doctrine has experienced significant changes and varying interpretations in that time, its primary purpose has remained the same: to protect unprotected elements of works for limited periods after publication. But the doctrine remains controversial because it comes dangerously close to giving creators property rights in facts that copyright law has dedicated to the public domain. With the advent of digital technologies in particular, the concern is that creators will lay claim to the fundamental building blocks of such technology: the individual units of data that copyright law says must be left free to roam for use in new works. But without additional protections, database providers argue, the risk of piracy remains strong and the incentive for them to create, low.

The doctrine's development has been as much a result of historical and social forces as it has been the result of strict legal interpretation. In this study, those factors ranged from the legislative response (or lack thereof), to the judiciary's protection of business interests during The Progressive Era, to changes in communications technology, to the specific facts surrounding case law, including the nature of the disputes between the parties, their customs, philosophies, business strengths (and weaknesses), employees, and leadership.

In this study, the evolution of the hot news doctrine was most especially affected by technological change and the response to that change by the legislature and the courts. Where the legislature failed to act, the courts responded, creating for the legislature a template for emerging statutory protections. When the legislature did act – as the U.S. Congress did in the 1960s and 70s to pass the 1976 Copyright Act – the courts stepped back, shrinking their role as protector of unprotected content.

Which leaves scholars and observers in the difficult position of passing judgment on the doctrine's continued usefulness and the form it should take going forward. On the basis of the social and historical factors outlined in this study, the doctrine, though narrowed, is still useful. But history advocates that at this stage, the doctrine is best kept as common law, where the courts have tackled the challenges presented by hot news, until the legislatures have fully understood the ramifications of codifying protections for new classes of communications.

The hot news doctrine continues to serve creators and the public for three reasons: (1) It exists on the cutting-edge of new forms of communication that have yet to fully establish their potential but which may require additional protections; (2) It serves as one mechanism by which society, through the courts, argues the merits of additional property protections for these developing communications; and (3) As defined by *NBA* and cases since, it is narrow enough not to pose significant threats to the public domain, though greater clarity in the requirements for hot news is warranted.

HOT NEWS AND NEW COMMUNICATIONS

There were several factors that contributed to the development of the hot news doctrine and the dispute in *INS v. AP*. Combined, these factors helped to define a new era in the delivery and content of news. First, the customs of newsgathering in the nineteenth century did not initially punish those publishers who stole news from others. Indeed, some publishers saw the taking of their news as a compliment, and the mail exchanges encouraged news sharing. But as telegraphy sped news around the country and encouraged news organizations to send their reports in smaller and more updated packages, the news became commoditized, and the most updated news became the most commercially valuable. This encouraged the fastest news providers, among them news agencies like AP, to grow increasingly protective of their work despite the persistence of news sharing customs.

The AP's growing power and influence over news in the United States brought it into conflict with smaller news operations that either sought to collude with AP or that attempted to drag AP into court under new antitrust regulations. In the wake of these developments, AP's first general manager, Melville Stone, sought to protect AP's news. He waged a campaign to establish, through the courts, a property right in news. When his deputy, Kent Cooper, discovered that INS was taking AP war news with help from a telegrapher at the *Cleveland News*, Stone saw his opportunity to establish such a right in court.

INS Chief William Randolph Hearst was unable to match muscle with Stone's crusade. The lawsuit was in part the result of Hearst's pro-German views, which resulted in a fierce backlash from the European allies during World War I. Hearst and INS were kicked out of Europe and left unable to cover the war. Without access, INS was forced to look elsewhere for news and turned to the AP report. Hearst claimed that he was not pro-German as much as he was simply speaking the truth. Suspicions that Hearst had ties to the Germans landed him in front of Congress shortly before the Supreme Court heard *INS*. This sequence of events made it virtually impossible for Hearst to battle the AP successfully in the suit and difficult for the Court to find in his favor.

The record of briefs and affidavits in *INS* demonstrated the clear advantage AP had in preparing its case and the likelihood that both news organizations aggressively sought – and even stole – each other's breaking news. Because AP had long planned to seek a property right in news through the courts, though, it was better prepared to show the court examples of INS's theft of AP news. The record was replete with damaging examples of INS's direct theft of AP news. INS was not similarly prepared, despite significant testimony from telegraphers regarding AP's similar efforts to pirate INS news. Such knowledge was made possible by the insiders of newsgathering at the time: The telegraphers, who often jumped from wire service to wire service, making it easier to know how to steal the other's news. Wire services also often placed their own local operations at a member paper or paid a member telegrapher to act as an agent, making it easy for wire service to have access to competitor news. The analysis of the record in the case revealed two aggressive news competitors on a new playing field of news, advancing the use of telegraphy and all the new benefits it provided to reporting the news.

Nearly 80 years later, the NBA and Motorola found themselves similarly engaged in a technological race to deliver information, though this time the focus was on up-to-the-minute scores delivered on pager systems. The history of Motorola showed a highly successful technology company with a decentralized management philosophy that emphasized creativity and fast, but error-free, product development. The history of the NBA demonstrated a hard-fought battle for success and profitability. Once achieved, however, the NBA jealously guarded such gains and was particularly protective of its intellectual property. Thus, it was not surprising that the two companies wound up in court after Motorola took the NBA's scores without permission when negotiations between the two companies to develop a basketball sports pager stalled.

In both these well-known cases – and the hot news cases representing the battles in radio, cable television, tape recordings and computers – the companies involved pushed the outer limits of the technology's capabilities to redistribute news, information, and other content. The hot news doctrine in these cases helped to manage exploration that appeared to go too far by "free-riding" on one competitor's work. The emergence of these new technologies warrants such a "managed" approach. It is at these emerging technological outposts – the expanded use of the telegraph, the use of magnetic tape recording, the introduction of cable television, the introduction of pager systems – that the hot news doctrine, as common law, offers flexibility to the "innovator/aggressor" while still protecting the work of the original creator. Stanford's Lawrence Lessig has argued for courts to acknowledge that some questions of technology are not plainly answered by the law, but that courts should nonetheless proceed and conduct the most democratic review possible toward a conclusion.[1] The case evidence shows that as common law, the hot news doctrine has helped courts serve in that role for the last 80 years.

HOT NEWS AND THE JUDICIAL FORUM

With this built-in flexibility, the hot news doctrine has undergone significant changes in the courts. An analysis of decisions since *INS* showed that courts have faced challenges interpreting *INS*, primarily because the Supreme Court did not outline a specific test for the hot news doctrine and did not comment on whether the doctrine could be applied to works other than news. Although it is not unusual for courts to leave new tests without specifics, the result has been widely varying interpretations of the doctrine. But the doctrine's flexibility has also been one of its strengths: When new communications warranted protection, the courts were able to provide it under the mantle of misappropriation/hot news. It is unlikely such flexibility would have been available had hot news been codified early on.

At first, courts were reluctant to apply the doctrine to cases that weren't factually similar to *INS*. But that changed as new technologies delivered content that was similarly left unprotected by copyright law. The advent of radio, in particular, challenged courts to decide whether musicians and their publishers, newspapers, and the organizers of sporting events had rights to the broadcasts of their products. These creators vehemently objected to the broadcast of their products without permission by raising misappropriation claims, and the courts were sympathetic. In deciding that these creators possessed some right to protect the broadcast of their works under misappropriation, the courts placed emphasis on two *INS* elements: the elements of the plaintiff's labor and investment and the element of the defendant's free-riding on the labor and investment. In some cases, courts expanded these elements to include ethical notions of "commercial immorality" – that commercially valuable property rights would be protected from any form of unfairness in business. Of lesser importance to these courts were the elements of competition, time, and harm. Overall, interpretation of the doctrine favored plaintiffs looking to punish radio stations.

Eventually, Congress intervened and created statutory rights for those whose work was redistributed by broadcasters, having the work of the courts on which to base the parameters of the new laws. In the meantime, the courts began to question the extent to which the states and the courts themselves could create intellectual property protections that under the Constitution were supposed to be legislated by Congress. The Supreme Court's decision in *Sears/Compco* warned courts that state law governing intellectual property was limited in the face of

Constitution. This led some courts after *Sears/Compco* to decide that the misappropriation doctrine had been abolished.

But emerging technologies such as cable television and tape recording – and the rampant piracy that took place in these media – pressured courts to find ways around *Sears/Compco* and offer greater protections to the creators of works who were exploited by these technologies. Finally, the Supreme Court's decision in *Goldstein v. California*, a 1972 case that addressed the constitutionality of a state law designed to prosecute those who copied music onto magnetic tapes, said that states could create intellectual property law in those areas in which Congress had not chosen to act. In addition, Congress passed legislation protecting broadcasted works and tape recordings and also passed the 1976 Copyright Act, which defined the extent to which copyright law preempted state law intellectual property protections.

Throughout this period, the concern for the hot news doctrine was for its survival in the face of federal law. Creators continued to raise misappropriation claims, but courts were less likely to find in favor of plaintiffs if the courts were persuaded that such claims were obstructed by the Constitution as defined by *Sears/Compco*. Thus, application of the doctrine was narrowed and would continue to be narrowed as Congress intervened.

The last era of cases examined in this section of the study – those cases between 1976 and 1996 – demonstrated that courts did indeed limit application of the hot news doctrine after passage of the 1976 Copyright Act and its preemption section. Courts continued to emphasize the element of labor and investment and the element of free-riding in misappropriation cases but began to emphasize more the elements of competition, time, and harm.

By the mid-1990s, the hot news doctrine had survived but had been narrowed. There was little consensus regarding which of the original *INS* elements were critical to the success of a misappropriation claim. The elements of time, competition, and harm were particularly unclear. Did the element of time in misappropriation claims refer to the timeliness or time sensitivity of the work or the timing of the publication? Did the element of competition require direct competition or not, and how was that defined? How much evidence of harm was required, and was future harm enough for a successful claim? These questions remained unanswered.

Conclusion

The legal record in *NBA v. Motorola* demonstrated that the essential elements of the hot news doctrine were so unclear by 1996 that both parties in the case were able to – with varying degrees of success – make good arguments that the doctrine either supported or rejected the NBA's misappropriation claim. *NBA v. Motorola* represented the first time in the digital era that a court was asked to better define the boundaries of the hot news doctrine. Motorola's use of NBA game scores brought into focus some of the key issues that had challenged courts since *INS*. Those issues included whether the ruling in *INS* was confined to its facts, how conflicting precedent since *INS* should be regarded, whether changes in copyright law affected the strength of the doctrine, and whether the growth of First Amendment law since 1918 affected the constitutionality of the doctrine in any way.

The U.S. Court of Appeals for the Second Circuit addressed some, but not all of these issues. For instance, it chose not to rule on the question of whether an injunction granted on the basis of the doctrine was an unconstitutional prior restraint under the First Amendment. It did, however, acknowledge that copyright law's preemption section had a significant effect on the strength of the doctrine and ruled that in order for a hot news claim to stand, five elements were necessary:

(i) a plaintiff generates or gathers information at a cost;
(ii) the information is time-sensitive;
(iii) a defendant's use of the information constitutes free-riding on the plaintiff's efforts;
(iv) the defendant is in direct competition with a product or service offered by the plaintiffs; and
(v) the ability of other parties to free-ride on the efforts of the plaintiff or others would so reduce the incentive to produce the product or services that its existence or quality would be substantially threatened.[2]

The *NBA* test was a clearer articulation of the hot news elements first defined by the *INS* Court, and for the first time, made those elements mandatory.

This evolution of the doctrine in the courts demonstrates a constructive, ongoing dialogue about protecting content left unprotected by copyright law – that is, filling the "gaps" in copyright law. Scholars like Jessica Litman have argued that gaps in copyright are fundamental to the "copyright balance." Some works are protected under copyright for a limited time, and others are left unprotected on purpose:

> Copyright was seen as designed to be full of holes. The balance underlying the view of the copyright system treated the interests of the owners of particular works (and often those owners were not the actual authors) as potentially in tension with the interests of the general public, including the authors of the future; the theory of the system was to adjust that balance so that each of the two sides got at least as much as it needed.[3]

The cases examined in this study suggest that hot news courts have served as an important forum for debate about the extent to which new kinds of works should be candidates for statutory protection – for debate about "plugging the gaps." As common law, the hot news doctrine plugs gaps without sealing them shut. And when the gaps have been appropriately "plugged" by the courts, the legislatures have responded in kind: with laws to halt the broadcast of sound recordings without permission; with laws to stop the piracy of recorded music; and with laws to halt the rebroadcast of broadcast signals on cable without permission. But that has happened with input from the courts as well as the industries affected and serves as a reminder that new legislation benefits from time spent debating in the courts as well as in the legislature.

THE PARAMETERS OF HOT NEWS

The hot news debate is ongoing. Today, the struggle is over protecting discrete, individual units of data from digital pirates looking to capitalize on the work of database providers.

With only a handful of cases to examine following *NBA*, that debate is still in its infancy – a significant argument against rushing to create statutory protections for databases just yet. Legislative proposals in Congress show an interest in following the *NBA* court's lead on defining a hot news right in digital data,[4] but data differ significantly from sports scores, radio broadcasts, cable transmissions and sound recordings, a major reason why the *NBA* court narrowed the hot news test so dramatically. Data are the building blocks, the facts, from which new works are created, and it is these that copyright law ardently protects from ownership. If Congress offers legislative protections for data, the language would need careful crafting not to impose on this fundamental tenet of intellectual property law.

The *NBA* test itself offers database creators protections under common law. But, indeed, this new hot news test needs further consideration. Of the five parts of the new *NBA* hot news test, the two that received the most consideration by courts after *NBA* were the third element (free-riding) and the fifth element (the effect of the free-riding on the content provider's business so that its existence or quality was substantially threatened). Despite the perception that free-riding is easily identified (the defendant either "reaped" where he shouldn't have or he didn't), the issue can be complicated by mitigating circumstances, such as reduced or obstructed access to information, as Morris argued in *PGA*. If access to information is denied to all competitors except one, the potential for anticompetitive behavior may be a more important consideration for courts than a hot news claim.

The concern over the threat to the plaintiff's business, as defined in the fifth part of the *NBA* test, is problematic for courts and plaintiffs. In *INS*, the Court expressed concern that INS's behavior would "render publication profitless" or "so little profitable as in effect *to cut off the service* by rendering the cost prohibitive in comparison with the return."[5] That evolved in *NBA* to the reduction of incentives "to produce the product or service that its existence or quality would be *substantially threatened*."[6] More recently, in *Fred Wehrenberg Circuit of Theatres v. Moviefone*, the actions must make the plaintiff *"virtually cease to participate"* in the business in question.[7] If anything can be said about the risk to the plaintiff in a hot news claim, it is that the threat must be real. But just how serious the threat must be is not at all clear.

Nor did *NBA* completely define the time element (the second element). In *Pollstar v. Gigmania*,[8] the plaintiff, creator of a Web site with time sensitive concert information, sued Gigmania, a similar Web site, for taking its concert information and posting it on the Gigmania site. Pollstar argued its case using the *NBA* test, alleging that it produced commercially valuable information about the concert industry that was time-sensitive, among other claims.[9] The court ruled that Pollstar's claim "was pled with sufficiency as a hot news claim" but conceded that there was no similar case holding that concert information was protectible as time-sensitive hot news.[10] The court declined to decide this particular issue but allowed the claim to proceed based on the other elements.

The first element – the plaintiff generates or collects information at some cost or expense – has remained an easy hurdle for plaintiffs to demonstrate. The fourth element under *NBA* – the defendant's use of the information in direct competition with the plaintiff – now requires the plaintiff to be in direct competition, a distinction that wasn't clear in earlier cases. However, as demonstrated in the discussion about the fifth element's requirement that the plaintiff's business be substantially threatened, it is still not clear whether the fourth element requires both plaintiff and defendant to be in the same business or not.

Much of the problem with the *NBA* test boils down to measuring the harm caused to the plaintiff: Is it great enough to justify additional protections? This is essentially a business evaluation, something courts are often loathe to do. But scholars have attempted to tease out more specifics for courts and legislatures to evaluate in the discussion of hot news protections for database providers. Boston University law professor Wendy Gordon has proposed a non-exclusive list of factors to consider, including:

1. the costs of developing an information product;
2. the costs of copying;
3. whether copying yields a substantially identical product;
4. the price of sale offered by the copyist;
5. whether consumers believing the two products are substantially identical, decide to purchase the cheaper one (thereby inducing market failure because the first entity is unable to recoup its expenses); and
6. whether such a market failure could have been averted by a period of protection that would allow the first entity to recoup its expenses and justify its investment in developing the information product.[11]

Gordon would support greater protection in instances where the costs of developing a product are high, the costs of copying are low, the products are nearly identical and consumers purchase the cheaper copy, the price offered by the copyist is low, and protection would have allowed the creator to recoup its expenses.

In addition, Pam Samuelson, a law and information management professor at the University of California – Berkeley, and Jerry Reichman, a law professor at Duke University, proposed that the following market criteria be included in any legislation prosecuting database pirates:

1. the quantum of data appropriated by the user
2. the nature of the data appropriated
3. the purpose for which the user appropriated them
4. the degree of investment initially required to bring that data into being
5. the degree of dependence or independence of the user's own development and the substantiality of the user's own investments in these efforts
6. the degree of similarity between the contents of the database and a product developed by the user – even if only privately consumed
7. the proximity or remoteness of the markets in which the database owner and the user are operating and
8. how quickly the user was able to come into the market with his or her product, as compared with the time required to develop the original database.[12]

These specifics offer an important start to the discussion over federalizing hot news, particularly for database providers, and specifying the harm, an element that continues to challenge courts. To date, these specifics have not been addressed in proposed Congressional legislation.

The risks of jumping forward with legislation without this kind of careful consideration at this juncture are significant. A poorly designed statute to protect data threatens to impose on the public domain in a way that the hot news doctrine, under the *NBA* test, does not. The history of the hot news doctrine serves as an important reminder that common law, though imperfect and sometimes ill-defined, offers a measured approach to protections for the works delivered by new technologies, until the debate is fully argued.

Endnotes

CHAPTER 1

[1] Morris Communications Corp. v. PGA Tour Inc., 235 F.Supp. 2d 1269 (M.D. Fla. 2002).

[2] 364 F.3d 1288 (11th Cir. 2004).

[3] Bidder's Edge shut down its Web site in February 2001, almost a year after a judge issued a preliminary injunction barring Bidder's Edge from using eBay data. *See* Troy Wolverton, *Bidder's Edge pushes Web site over cliff, at* http://news.cnet.com (visited Sept. 6, 2004).

[4] *Morning Edition* (NPR radio broadcast, April 19, 2000) (transcript on file with Burrelle's Information Services).

[5] Anick Jesadanun, *Web Sites Leak Voting Results*, The Associated Press, Nov. 7, 2000.

[6] *Id.*

[7] "From colonial days onward, printers exchanged newspapers free through the mails, a mechanism that dictated the major exchanges of news until the telegraph and the press associations assumed that function in the mid-1800s." *See* JEAN FOLKERTS & DWIGHT L. TEETER JR., VOICES OF A NATION 97 (1998).

[8] Barbara Cloud, *News: Public Service or Profitable Property*, AMERICAN JOURNALISM, Spring 1996, at 143.

[9] *Id.* at 141.

[10] *Id.* at 143-56.

[11] *U.S. Software State Piracy Study,*, Business Software Alliance, *at* http://www.bsa.org/globalstudy/2003_SPS.pdf (last visited July 7, 2004).

[12] Laura D'Andrea Tyson & Edward F. Sherry, *Statutory Protection for Databases: Economic Public Policy Issues, at* http://www.house.gov/judiciary/41118.htm (last visited Sept. 6, 2004). Estimates of the database market vary, but some report it close to $55

billion. *See* Charles Brill, *Legal Protection of Collection of Facts*, COMP. L. REV. & TECH. J. 1 (1998).

[13] J.D. Lasica, *Preventing Content from Being Napsterized*, Newspaper Association of America, at http://216.182.209.78/preview.cfm?AID=2226 (last visited June 16, 2004).

[14] Stanford Law professor Larry Lessig points out that not all file sharing constitutes piracy, and we should be careful not to condemn or over-regulate all aspects of file sharing technology. *See* LARRY LESSIG, FREE CULTURE: HOW BIG MEDIA USES TECHNOLOGY AND THE LAW TO LOCK DOWN CULTURE AND CONTROL CREATIVITY 68-9 (2004).

[15] 248 U.S. 215 (1918).

[16] 105 F.3d 841 (2d Cir. 1997).

[17] U.S. CONST. Art. I §8 provides that Congress "shall have the power to promote the Progress of Science and the useful Arts, by securing for limited Times to Authors and Inventors the exclusive Right to their respective Writings and Discoveries."

[18] 499 U.S. 340 (1991).

[19] *Id.* at 349-50.

[20] The Court wrote: "Originality is a constitutional requirement. The source of Congress' power to enact copyright laws is Article I, §8, cl. 8, of the Constitution, which authorizes Congress to 'secure for limited Times to Authors . . . the exclusive Right to their respective Writings.' In two decisions from the late 19th century -- The Trade-Mark Cases, 100 U.S. 82 (1879); and Burrow-Giles Lithographic Co. v. Sarony, 111 U.S. 53 (1884) -- this Court defined the crucial terms 'authors' and 'writings.' In so doing, the Court made it unmistakably clear that these terms presuppose a degree of originality." *Id.* at 346.

[21] *Id.* at 358.

[22] "English and American courts created the sweat of the brow theory of copyright in an effort to determine when a collection of facts crosses the threshold and becomes protected by copyright laws. The sweat of the brow theory is attractive due to its ability to arrive at what seems like a just result. Under the sweat of the brow theory, an author of a compilation of facts can protect her sometimes tremendous investment of labor from blatant copying by later authors." *See* Charles Brill, *Legal Protection of Collections of Facts*, COMP. L REV. & TECH. J. 1, 11 (1998).

[23] 499 U.S. at 354.

[24] 499 U.S. at 347, quoting Miller v. Universal Studios, 650 F.2d 1365, 1369 (5th Cir. 1981).

[25] *Id.* at 350.

[26] Section 102(b) of the 1976 Copyright Act specifically states: "In no case does copyright protection for an original work of authorship extend to any idea, procedure, process, system, method of operation, concept, principle, or discovery, regardless of the form in which it is described, explained, illustrated, or embodied in such a work."

[27] Section 101 of the 1976 Copyright Act defines a compilation as a "work formed by the collection and assembling of preexisting materials or of data that are selected, coordinated, or arranged in such a way that the resulting work as a whole constitutes an original work of authorship."

[28] 499 U.S. at 348, quoting Miller v. Universal Studios, 650 F.2d 1365, 1369 (5th Cir.1981).

[29] The Feist court refused to address the apparent contradictions between copyright and the hot news doctrine, saying only that the INS court had "rendered judgment for The Associated Press on non-copyright grounds that are not relevant here." 499 U.S. at 354, see footnote.

[30] 248 U.S. 215 (1918).

[31] For example, misappropriation can protect trade secrets and the commercial value of a person's identity. *See* RESTATEMENT (THIRD) OF UNFAIR COMPETITION §38 (1995).

[32] Today, the hot news doctrine is part of state common law. The U.S. Supreme Court abolished federal common law in Erie Railroad Co. v. Tompkins, 304 U.S. 64 (1938). In addition to New York, those states that have adopted the doctrine are Pennsylvania, California, Alaska, Colorado, Illinois, North Carolina, South Carolina, Wisconsin, New Jersey, Missouri, Texas, Maryland, and Delaware. Legal scholars and this author often use "hot news doctrine," "hot news," "misappropriation" and "hot news misappropriation" interchangeably to refer to the doctrine. *See* Edmund Sease, *Misappropriation is Seventy-Five Years Old; Should we Bury it or Revive it?* 70 N. DAK. L. REV. 781 (1994).

[33] Separate Brief for Complainant at 2, INS v. AP, 248 U.S. 215 (1918). The AP asked the district court for an injunction to restrain INS from continuing its practices. The district court's review of the facts

and testimony led it to rule for AP on the first two claims and to grant the injunction. The court also thought the third claim was deserving of the injunction, but referred the legal question to the Second Circuit U.S. Court of Appeals. That court decided the injunction should apply to the third claim as well. INS appealed to the U.S. Supreme Court.

[34] Today, however, news wire stories are copyrighted the moment they are "fixed in a tangible medium of expression." *See* 17 U.S.C. §101 (2000).

[35] Brief for Complainant at 34. Under the 1909 Copyright Act, creators were required to register their work with the Copyright Office to receive copyright protection. Since the passage of the 1976 Copyright Act, that is no longer the case.

[36] Justice John Clarke excused himself from the case because of his financial interests in newspapers.

[37] 248 U.S. at 239.

[38] *Id.* at 240.

[39] *Id.* at 241.

[40] *Id.* at 248.

[41] *Id.* at 242.

[42] Brandeis argued that the leading unfair competition cases relied on a breach of contract or trust to award relief and that none was evident in the case. He also argued that under the principles of common law copyright, all rights in the news ceased upon publication. *Id.* at 251.

[43] *Id.* at 250.

[44] *Id.* at 264.

[45] *Id.* at 263.

[46] INS was banned from reporting in Great Britain, France, Portugal, and Japan during World War I. The British government cited INS for "continued garbling of messages and breach of faith," but the common belief is that the Hearst-owned service's pro-German views led to its newsgathering troubles. *See* OLIVER GRAMLING, AP: THE STORY OF NEWS 285 (1940).

[47] 248 U.S. at 263.

[48] A "bot" is short for "robot," a "computer program that runs automatically." *See* http://www.webopedia.com.

[49] *See* Eben Moglen, The DotCommunist Manifesto: How Culture Became Property and What We're Going to Do About It, Address at

the University of North Carolina — Chapel Hill (Nov. 8, 2001) (transcript available at http:// moglen.law.columbia.edu/).

[50] *See* LAWRENCE LESSIG, THE FUTURE OF IDEAS: THE FATE OF THE COMMONS IN A CONNECTED WORLD (2001).

[51] 105 F.3d 841 (2d Cir. 1997).

[52] 939 F.Supp. 1071 (S.D.N.Y. 1996).

[53] 17 U.S.C. §301 (2000).

[54] *See* Frank Gomez, *Copyright: preemption – misappropriation (Washington Post v. Total News, Inc.)*, 13 BERKELEY TECH. L.J. 21 (1998).

[55] 105 F.3d at 845.

[56] *Id.*

[57] H.R. 3531, 103rd Cong. (1996).

[58] *See* John M. Conley et al, *Database Protection in a Digital World*, 6 RICH J.L. & TECH. 2 (1999).

[59] *See* 17 U.S.C. §107 (Foundation Press 2000). The provisions of fair use in copyright law allow users of copyrighted material to use the work without permission "for purposes such as criticism, comment, news reporting, teaching, scholarship, or research."

[60] H.R. 2652, 104th Cong. (1997).

[61] *Id.*

[62] 17 U.S.C. §1201 (2000).

[63] *See* Conley, *supra* note 58.

[64] H.R. 354, 106th Cong. (1999).

[65] *See* Conley, *supra* note 58.

[66] H.R. 1858, 106th Cong. (1999).

[67] H.R. 1858, *The Consumer and Investor Access to Information Act of 1999*, 145 Cong Rec E 1055, May 20, 1999 (statement of Rep. Tom Bliley).

[68] H.R. 354, 106th Cong. (1999).

[69] H.R. 1858 §101(5)(a)(b) (1999).

[70] Not surprisingly, out of the eleven organizations that testified in support of the measure, six were financial markets institutions.

[71] "After the House Commerce Committee passed H.R. 1858 in August 1999, database legislation in the 106th Congress ground to a halt. Rather than choosing between H.R. 354 and H.R. 1858, the House Rules Committee and the House Republican leadership urged the two committees to reach a consensus. Intermittent negotiations between the

committee staffs failed to produce a compromise and both bills died with the end of the 106th Congress." *See* Jonathan Band & Makoto Kono, *The Database Protection Debate in the 106th Congress*, 62 OHIO ST. L.J. 869 (2001).

[72] H.R. 3261 108th Cong. (2003).
[73] H.R. 3261 §3(b) (2003).
[74] H.R. 3261 §3(c) (2003).
[75] H.R. 3261 §9(a) (2003).
[76] Jonathan Band, *Response to the Coalition against Database Privacy Memorandum*, THE COMPUTER & INTERNET LAWYER, May 2004.
[77] *Id.* Opponents argue that database protection legislation cannot be passed by Congress' powers under the Intellectual Property Clause or the Commerce Clause. These critics cite the U.S. Supreme Court's decision in *Feist v. Rural Telephone* as support for Congress' lack of authority to give facts protection under copyright. They argue that a recent Supreme Court decision, *Dastar Corp. v. Twentieth Century Fox Film Corp.*, stands for the notion that "Congress could not rely on its power under the Commerce Clause to enact legislation that in effect creates a perpetual patent or copyright prohibited by the Intellectual Property Clause." *Id.* In *Dastar*, a film company purchased a public domain TV series, edited and republished the series without giving credit to the first producers of the series, who had allowed the original series' copyright to lapse. The original producers sued under federal trademark law, which was created under Congress' Commerce Clause powers, and lost.
[78] *See* RESTATEMENT (THIRD) OF UNFAIR COMPETITION §38 (1995). *See also* Louis Klein, *Copyright — Misappropriation Doctrine: National Basketball Association v. Motorola, Inc.: Future Prospects for Protecting Real-Time Information*, 64 BROOKLYN L. REV. 585, 588 (1998); and David Djavaherian, *Hot News and No Cold Facts: NBA v. Motorola and the Protection of Database Contents*, 5 RICH J.L. & TECH. 8 (1998).
[79] *See* Bruce Keller, *Condemned to Repeat the Past: The Reemergence of Misappropriation and Other Common Law Theories of Protection for Intellectual Property*, 11 HARV. J. LAW & TEC 401, 403 (1998). *See also* Dale P. Olson, *Common Law Misappropriation in the Digital Era*, 64 MO. L. REV. 837 (1999);

[80] See Gary Myers, *The Restatement's Rejection of the Misappropriation Tort: A Victory for the Public Domain*, 47 S.C. L. REV. 673, 674 (1996). See also Rex Y. Fujichaku, *The misappropriation doctrine in cyberspace: protecting the commercial value of "hot news,"* 20 U. HAW. L. REV. 421, 425 (1998).

[81] Richard A. Posner, *Essay: Misappropriation: A Dirge*, 40 HOUS. L. REV. 621 (2003).

[82] *Id.* at 625.

[83] *Id.* at 638.

[84] See Michael Freno, *Database Protection: Resolving the U.S. Database Dilemma with an Eye Toward International Protection*, 34 CORNELL INT'L L.J. 165, 185 (2001). "The EU's Database Directive calls for the creation of a sui generis property right in the factual contents of any database that has been created through 'substantial investment.' This right, which lasts for fifteen years, is to protect database owners from acts of "extraction" and "re-utilization" of the facts in their databases, but this term of protection could be extended indefinitely if there was substantial investment." *See also* John Tessensohn, *The Devil's in the Details: The Quest for Legal Protection of Computer Databases and the Collections of Information Act, H.R. 2652*, 38 IDEA 439, 465 (1998).

[85] *See* C. Boyden Gray, Jamie Gorelick, and Randolph Moss, *Memorandum on the Legal Need for H.R. 3261, the "Database and Collections of Information Misappropriation Act,"* THE COMPUTER & INTERNET LAWYER, May 2004, at 2; John Tessensohn, *The Devil's in the Details: The Quest for Legal Protection of Computer Databases and the Collections of Information Act, H.R. 2652*, 38 IDEA 439, 465 (1998). *See also* Jeffrey C. Wolken, *Just the Facts, Ma'am. A Case for Uniform Federal Regulation of Information Databases in the New Information Age*, 48 SYRACUSE L. REV. 1263, 1279 (1998); Jason R. Boyarski, *The Heist of Feist: Protection for Collections of Information and the Possible Federalization of "Hot News,"* 21 CARDOZO L. REV. 871, 902 (1999); and Cynthia M. Bott, *Protection of Information Products: Balancing Commercial Reality and the Public Domain*, 67 U. CIN. L. REV. 237 (1998).

[86] J.H. Reichman & Pamela Samuelson, *Intellectual Property Rights in Data?* 50 VAND. L. REV. 51 (1997); Charles Brill, *Legal*

Protections of Collections of Facts, COMP. L REV. & TECH. J. 1,17 (1998).

[87] Malla Pollack, *The Right to Know?: Delimiting Database Protection at the Juncture of the Commerce Clause, the Intellectual Property Clause and the First Amendment*,17 CARDOZO ARTS & ENT L.J. 47, 93 (1999); Yochai Benkler, *Free as the Air to Common Use: First Amendment Constraints on Enclosure of the Public Domain*, 74 N.Y.U.L. REV. 354 (1999); *See also* Yochai Benkler, *Constitutional Bounds of Database Protection: The Role of Judicial Review in the Creation and Definition of Private Rights in Information*, 15 BERKELEY TECH. L.J. 535 (2000).

[88] Jonathan Band, *Response to the Coalition Against Database Privacy Memorandum*, THE COMPUTER & INTERNET LAWYER, May 2004.

[89] See Wendy J. Gordon, *On Owning Information: Intellectual Property and the Restitutionary Impulse*, 78 VA. L. REV. 149, 167 (1992). *See also* Wendy Gordon, *Asymmetric Market Failure and Prisoner's Dilemma in Intellectual Property*, 17 U. DAYTON L. REV. 853, 854 (1992); J.H. Reichman & Pamela Samuelson, *Intellectual Property Rights in Data?* 50 VAND. L. REV. 51 (1997); Edmund Sease, *Misappropriation is Seventy-Five Years Old; Should we Bury it or Revive it?* 70 N. DAK. L. REV. 781 (1994); and Leo J. Raskind, *The Misappropriation Doctrine as a Competitive Norm of Intellectual Property Law*, 75 MIN. L. REV. 875, 886 (1991).

CHAPTER 2

[1] Edward Campbell Aff. at 147, Jan. 12, 1917. INS v. AP, 240 F. 983 (S.D.N.Y. 1917).

[2] *Id.*

[3] *Id.*

[4] KENT COOPER, KENT COOPER AND THE ASSOCIATED PRESS 198 (1959).

[5] 240 F. 983 (S.D.N.Y. 1917).

[6] 240 U.S. 215 (1918).

[7] While there is some debate about the exact date of AP's founding, it is generally thought to have been founded between 1848 and 1849. For a detailed discussion on AP's founding, *see* RICHARD SCHWARZLOSE, THE NATION'S NEWSBROKERS, VOL. 1, 89-119 (1989).

[8] *Id.* at 121.

[9] RICHARD SCHWARZLOSE, THE NATION'S NEWSBROKERS, VOL. 2, 24 (1989).
[10] Barbara Cloud, *News: Public Service or Profitable Property*, AMERICAN JOURNALISM, Spring 1996, at 141.
[11] OLIVER GRAMLING, AP: THE STORY OF NEWS 284 (1940).
[12] VICTOR ROSEWATER, HISTORY OF COOPERATIVE NEWSGATHERING IN THE UNITED STATES 279 (1930).
[13] MENAHEM BLONDHEIM, NEWS OVER THE WIRES: THE TELEGRAPH AND THE FLOW OF PUBLIC INFORMATION IN AMERICA, 1844-1897, 75 (1994).
[14] Cloud, *supra* note 10, at 141.
[15] BLONDHEIM, *supra* note 13, at 75.
[16] Cloud, *supra* note 10, at 144.
[17] ROSEWATER, *supra* note 12, at 118.
[18] For a complete discussion of the conflict, *see* Peter R. Knights, *The Press Association War of 1866-1867*, JOURNALISM MONOGRAPHS, December (1967).
[19] SCHWARZLOSE, *supra* note 7, at 19.
[20] *Regulations of the General News Association of the City of New York*, 1856, *reprinted in* VICTOR ROSEWATER, *supra* note 12, at 381-88.
[21] *Id.* at 248. "A members" were voting members of the Associated Press corporation. At the time this rule was adopted, the AP was a for-profit stock company, incorporated in Illinois in 1892.
[22] *Id.* at 249.
[23] BLONDHEIM, *supra* note 13, at 162.
[24] *Id.*
[25] Cloud, *supra* note 10, at 147-48 (quoting Henry Watterson).
[26] H.R. 62, 48th Cong. (1884); H.R. 4160, 48th Cong. (1884); H.R. 5850, 48th Cong. (1884); and H.R. 1728, 48th Cong. (1884).
[27] Cloud, *supra* note 10, at 145.
[28] Cloud's research showed that H.R. 1728, 48th Cong., provided:
"That any daily or weekly newspaper, or any association of daily or weekly newspapers, published in the United States or any of the Territories thereof, shall have the sole right to print, issue, and sell, for the term of eight hours, dating from the hour of going to press, the contents of said daily or weekly newspaper, or the collected news of said newspaper association, exceeding one hundred words.

"Sec. 2. That for any infringement of the copyright granted by the first section of this act the party injured may sue in any court of competent jurisdiction and recover in any proper action the damages sustained by him from the person making such infringement, together with the costs of suit."

[29] Cloud, *supra* note 10, at 156.
[30] *Id.* at 154.
[31] *Id.* at 150.
[32] ROSEWATER, *supra* note 12, at 280.
[33] SCHWARZLOSE, *supra* note 7, at 139.
[34] In this context, a "trust" is an "intercorporate organization designed to restrict competition within specific areas and industries over a long period." Trusts were common until 1890, when they were outlawed under the Sherman Antitrust Act of 1890. By contrast, a monopoly is generally a "company or group having exclusive control over a commercial activity." A monopoly may or may not be legal. THE AMERICAN HERITAGE DICTIONARY, NEW COLLEGE EDITION (1978).
[35] For a discussion of the UP-AP trust agreements, *see* SCHWARZLOSE, *supra* note 7, at 109-47 and ROSEWATER, *supra* note 12, at 182-89.
[36] SCHWARZLOSE, *supra* note 7, at 145.
[37] *Id.* at 179.
[38] SCHWARZLOSE, *supra* note 7, at 192.
[39] MELVILLE E. STONE, FIFTY YEARS AS A JOURNALIST 357-61 (1921).
[40] ASSOCIATED PRESS, LAW OF THE ASSOCIATED PRESS, VOLS. 1-2 (1914-19).
[41] *Antitrust: An Overview*, Legal Information Institute, at http://www.law.cornell.edu/topics/antitrust.html (last visited May 6, 2002).
[42] *See* State of Missouri v. AP (Oct. 1900), *reprinted in* LAW OF THE ASSOCIATED PRESS, VOL. 1, 275 (1914).
[43] *See* Matthews v. AP, 61 Hun. 199 (1891); and New York Sun v. AP (1897) *reprinted in* LAW OF THE ASSOCIATED PRESS, VOL. 1, 277, 289 (1914). Citations are incompletely reported in the LAW OF THE ASSOCIATED PRESS and could not be independently established.
[44] AP v. Washington News; Minnesota Tribune v. AP, 83 F. 350 (8th Cir. 1897); Helena Record v. Helena Independent; Dunlap's Cable News Co. v. Stone, 60 Hun. 583 (1891), Ohio State Journal v. AP, Publisher's Press v. AP, 58 NYS 186 (decision of attorney general of

New York, 1904) *reprinted in* LAW OF THE ASSOCIATED PRESS, VOL. 1 (1914). Citations are incompletely reported in the LAW OF THE ASSOCIATED PRESS and could not be independently established.

[45] AP v. Washington News, *reprinted in* LAW OF THE ASSOCIATED PRESS, VOL. 1, 447 (1914).

[46] 184 Ill. 438 (1900).

[47] The *New York Sun* was part of the original New York AP, but after the UP scandal, it split from the new AP. Relations between the *Sun* and the AP were never the same. The *Sun* relied on its own news agency, the Laffan News Bureau. It lost its own case against AP's bylaws in 1897. In 1914, the paper filed a complaint with the U.S. Justice Department against AP, accusing AP of unfair trade practices. *See In the Matter of the Complaint of the Sun Printing and Publishing Association against the Associated Press, reprinted in* LAW OF THE ASSOCIATED PRESS, VOL. 1 (1914). The Justice Department dismissed the complaint, but recommended that AP eliminate its bylaw that expelled members who allowed non-AP operators and competitor wire services into AP member newsrooms. The AP board rescinded that bylaw in 1915. *See* SCHWARZLOSE, *supra* note 7, at 240. Incidentally, the decision to repeal this bylaw was a contributing factor in INS v. AP. The employee of the *Cleveland News* — who secretly shared AP news with INS — monitored the AP and INS wires, both of which were in place at the paper.

[48] 184 Ill. 438, 449 (1900).

[49] *Id.* at 453.

[50] ROSEWATER, *supra* note 12, at 274.

[51] STONE, *supra* note 39, at 357.

[52] Cloud, *supra* note 10, at 145.

[53] STONE, *supra* note 39, at 359. A chancellor is "a judge in a court of chancery or equity in various states of the United States." WEBSTER'S NINTH NEW COLLEGIATE DICTIONARY (1989).

[54] STONE, *supra* note 39, at 360.

[55] *Id.*

[56] 119 F. 294 (7th Cir. 1902).

[57] Equity refers to "the body of principles constituting what is fair and right; natural law." It also is "the right to decide matters in equity." BLACK'S LAW DICTIONARY 560 (7TH ED. 1999).

[58] 119 F. at 299-300.

[59] *Id.*

[60] THE ASSOCIATED PRESS, M.E.S. HIS BOOK 70 (1918).

[61] 248 U.S. 215, 237-38 (1918).
[62] THE ASSOCIATED PRESS, *supra* note 60, at 64.
[63] STONE, *supra* note 39, at 361.
[64] *Id.*
[65] DAVID NASAW, THE CHIEF: THE LIFE OF WILLIAM RANDOLPH HEARST, 234 (2000).
[66] *Id. See also* INTERNATIONAL NEWS SERVICE, HISTORY OF INS 1 (1946).
[67] HISTORY OF INS, *supra* note 66, at 3.
[68] JOHN K. WINKLER, WILLIAM RANDOLPH HEARST: A NEW APPRAISAL 192-93 (1955).
[69] OLIVER CARLSON & ERNEST SUTHERLAND BATES, HEARST: LORD OF SAN SIMEON 187 (1936).
[70] NASAW, *supra* note 65, at 244.
[71] *Id.*; CARLSON & BATES, *supra* note 69, at 188; WINKLER, *supra* note 68, at 193.
[72] Fred J. Wilson Aff., at 126, Jan. 15, 1917. INS v. AP, 240 F. 983 (S.D.N.Y. 1917).
[73] The Jutland Naval Battle in May of 1916 was "the first and last great engagement between the British and German Fleets. Although the British Fleet suffered serious losses, the German High Seas Fleet never faced them again." *See* JAY WINTER & BLAINE BAGGETT, THE GREAT WAR AND THE SHAPING OF THE 20TH CENTURY 161 (1996).
[74] Wilson Aff., *supra* note 72, at 126.
[75] WINKLER, *supra* note 68, at 12-13.
[76] *Id.* at 193.
[77] NASAW, *supra* note 65, at 247.
[78] *Id.* at 258.
[79] The United States entered World War I on April 6, 1917.
[80] NASAW, *supra* note 65, at 259.
[81] *Id.* at 261.
[82] *Id.* at 247-48.
[83] *Id.* at 265.
[84] *Id.* at 272.
[85] CARLSON & BATES, *supra* note 69, at 192.
[86] *Senate Told About Loan by Brisbane*, SAN FRANCISCO EXAMINER, Dec. 6, 1918, at 6; *Hale Named As Agent of Germany*, SAN FRANCISCO EXAMINER, Dec. 7, 1918, at 4; *Hale Sent to Berlin as Neutral German Connection Unsuspected*, SAN FRANCISCO EXAMINER, Dec. 7, 1918, at 4; *Propaganda for Germany Fails in U.S.*, SAN

FRANCISCO EXAMINER, Dec. 8, 1918, at 12; *Enemy Raises $27,850,000 in This Country*, SAN FRANCISCO EXAMINER, Dec. 10, 1918, at 6; *Mr. Hearst Opposed to Espionage*, SAN FRANCISCO EXAMINER, Dec. 11, 1918, at 1,6; Editorial, *Some Information That May Be Of Use to the Senate Committee That is Investigating Pre-War Propaganda*, SAN FRANCISCO EXAMINER, Dec. 12, 1918, at 20; *Hearst Holds To Policy of America First*, SAN FRANCISCO EXAMINER, Dec. 13, 1918, at 9; *German Propagandists Sent to America Before This Nation Entered War*, SAN FRANCISCO EXAMINER, Dec. 14, 1918, at 6; *Edward Lyell Fox, Correspondent Was Never in Employ of Mr. Hearst*, SAN FRANCISCO EXAMINER, Dec. 14, 1918, at 6; Editorial, *Nevada Defense Council Attack Upon Hearst Papers Fittingly Meets an Ignominious End*, SAN FRANCISCO EXAMINER, Dec. 14, 1918, at 18; *Capt. Lester in Tangle of Denials*, SAN FRANCISCO EXAMINER, Dec. 15, 1918, at 5; Editorial, *What Do You Folks Think of This Last Futile Attack of the Interests and Their Paid Tools?* SAN FRANCISCO EXAMINER, Dec. 17, 1918, at 20; Albert E. Bryan, *Innuendos on U.S. Loyalty Are Exposed*, SAN FRANCISCO EXAMINER, Dec. 18, 1918, at 4; *Capt. Lester's Conclusions, Insinuations Are Scored*, SAN FRANCISCO EXAMINER, Dec. 19, 1918, at 6; *Winsor McCay Writes About His American Cartoons and Mr. Hearst*, SAN FRANCISCO EXAMINER, Dec. 19, 1918, at 6; Albert E. Bryan, *U.S. Senators Make Witness Admit Truth*, SAN FRANCISCO EXAMINER, Dec. 20, 1918, at 1,3; Editorial, *Henry Ford's Attack on the Chicago "Tribune,"* SAN FRANCISCO EXAMINER, Dec. 20, 1918, at 20; *Officers Play Politics With Bolo Papers*, SAN FRANCISCO EXAMINER, Dec. 21, 1918, at 1, 6; Albert E. Bryan, *Becker Case 'Mere Scraps' Asserts Reed*, SAN FRANCISCO EXAMINER, Dec. 22, 1918, at 1, 6.

[87] *Mr. Hearst Opposed to Espionage*, SAN FRANCISCO EXAMINER, Dec. 11, 1918, at 1, 6.

[88] *High Court Decides on News Rights*, SAN FRANCISCO EXAMINER, Dec. 24, 1918, at 13. The article was decidedly pro-INS, emphasizing Justice Brandeis' dissent in the case and the Court's rejection of an outright property right in news. It failed, however, to explain the limited right awarded by the Court to hot news following publication.

[89] *'Examiner,' Unsurpassed, Will Cover World's News*, SAN FRANCISCO EXAMINER, Dec. 22, 1918, at 8N. Hearst made a similar announcement following the U.S. Court of Appeals decision in INS v. AP on July 17, 1917. In a story appearing the following day, Hearst

announced a new alliance with Agence Radio of Paris for war news. *See I.N.S. Opens Great War News Service*, SAN FRANCISCO EXAMINER, July 18, 1917, at 1.

[90] NASAW, *supra* note 65, at 106-10.

[91] *Id.* at 112.

[92] CARLSON & BATES, *supra* note 69, at 86.

[93] NASAW, *supra* note 65, at 110.

[94] *Id.* at 149.

[95] CARLSON & BATES, *supra* note 69, at 181.

[96] COOPER, *supra* note 4, at 195.

[97] *Id.* at 197.

[98] Melvin I. Urofsky, *Proposed Federal Incorporation in the Progressive Era, in* GROWTH OF THE REGULATORY STATE, 1900-1917: STATE AND FEDERAL REGULATION OF RAILROADS AND OTHER ENTERPRISES 304 (ROBERT F. HIMMELBERG, ED., 1994).

[99] JOHN WHITECLAY CHAMBERS II, THE TYRANNY OF CHANGE: AMERICA IN THE PROGRESSIVE ERA 2 (2000).

[100] *Id.*

[101] *Id.* at xx.

[102] DAVID M. KENNEDY, PROGRESSIVISM: THE CRITICAL ISSUES VIII (1971).

[103] Gabriel Kolko, *The Triumph of Conservatism*, in PROGRESSIVISM: THE CRITICAL ISSUES 109-21 (DAVID M. KENNEDY, ED., 1971); MARTIN SKLAR, THE CORPORATE RECONSTRUCTION OF AMERICAN CAPITALISM, 1890-1916: THE MARKET, THE LAW, AND POLITICS (1988).

[104] U.S. Const. amend. XIV, §1.

[105] JOHN SEMONCHE, KEEPING THE FAITH: A CULTURAL HISTORY OF THE U.S. SUPREME COURT 139 (1998). The Supreme Court first gave corporations the rights of individuals in *Santa Clara County v. Southern Pacific Railroad*, 188 U.S. 394 (1886). It "extended to corporations, at first to their stockholders as associated property owners, ultimately to the corporation itself as a 'natural entity,' the legal status of a person within the meaning of the Fifth and Fourteenth Amendments of the United States Constitution." *See* SKLAR, *supra* note 103, at 49.

[106] JOHN R. COMMONS, LEGAL FOUNDATIONS OF CAPITALISM 11-18 (1924), *quoted in* SKLAR, *supra* note 103, at 49-50.

[107] Semonche, *supra* note 105, at 146.

[108] *Id.* at 135-68.

[109] *Id.* at 144.

[110] The INS Court wrote: "Regarding the news, therefore, as but the material out of which both parties are seeking to make profits at the same time and in the same filed, we hardly can fail to recognize that for this purpose, as between them, it must be regarded as quasi property, irrespective of the rights of either as against the public." 248 U.S. 215, 236 (1918).

[111] CHAMBERS, *supra* note 99, at 40.

[112] *Antitrust: An Overview*, Legal Information Institute, *at* http://www.law.cornell.edu/topics/antitrust.html (last visited May 6, 2002).

[113] CHAMBERS, *supra* note 99, at 55-61; SKLAR, *supra* note 103, at 4-14; Kolko, *supra* note 103, at 134.

[114] SKLAR, *supra* note 103, at 48.

[115] United States v. Trans-Missouri Freight Ass'n, 166 U.S. 290 (1897). In 1892, the U.S. government filed suit against 18 railroad companies charging them with illegal monopolistic practices. The Supreme Court ruled that the railroads' trust agreement was an illegal restraint of trade.

[116] Standard Oil Co. v. U.S., 221 U.S. 1 (1911); U.S. v. American Tobacco Co., 221 U.S. 106 (1911). The Supreme Court found the Standard Oil and American Tobacco trusts to be illegal monopolies and ordered their breakups.

[117] Richard M. Steuer, *Executive Summary of the Antitrust Laws, Rule of Reason and Per Se Offenses*, *at* http://profs.lp.findlaw.com/antitrust/antitrust_2.html (last visited May 7, 2002).

[118] 248 U.S. 215, 241 (1918).

[119] In 1940, the U.S. Supreme Court ruled that AP bylaws restricting the entrance of news members into the cooperative violated antitrust laws. *See* Margaret Blanchard, *The Associated Press Antitrust Suit: A Philosophical Clash Over Ownership of First Amendment Rights*, BUSINESS HISTORY REVIEW, Vol. 61, Spring, 43 (1987).

[120] J. THOMASMCCARTHY, MCCARTHY ON TRADEMARKS AND UNFAIR COMPETITION, §1:8 (4th ed. 2002); HARRY D. NIMS, THE LAW OF UNFAIR COMPETITION AND TRADEMARKS §1 (4th ed. 1947).

[121] INS v. AP, 248 U.S. 215 (1918)

[122] Brooks Bros. v. Brooks Clothing of California, Ltd., 60 F.Supp. 442 (D.Cal. 1945), *quoted in* MCCARTHY, *supra* note 120, at §1:9.

[123] Johnson & Johnson v. Quality Pure Mfg., 484 F. Supp. 975 (D.N.J. 1979), *quoted in* MCCARTHY, *supra* note 120, at §1:9.
[124] American Heritage Life Ins. Co. v. Heritage Life Ins. Co., 494 F.2d 3 (5th Cir. 1974), *quoted in* MCCARTHY, *supra* note 120, §1:9.
[125] MCCARTHY, *supra* note 120, at §1:13.
[126] NIMS, *supra* note 120, at §2.
[127] MCCARTHY, *supra* note 120, at §1:12.
[128] *Id.* at §4:4.
[129] Today, both kinds of trademark are protected by federal statute.
[130] Today, passing off is still unfair competition but is "reserved for those cases where defendant has made an unauthorized substitution of the goods of one manufacturer when the goods of another manufacturer were ordered by the customer." MCCARTHY, *supra* note 120, at §1:12.
[131] *Id.* at §1:23.
[132] INS v. AP, 248 U.S. 215, 240 (1918).
[133] "No doubt news articles often possess a literary quality, and are the subject of literary property at the common law; nor do we question that such an article, as a literary production, is the subject of copyright by the terms of the act as it now stands." 248 U.S. at 234.
[134] U.S. CONST., ART I., § 8.
[135] *See* LYMAN RAY PATTERSON, COPYRIGHT IN HISTORICAL PERSPECTIVE 144 (1968).
[136] EDWARD SAMUELS, THE ILLUSTRATED STORY OF COPYRIGHT 15 (2000).
[137] British statute recognized copyright protections for periodicals, and British courts recognized a copyright in periodicals, whether a work was registered or not. *See* EATON S. DRONE, A TREATISE ON THE LAW OF PROPERTY IN INTELLECTUAL PRODUCTIONS IN GREAT BRITAIN AND THE UNTIED STATES 170-74 (1879).
[138] *Id.* at 169.
[139] SAMUELS, *supra* note 136, at 234-38. *See also* RICHARD ROGERS BOWKER, COPYRIGHT: ITS HISTORY AND ITS LAW 341-72 (1912).
[140] BOWKER, *supra* note 139, at 39.
[141] *Id.*
[142] Copyright Act of 1909, §5, *reprinted in* BOWKER, *supra* note 139, at 467.
[143] BOWKER, *supra* note 139, at 88.
[144] Interestingly, the first Berne Convention, the leading international copyright treaty of the late nineteenth and early twentieth

centuries, specifically provided that the facts of news were free for others to take. The Berne Convention was passed in 1886, and was adopted by Great Britain, Germany, Belgium, Spain, France, Haiti, Italy, Switzerland, Tunis, and Liberia. The United States did not become a member of the Berne Convention until 1998. *See* BOWKER, *supra* note 139, at 320. *See also* Berne Convention, Sept. 9, 1886, art. VII, reprinted in BOWKER, *supra* note 139, at 611-12.

[145] Copyright Act of 1909, §5, *reprinted in* BOWKER, *supra* note 139, at 467.

[146] 17 U.S. §102, §106 (Foundation Press 2000).

[147] Copyright Act of 1909, §9, §10, *reprinted in* BOWKER, *supra* note 139, at 469.

[148] 17 U.S. §102 (Foundation Press 2000).

[149] *See* PAUL GOLDSTEIN, COPYRIGHT, PATENT, TRADEMARK AND RELATED STATE DOCTRINES 173 (4th ed. 1997).

[150] MARK ROSE, AUTHORS AND OWNERS: THE INVENTION OF COPYRIGHT 67 (1993).

[151] Donaldson v. Beckett, a 1772 British case, "is generally cited for the proposition that it abolished the author's common law copyright, and thus limited the author's rights in connection with his published works to rights granted by statute." However, some scholars have argued that the Donaldson case took only the author's common law right to "print, publish, and vend" his work and did not take away whatever other common law rights the author had in the work. *See* PATTERSON, *supra* note 135, at 173-75. In 1834, the U.S. Supreme Court ruled in Wheaton v. Peters that authors do not have a common law copyright in their work after publication. *Id.* at 203-12.

[152] BOWKER, *supra* note 139, at 53.

[153] *See generally* DRONE, *supra* note 137, at 283-97. *See also* BOWKER, *supra* note 139, at 52-3.

[154] Kiernan v. Manhattan Quotation, 50 How. Pr. 194 (1876); Bd. of Trade v. Thomson, 103 F. 902 (E.D. Wis. 1900); Tribune Co. v. AP, 116 F. 126 (N.D. Ill. 1900); Bd. of Trade v. Hadden-Krull Co., 109 F. 705 (E.D. Wis. 1901); Nat'l Telegraph News v. Western Union, 119 F. 294 (7th Cir. 1902); Bd. of Trade v. Kinsey, 130 F. 507 (7th Cir. 1904); Bd. of Trade v. Christie Grain & Stock Co., 198 U.S. 236 (1905); Hunt v. New York Cotton Exch., 205 U.S. 322 (1907); Bd. of Trade v. Tucker, 221 F. 305 (2d Cir. 1915).

[155] 50 How Pr. 194 (1876).

[156] *Id.* at 194.

[157] *Id.* at 196.

[158] *Id.* at 196-97.

[159] *Id.* at 199.

[160] *Id.* at 201.

[161] Like *Kiernan*, these courts also held that market quotations were property: *See* Bd. of Trade v. Thomson, 103 F. 902 (E.D. Wis. 1900); Bd. of Trade v. Hadden-Krull Co., 109 F. 705 (E.D. Wis. 1901); Bd. of Trade v. Kinsey 130 F. 507 (7th Cir. 1904); Bd. of Trade v. Christie Grain & Stock Co., 198 U.S. 236 (1905); Hunt v. New York Cotton Exch., 205 U.S. 322 (1907); Bd. of Trade v. Tucker, 221 F. 305 (2d Cir. 1915). Some of these courts also held held that quotations sent to subscribers — and not yet to the public — did not constitute publication. *See* Bd. of Trade v. Hadden-Krull Co., 109 F. 705 (E.D. Wis. 1901); Bd. of Trade v. Tucker, 221 F. 305 (2d Cir. 1915). In only one case, Tribune Co. v. AP, 116 F. 126 (N.D. Ill. 1900), was the news published. In that case, the Tribune Co. had a contract with a London newspaper for use of its foreign news, but the AP transmitted that news once published in the London paper. The court ruled that it could not restrain AP from taking news published in England and wrote that Tribune's "exclusive right terminates with publication in London." 116 F. at 128.

[162] 198 U.S. 236 (1905).

[163] For more on the history of the Chicago Board of Trade, *see* WILLIAM G. FERRIS, THE GRAIN TRADERS: THE STORY OF THE CHICAGO BOARD OF TRADE (1988). *See also* Chicago Board of Trade, at http://www.cbot.com/cbot/www/page/0,1398,10+10+83,00.html.

[164] FERRIS, *supra* note 163, at 118.

[165] *Id.* at 121. Key cases included: Bd. of Trade v. Thomson, 103 F. 902 (E.D. Wis. 1900); Bd. of Trade v. Hadden-Krull Co., 109 F. 705 (E.D. Wis. 1901); Bd. of Trade v. Kinsey, 130 F. 507 (7th Cir. 1904); Bd. of Trade v. Christie Grain & Stock Co., 198 U.S. 236 (1905); Bd. of Trade v. Tucker, 221 F. 305 (2d Cir. 1915). *See also* Hunt v. New York Cotton Exch., 205 U.S. 322 (1907).

[166] FERRIS, *supra* note 163, at 122.

[167] Bd. of Trade v. Christie, 198 U.S. 236, 250 (1905).

[168] 119 F. 294 (7th Cir. 1902).

[169] Indeed, Grosscup expressed concern that too much was eligible for copyright and that news should never be copyrighted: "There is a point at which this process of expansion must cease. It would be both inequitable and impracticable to give copyright to every printed article.

Much of current publication — in fact the greater portion — is nothing beyond the mere notation of events transpiring, which, if transpiring at all, are accessible by all. It is inconceivable that the copyright grant of the constitution, and the statutes in pursuance thereof, were meant to give a monopoly of narrative to him, who, putting the bare recital of events in print, went through the routine formulas of the copyright statutes." 119 F. at 297.

[170] On the immediacy of news, Grosscup wrote: "The value of the tape to the patron is almost wholly in the fact that the knowledge thus communicated is earlier, in point of time, than knowledge communicated through other means, or to persons other than those having a like service. In just this quality — to coin a word, the precommunicatedness of the information — is the essence of appellee's service; the quality that wins from the patron his patronage." *Id.* at 298.

[171] *Id.* at 296.

[172] Some of these courts held that information sent to subscribers — and not yet to the public — did not constitute publication. *See* Bd. of Trade v.Hadden-Krull Co., 109 F. 705 (E.D. Wis. 1901); Bd. of Trade v. Tucker, 221 F. 305 (2d Cir. 1915).

CHAPTER 3

[1] George H. Eke Aff. at 41, Jan. 3, 1917. AP v. INS, 240 F. 983 (S.D.N.Y. 1917).

[2] E.P. Koukol Aff. at 42, Jan. 3, 1917; James Finnerty Aff. at 43, Jan. 3, 1917. *AP*.

[3] Melville Stone Aff. at 23, Jan. 3, 1917. *AP*.

[4] *Id.* at 25-6.

[5] *Id.* at 26.

[6] Edward Campbell Aff. at 147, Jan. 12, 1917. *AP*.

[7] *Id.*

[8] *Id.*

[9] George T. Hattie Aff. at 148, Jan. 12, 1917. *AP*.

[10] KENT COOPER, KENT COOPER AND THE ASSOCIATED PRESS 198 (1959).

[11] *Id.*

[12] Edward Campbell Aff., *supra* note 6, at 145.

[13] Fred Agnew Aff. at 32-33, Dec. 28, 1916. *AP*.

[14] Fred Agnew Aff. at 31-32, Dec. 28, 1916.

[15] Today, it is more common to see a news organization independently report the story and/or credit another news source. While this doesn't necessarily absolve the news organization from a claim of misappropriation, it is often less likely that the news organization will pursue a hot news claim if a competing organization attributes news to it.

[16] E.A. Smiley Aff. at 136, Jan. 11, 1917; Ollie Jospy Aff. at 47, Jan. 8, 1917. *AP*.

[17] Benjamin Cushing Aff. at 45, Jan. 8, 1917.

[18] *Id.*

[19] *Id.*

[20] Frank H. Ward Aff. at 131, Jan. 10, 1917. *AP*.

[21] Barry Faris Aff. at 128, Jan. 15, 1917.

[22] E.A. Smiley Aff., *supra* note 16, at 137.

[23] Frederick Roy Martin Aff. at 77, Jan. 17, 1917. *AP*.

[24] Benjamin F. Field Aff. at 141, Jan. 12, 1917.

[25] *See Id.* at 142; Sam B. Anson Aff. at 143, Jan. 13, 1917; Karl Shimansky Aff. at 144, Jan. 15, 1917.

[26] William Warnock Aff. at 151, Jan. 11, 1917. *AP*.

[27] Henry E. Leary Aff. at 153, Jan. 13, 1917.

[28] *See* Carlyle E. Cox Aff. at 160, Jan. 16, 1917.

[29] Kent Cochran Aff. at 157, Jan. 13, 1917.

[30] Edward R. Sartwell Aff. at 161, Jan. 15, 1917. *AP*.

[31] William Schwinger Aff. at 166, Jan. 12, 1917; William M. Baskervill Aff. at 163, Jan. 12, 1917; Fred Harvey Aff. at 167, Jan. 12, 1917.

[32] Fred Harvey Aff. at 167, Jan. 12, 1917.

[33] Kent Cooper Aff. at 84, Jan. 22, 1917; Frederick Roy Martin Aff. at 77, Jan. 17, 1917; Arthur Copp Aff. at 86, Jan. 22, 1917; Harold Martin Aff. at 93, Jan. 22, 1917; Paul Cowles Aff. at 96, Jan. 19, 1917. *AP*.

[34] *See* J.W. McGuire Aff. at 71, Jan. 18, 1917; Alfred M. Corrigan Aff. at 72, Jan. 19, 1917; Albert J. Hain Aff. at 73, Jan. 19, 1917; H.J. Weidenthal Aff. at 75, Jan. 19, 1917; C.A. Wellmann Aff. at 76, Jan. 19, 1917; Joseph Williams Aff. at 77, Jan. 19, 1917; T.J. Thomas Aff. at 74, Jan. 19, 1917; Charles E. Kloeber Aff. at 78, Jan. 17, 1917; Frank Wilson Aff. at 80, Jan. 19, 1917; Arthur W. Copp Aff., *supra* note 33, at 87; Jesse Crosswy Aff. at 88, Jan. 20, 1917; Jackson S. Elliott Aff. at 89, Jan. 20, 1917; C.G. Marshall Aff. at 92, Jan. 20, 1917; Henry L. Rennick Aff. at 93, Jan. 19, 1917; Harold Martin Aff. at

Endnotes *185*

93, Jan. 22, 1917; Paul Cowles Aff. at 96, Jan. 19, 1917; Basil G. Wyrick Aff. at 97, Jan. 19, 1917.

[35] Kent Cooper Aff., *supra* note 33, at 85.
[36] Jackson S. Elliott Aff. at 88, Jan. 20, 1917.
[37] AP v. INS, 240 F. 983, 985 (S.D.N.Y. 1917).
[38] *Id.*
[39] *Id.* at 988.
[40] *Id.* at 986.
[41] *Id.* at 988.
[42] *Id.* at 989.
[43] BLACK'S LAW DICTIONARY 7TH ED. 244 (1999).
[44] 240 F. at 989.
[45] *Id.* at 990.
[46] *Id.* at 989.
[47] *Id.* at 991.
[48] *Id.* at 991-92.
[49] 240 F. at 992.
[50] *Id.* at 993.
[51] 240 F. at 994-95.
[52] *Id.* at 996.
[53] 245 F. 244, 248 (2d Cir. 1917).
[54] *Id.* at 248.
[55] *Id.* at 250.
[56] *Id.* at 248.
[57] *Id.* at 249.
[58] *Id.* at 250.
[59] *Id.*
[60] 245 F. 244, 247 (2d Cir. 1917).
[61] *Id.* at 253.
[62] *Id.* at 252.
[63] *Id.* at 254.
[64] Brief for Respondent at 11, INS v. AP, 248 U.S. 215 (1918).
[65] *Id.* at 20.
[66] *Id.* at 44.
[67] *Id.* at 55.
[68] Brief for Petitioner at 17, *INS*.
[69] *Id.* at 65.
[70] *Id.* at 71.

[71] *Id.* at 74.
[72] 248 U.S. 215, 232 (1918).
[73] Other examples of unprotected works at that time included sound recordings, designs, and performances.
[74] Separate Brief for Complainant at 31-32, *INS*.
[75] Brief for Complainant at 35, *INS*.
[76] *Id.*
[77] Separate Brief for Complainant at 8. *INS*.
[78] Brief for Complainant at 35.
[79] *Id.* at 36.
[80] Separate Brief for Complainant at 6-8, *INS*.
[81] Here, a commodity is "an article of trade or commerce that can be transported." *See* THE AMERICAN HERITAGE DICTIONARY 268 (1978).
[82] Brief for Complainant at 11.
[83] *Id.* at 12-20.
[84] 198 U.S. 236 (1905).
[85] 221 F. 305 (2d. Cir. 1915).
[86] 119 F. 294 (7th Cir. 1902).
[87] Brief for Respondent at 39, *INS*.
[88] *Id.* at 49.
[89] Brief for Petitioner at 38, *INS*.
[90] Brief for Respondent at 46.
[91] *Id.* at 47.
[92] Brief for Respondent at 43, *INS*.
[93] *Id.* at 4.
[94] Brief for Petitioner at 44.
[95] *Id.* at 43.
[96] *Id.* at 18-19.
[97] *Id.* at 234.
[98] *Id.*
[99] *Id.* at 235. "We need spend no time, however, upon the general question of property in news matter at common law, or the application of the copyright, since it seems to us the case must turn upon the question of unfair competition in business."
[100] *Id.*
[101] *Id.* at 236.
[102] *Id.* at 4.
[103] Separate Brief for Respondent at 8, *INS*.

[104] *Id.* at 10.
[105] Brief for Respondent at 11-12, *INS*.
[106] Brief for Petitioner at 47.
[107] *Id.* at 47-8.
[108] Brief for Respondent at 23.
[109] Brief for Petitioner at 49, *INS*.
[110] 248 U.S. 215, 238 (1918).
[111] Separate Brief for Respondent at 28, *INS*.
[112] Brief for Petitioner at 4.
[113] *Id.* at 40.
[114] 248 U.S. at 239.
[115] *Id.* at 240.
[116] *Id.* at 240.
[117] *Id.* at 245.
[118] *Id.* at 264-65.
[119] *Id.* at 264.
[120] *Id.* at 266.
[121] *Id.* at 250.
[122] *Id.* at 259.
[123] VICTOR ROSEWATER, HISTORY OF COOPERATIVE NEWSGATHERING IN THE UNITED STATES 289 (1930).
[124] *Id.*
[125] *Id.*
[126] *Id.* at 289-98.
[127] *Id.* After significant debate following election results in 1924, the AP initially allowed member newspapers to rebroadcast "important" news on member-owned radio stations. The issue of radio station use of AP news and membership in the AP would be a source of contention for many years, until 1941, when the board voted to allow radio stations to join the cooperative.
[128] *Id.* at 297.
[129] *Predict Statutory Protection for News as Property*, EDITOR & PUBLISHER, Jan. 4, 1919, at 24.
[130] *Id.*
[131] Notes, *Equity Jurisdiction — Property in News — Unfair Competition*, 67 U PA. L. REV. 191, 194 (1919).
[132] Notes, *Property in News*, 32 HARV. L. REV. 566 (1918-19).

[133] Editorials, *The Associated Press Case — Literary Property in News — "Pirating" News as Unfair Competition*, IV VA. L. REG. 847, 851 (1918-19).

[134] Notes, *Injunction to Protect the Right of Property in News*, 18 COLUM. L. REV. 257, 261 (1918).

[135] Comments, *The Associated Press Case*, 28 YALE L. J. 387, 390-91 (1918-19).

[136] A.K., *Comment on Recent Cases*, 13 ILL. L. REV. 708, 716 (1918).

CHAPTER 4

[1] These decisions were selected from a larger universe of 475 state and federal decisions that were obtained by Shepardizing *INS v. AP*. The headnotes, case background, and legal conclusions within this larger sample were examined to select cases that had direct bearing on developing judicial interpretation of the misappropriation doctrine. Special attention was paid to those decisions that directly hinged on a determination of misappropriation, engaged in a discussion of *INS*, and/or identified the elements of a hot news claim. The other decisions usually mentioned some brief, colorful quote from *INS* in passing (the "reap where you have not sown" comment was a particular favorite of judges in many other types of actions) or simply cited the case without further discussion. These decisions and nearly all the decisions regarding the misappropriation of patents and trademarks were excluded because they were beyond the scope of this study.

[2] Nat'l Tel. Dir. Co. v. Dawson Mfg., 263 S.W. 483 (Mo. Ct. App. 1924); Gilmore v. Sammons, 269 S.W. 861 (Tex. Civ. App. 1925). Two decisions "favored" a finding of misappropriation; That is, the judge generally issued a judgment finding misappropriation or issued an injunction preventing further misappropriation until a judgment was rendered.

[3] 263 S.W. 483 (Mo. Ct. App. 1924).

[4] *Id.* at 484.

[5] *Id.* at 485.

[6] Crump Co. v. Lindsay, 130 Va. 144 (1921).

[7] Hughes v. West Publ'g Co., 225 Ill. App. 58 (1922).

[8] Public Ledger v. New York Times, 275 F. 562 (S.D.N.Y. 1921).

[9] 35 F.2d 279 (2d Cir. 1929).

[10] *Id.* at 280.

[11] Associated Press v. KVOS, 9 F.Supp. 279 (W.D. Wash. 1934), 80 F.2d 575 (9th Cir. 1935), 299 U.S. 269 (1936); Veatch v. Wagner, 109 F.Supp. 537 (D. Alaska 1953), 116 F.Supp. 904 (D. Alaska 1953); Nat'l Exhibition Co. v. Fass, 143 N.Y.S.2d 767 (N.Y. Special Term 1955); Pittsburgh Athletic Co. v. KQV, 24 F.Supp. 490 (W.D. Pa. 1938); Twentieth Century Sporting Club v. Transradio Press Service, 300 N.Y.S. 159 (N.Y. Special Term 1937); Mutual Broadcasting Sys. v. Muzak Corp., 30 N.Y.S.2d 419 (N.Y. Special Term 1941); Loeb v. Turner, 257 S.W.2d 800 (Tex. Ct. App. 1953); RCA Mfg. Co. v. Whiteman, 28 F.Supp. 787 (S.D.N.Y. 1939), 114 F.2d 86 (2d Cir. 1940); Waring v. WDAS, 27 Pa. D.&C. 297 (1936), 327 Pa. 433 (1937): Metropolitan Opera Ass'n v. Wagner-Nichols Recorder Corp., 101 N.Y.S.2d 483 (App. Div. 1950); Uproar Co. v. NBC, 8 F.Supp. 358 (D. Mass. 1934).

[12] The courts in the decisions listed in footnote 11 supported a misappropriation claim except for: Associated Press v. KVOS, 9 F.Supp. 279 (W.D. Wash. 1934); Loeb v. Turner, 257 S.W.2d 800 (Tex. Ct. App. 1953); and Veatch v. Wagner, 116 F.Supp. 904 (D. Alaska 1953).

[13] 9 F.Supp. 279 (W.D. Wash. 1934).

[14] *Id.* at 286.

[15] *Id.* The court did not consider the station's sponsorships in its ruling.

[16] *Id.* at 287-88.

[17] 80 F.2d 575, 577 (9th Cir. 1935).

[18] *Id.* at 578.

[19] *Id.* at 581.

[20] KVOS v. Associated Press, 299 U.S. 269 (1936).

[21] *Id.* at 279.

[22] *Id.*

[23] *Id.*

[24] Waring v. WDAS Broadcasting Station, Inc., 27 Pa. D.&C. 297, 301 (1936).

[25] Madison Square Garden Corp. v. Universal Pictures, 7 N.Y.S. 2d 845 (App. Div. 1938) (ruling that a motion picture producer misappropriated scenes of the New York Rangers hockey team in action at Madison Square Garden because the team had built up goodwill at considerable expense and had a right to market that interest

in return for "substantial revenue"); Beecham v. London Gramophone Corp., 104 N.Y.S.2d 473 (N.Y. Special Term 1951) (ruling that a phonographic record company misappropriated the sound track from the plaintiff's motion picture and relief could be granted based on the "subterfuge, piracy, wrongdoing, or unfair tactics of the competitor"); McCord Co. v. Plotnick, 239 P.2d 32 (Cal. Dist. Ct. App. 1951) (ruling that the publisher of a trade publication containing credit items of interest to financial institutions and other businesses misappropriated credit information from a competing trade publication); Dior v. Milton, 155 N.Y.S.2d 443 (N.Y. Special Term 1956) (ruling that a competitor misappropriated Dior fashion designs because it caused "irreparable harm" and was the result of "unconscionable business practices…and moral standards.")

[26] Triangle Publ'ns, Inc. v. New England Newspaper Pub. Co., 46 F.Supp. 198 (D. Mass. 1942) (ruling that the use of racing statistics from a daily racing publication of another publisher was probably not misappropriation because the practice resembled a "tip," and it was not unfair to use information assembled by a competitor); Nat'l Exhibition Co. v. Teleflash, Inc., 24 F.Supp. 488 (S.D.N.Y. 1936) (ruling that the dissemination of play-by-play descriptions of a sporting event by telephone from the game is not misappropriation because there was no competition between "the game itself and the words concerning it used by the defendants"); New England Tel. & Tel. Co. v. Nat'l Merch. Corp., 335 Mass. 658 (1957) (ruling that the use of the defendant's covers on the plaintiff's telephone directories was not misappropriation because "what is being supplied is a convenient, attractive, and ingenious accessory for use with telephone directories" and there was no proof "of substantial damage to the public interest"); Supreme Records v. Decca Records, 90 F.Supp. 904 (S.D. Cal. 1950) (ruling that the defendant's sale of recordings of a musical arrangement of a song first arranged by the plaintiff was not misappropriation because there is no property right in an arrangement and "Congress did not intend to give recognition to the right of arrangement.").

[27] 25 F.Supp. 787 (S.D.N.Y. 1939); 114 F.2d 86 (2nd Cir. 1940).
[28] 114 F.2d 86, 90 (2nd Cir. 1940).
[29] 327 Pa. 433 (1937).
[30] *Id.* at 454.
[31] 8 F.Supp. 358 (D. Mass. 1934).
[32] *Id.* at 362.

[33] *Id.*
[34] 101 N.Y.S.2d 483 (App. Div. 1950), *aff'd* 107 N.Y.S.2d 795 (App. Div. 1951).
[35] While Congress had given creators a copyright in public performances of their works in 1897, a composer's right extended only to public performances that were for profit. Courts struggled for many years attempting to decide whether radio music performances were "for profit." Eventually, the American Society of Composers, Authors and Publishers (ASCAP) and others brought enough cases against radio broadcasters to convince them to pay ASCAP a licensing fee for broadcasting music. *See* EDWARD SAMUELS, THE ILLUSTRATED STORY OF COPYRIGHT 39-44 (2000).
[36] 101 N.Y.S. 2d 483, 492 (App. Div. 1950).
[37] *Id.*
[38] 300 N.Y.S. 159 (N.Y. Special Term 1937).
[39] *Id.* at 160.
[40] *Id.* at 161.
[41] *Id.*
[42] 24 F.Supp. 490 (W.D. Pa. 1938).
[43] *Id.* at 493-94.
[44] 143 N.Y.S.2d 767 (N.Y. Special Term 1955).
[45] *Id.* at 777.
[46] *Id.* at 770.
[47] *Id.* at 776.
[48] 30 N.Y.S.2d 419 (N.Y. Special Term 1941).
[49] *Id.* at 420.
[50] *Id.*
[51] 257 S.W.2d 800 (Tex. Ct. App. 1953).
[52] *Id.* at 802-3.
[53] The development of ASCAP, the American Society of Composers, Authors and Publishers, helped musicians receive licensing fees for the broadcast of their music on the radio. It wasn't until 1972 that Congress awarded separate federal rights for sound recordings. *See* SAMUELS, *supra* note 35, at 44-5. In addition, private entities, such as sports arenas, increasingly relied on the use of exclusive contracts with broadcasters and placed greater restrictions on those attending, listening, or viewing a game.
[54] *Id.* at 36.

[55] JESSICA LITMAN, DIGITAL COPYRIGHT 36, 43 (2001).
[56] *Id.* at 45.
[57] *Id.* at 48-9.
[58] *Id.* at 51.
[59] *Id.*
[60] 304 U.S. 64 (1938).
[61] *Id.* at 78.
[62] Those states are Missouri, Texas, New York, Pennsylvania, California, Alaska, Colorado, Illinois, North Carolina, South Carolina, Wisconsin, New Jersey, Maryland, and Delaware. *See* Edmund Sease, *Misappropriation is Seventy-Five Years Old; Should we Bury it or Revive It?* 70 N.D. L. REV. 788, 802 (1994).
[63] 376 U.S. 225 (1964).
[64] 376 U.S. 234 (1964).
[65] 376 U.S. at 231-32.
[66] 412 U.S. 546 (1973).
[67] Of twenty-eight decisions in the study between 1960 and 1976, fifteen decisions addressed the misappropriation of sound recordings by tape and four addressed the misappropriation of television programming by cable operations. The remaining decisions addressed the misappropriation of comics, news stories, listings, ideas, and ads.
[68] 196 F.Supp. 315 (D. Idaho 1961).
[69] *Id.* at 325.
[70] *Id.* at 326.
[71] 211 F.Supp. 47 (D. Idaho 1962).
[72] *Id.* at 56.
[73] Cable Vision, Inc. v. KUTV, Inc., 335 F.2d 348 (9th Cir. 1964).
[74] *Id.* at 351.
[75] *Id.* at 353.
[76] 173 So.2d 469 (Fla. Dist. Ct. App. 1965).
[77] *Id.* at 472.
[78] 392 U.S. 390 (1968).
[79] 415 U.S. 394 (1974).
[80] "The funds raised by the compulsory license are distributed among all of the owners of copyright whose works have been picked up by cable. The allocation has become fairly standard from year to year. About 55-60 percent of all the money collected goes to program suppliers, primarily motion picture companies (through the Motion Picture Association of America); about 20-25 percent to professional

sports leagues; and the remainder to various other claimants." The revenues have risen to about $200 million in 2000. *See* SAMUELS, *supra* note 35, at 66.

[81] Capitol Records, Inc. v. Erickson, 82 Cal. Rptr. 798 (Cal. Dist. Ct. App. 1969); Capital Records v. Spies, 130 Ill.App.2d 429 (Ill. App. Ct. 1970); Tape Ind. Ass'n of America v. Younger, 316 F.Supp.340 (C.D. Cal. 1970); Liberty v. Eastern Tape Corp., 11 N.C.App. 20 (N.C. Ct. App. 1971); CBS v. Custom Recording Co., 258 S.C. 465 (1972); Goldstein v. California, 412 U.S. 546 (1973); Mercury Record Prod. v. Econ. Consultants, 64 Wis.2d 163 (1974); NBC v. Nance, 506 S.W.2d 483 (Mo. Ct. App. 1974); GAI Audio v. CBS, 340 A.2d 736 (Md. Ct. Spec. App. 1975); CBS v. Melody Recordings, 134 N.J.Super. 368 (App. Div. 1975).

[82] CBS v. Melody Recordings, 124 N.J. 322 (N.J. Ch. 1973); Int'l Tape Mfr. Ass'n v. Gerstein, 344 F.Supp. 38 (S.D. Fla. 1972); Walsh v. RCA, 275 F.2d 220 (2d Cir. 1960).

[83] SAMUELS, *supra* note 35, at 45.

[84] Tape Ind. Ass'n of America v. Younger, 316 F.Supp. 340, 351 (C.D. Cal. 1970).

[85] 11 N.C. App. 20 (N.C. Ct. App. 1971).

[86] *Id.* at 24.

[87] 130 Ill.App.2d 429 (Ill. App. Ct. 1970).

[88] 82 Cal. Rptr. 798 (Cal. Dist. Ct. App. 1969).

[89] 258 S.C. 465 (1972).

[90] 316 F.Supp.340 (C.D. Cal. 1970).

[91] *Id.* at 350.

[92] 344 F.Supp. 38 (S.D. Fla. 1972).

[93] 124 N.J. Super 322 (N.J. Ch. 1973).

[94] *Id.* at 329-30. The decision in this case was later reversed after the Supreme Court decision in Goldstein v. California clarified that Sears/Compco did not abolish such claims and after the U.S. Congress passed an amendment to copyright law protecting sound recordings. *See* 134 N.J.Super. 368 (App. Div. 1975).

[95] FLA. STAT. ch. 71-102 §543.041 (1971).

[96] CAL. PENAL CODE §653H (1971).

[97] 412 U.S. 546 (1973).

[98] 412 U.S. 546, 569-70 (1973).

[99] SAMUELS, *supra* note 35, at 45.

[100] 64 Wis.2d 163 (1974).

[101] *Id.* at 184.

[102] Ind. News v. Williams, 184 F.Supp. 877 (E.D. Pa. 1960), 293 F.2d 510 (3rd Cir. 1961) (ruling that a second-hand comic book dealer's use of coverless comic books sold by a waste dealer did not constitute misappropriation); Desclee & Cie v. Nemmers, 190 F.Supp. 381 (E.D. Wis. 1961) (ruling that the use of Gregorian chants did not constitute misappropriation); Pottstown Daily News v. Pottstown Broad., 411 Pa. 383 (1963), 247 F.Supp. 578 (E.D. Pa. 1965) (ruling that use of content from a newspaper by a competitor local radio station constitutes misappropriation); Flexitized Inc. v. Nat'l Flexitized Corp., 335 F.2d 774 (2d Cir. 1964) (ruling that the use of flexible collars by the defendants constituted commercial immorality); KMLA v. Twentieth Century Cigarette Vendors, 264 F.Supp. 35 (C.D. Calif. 1967) (ruling that the use of radio station music as background music constituted commercial immorality); Bond Buyer v. Dealers Digest, 267 N.Y.S.2d 944 (N.Y. App. Div. 1966) (ruling that use of market information constituted commercial immorality); Press Publ'g Co. v. Atlantic County Advertiser, Inc., 108 N.J. Super 75 (1969) (ruling that the copying of ads did not constitute misappropriation); Jacobs v. Robitaille, 406 F.Supp. 1145 (D.N.H. 1976) (ruling that the copying of classified ads did not constitute misappropriation); Triangle Publ'ns v. Sports Eye, 415 F.Supp. 682 (E.D. Pa. 1976) (ruling that the copying of racing forms did not constitute misappropriation).

[103] 411 Pa. 383 (1963).

[104] *Id.* at 393.

[105] 184 F.Supp. 877 (E.D. Pa. 1960), 293 F.2d 510 (3rd Cir. 1961).

[106] 184 F.Supp. 877, 880 (E.D. Pa. 1960).

[107] *Id.*

[108] 17 U.S.C. §102 (Foundation Press 2000).

[109] 17 U.S.C. §102(b) (Foundation Press 2000).

[110] Conference Report on the Copyright Act of 1976, *quoted in* SAMUELS, *supra* note 35, at 127.

[111] LITMAN, *supra* note 55, at 58-63.

[112] 17 U.S.C. §301 (Foundation Press 2000).

[113] H.R. No. 94-1476 at 132, *quoted in* NBA v. Motorola, 105 F.3d 841 at 850 (2d Cir. 1997).

[114] Storch v. Mergenthaler 1979 U.S. Dist. LEXIS 14582 (E.D.N.Y. Feb. 7, 1979); Prof'l Sys. v. Databank, 1979 U.S. Dist.

LEXIS 12849 (D. Okla. April 24, 1979); Roy Export v. CBS, 503 F.Supp. 1137 (S.D.N.Y 1980), 672 F.2d 1095 (2d Cir. 1982); Am. Tel. v. Manning, 651 P.2d 440 (Colo. Ct. App. 1982); Standard & Poor's Corp. v. Commodity Exch., 683 F.2d 704 (2d Cir. 1982); Universal City Studios v. Kamar, 1982 U.S. Dist. 15942 (S.D. Tex. Sept. 20, 1982); Bd. of Trade v. Dow Jones, 108 Ill. App. 3d 681 (1982), 98 Ill.2d 109 (1983); CBS v. Garrod, 622 F.Supp. 532 (D.C. Fla. 1985); Michael Anthony Jewelers v. Peacock, 795 F.Supp. 639 (S.D.N.Y. 1992).

[115] Section 102(b) states: "In no case does copyright protection for an original work of authorship extend to any idea, procedure, process, system, method of operation, concept, principle, or discovery, regardless of the form in which it is described, explained, illustrated, or embodied in such work."

[116] 683 F.2d 704 (2d Cir. 1982).

[117] *Id.* at 710-11.

[118] 108 Ill.App. 3d 681(1982), 98 Ill.2d 109 (1983).

[119] 108 Ill.App. 3d 681, 695 (1982).

[120] 98 Ill.2d 109, 120 (1983).

[121] *Id.* at 121.

[122] 1984 U.S. Dist. LEXIS 20579 (S.D.N.Y. Jan. 10, 1984).

[123] 808 F.2d 204 (2d Cir. 1986).

[124] *Id.* at 208.

[125] *Id.* at 209.

[126] 499 U.S. 340 (1991).

[127] The Court wrote: "Originality is a constitutional requirement. The source of Congress' power to enact copyright laws is Article I, §8, cl. 8, of the Constitution, which authorizes Congress to 'secure for limited Times to Authors . . . the exclusive Right to their respective Writings.' In two decisions from the late 19th century -- The Trade-Mark Cases, 100 U.S. 82 (1879); and Burrow-Giles Lithographic Co. v. Sarony, 111 U.S. 53 (1884) -- this Court defined the crucial terms "authors" and "writings." In so doing, the Court made it unmistakably clear that these terms presuppose a degree of originality." *Id.* at 346.

[128] 499 U.S. at 347, *quoting* Miller v. Universal Studios, 650 F.2d 1365, 1369 (5th Cir. 1981).

[129] *Id.* at 354.

[130] M. Nimmer, The Law of Copyright §1.01[B] at 1-12, *quoted in* Mayer v. Josiah Wedgwood & Sons, Ltd., 601 F.Supp. 1523, 1535 (S.D.N.Y. 1985).

[131] "Extra elements" have included state law contract claims, *see* ProCD v. Zeidenberg, 86 F. 3d 1447 (7th Cir. 1996); Selby v. New Line Cinema, 96 F.Supp.2d 1053 (C.D. Cal. 2000); Wrench v. Taco Bell Corp., No. 1:98-CV-45, 1998 US Dist. LEXIS 12710 (W.D. Mich. June 18, 1998); Lennon v. Seaman, 63 F.Supp.2d 428 (S.D.N.Y. 1999); state unfair competition statutes, *see* ETS v. Simon, 96 F.Supp.2d 1081 (C.D. Cal. 1999); and breaches of trust, *see* A. Brod Inc. v. SK&I Co., L.L.C., 998 F.Supp. 314 (S.D.N.Y. 1998).

[132] 601 F.Supp. 1523 (S.D.N.Y. 1985).

[133] *Id.* at 1535.

[134] 634 F.Supp. 1468 (S.D.N.Y. 1986).

[135] *Id.* at 1477.

[136] Nat'l Car Rental Sys., Inc. v. Computer Assoc. Int'l, 991 F.2d 426, 433 (8th Cir. 1993); Taquino v. Teledyne Monarch Rubber, 893 F.2d 1488, 1501 (5th Cir. 1990); Acorn Structures, Inc. v. Swantz, 846 F.2d 923, 926 (4th Cir. 1988).

[137] 86 F.3d 1447 (7th Cir. 1997).

[138] *Id.* at 1454.

[139] 1994 U.S. Dist. LEXIS 15736 (N.D. Ill. Oct. 24, 1994).

[140] *Id.* at *17.

[141] *Id.* at *18.

[142] 435 F.Supp. 1372 (D. Del. 1977).

[143] 749 F.2d 1028 (3rd Cir. 1984).

[144] NFL v. Governor of Delaware, 435 F.Supp. 1372, 1377 (D. Del. 1977).

[145] *Id.* at 1379.

[146] *Id.* at 1378.

[147] 749 F.2d 1028, 1030 (3rd Cir. 1984).

[148] *Id.* at 1038.

CHAPTER 5

[1] "Repurposing" is "the process of taking content from one medium (such as from a book, a newspaper, TV, or radio) and repackaging it for use in another medium (such as on the Web)." *See* http://www.netlingo.com.

Endnotes

[2] For more about the proposed database protection bills, *see* Victoria Smith Ekstrand, *Drawing Swords After Feist: Efforts to Legislate the Database Pirate*, 7 COMM L. & POL'Y 317 (2002).

[3] 105 F.3d 841 (2d Cir. 1997), 939 F.Supp. 1071 (S.D.N.Y. 1996).

[4] 939 F.Supp. 1071 (S.D.N.Y. 1996).

[5] *Motorola History Highlights*, *at* http://www.motorola.com (last visited Nov. 16, 2002).

[6] *Id.*

[7] A semiconductor is "a chemical substance or compound that conducts electricity under some conditions but not others, making it a good medium for the control of electrical current." *See "semiconductor,"* *at* http://whatis.techtarget.com.

[8] *Motorola History Highlights*, *at* http://www.motorola.com (last visited Nov. 16, 2002).

[9] John E. Walsh & William P. Coon, *Motorola's Attempts to Increase Market Share and Profits in Japan*, *in* INTERNATIONAL BUSINESS CASE STUDIES FOR THE MULTICULTURAL MARKETPLACE 212 (Robert T. Moran, David O. Braaten, & John E. Walsh, Jr., eds., 1994).

[10] *See* Dennis Sester, *Motorola: A Tradition of Quality*, QUALITY, Oct. 2001, at 30-34; Alex Poole, *Six-Sigma: Communication's Perfect Role*, STRATEGIC COMMUNICATION MANAGEMENT, Feb.-March 2000, at 34-35.

[11] Walsh & Coon, *supra* note 9, at 212.

[12] *Motorola History Highlights*, *at* http://www.motorola.com (last visited Sept. 20, 2004).

[13] *Id.*

[14] Roger O. Crockett & Peter Elstrom, *How Motorola Lost Its Way*, BUSINESS WEEK, May 4, 1998, at 143.

[15] *Id.* at 146.

[16] *Id.* at 140.

[17] *Id.* at 142.

[18] JOHN A. FORTUNATO, THE ULTIMATE ASSIST: THE RELATIONSHIP AND BROADCAST STRATEGIES OF THE NBA AND TELEVISION NETWORKS 14 (2001).

[19] Mike Monroe, *The Commissioners*, *at* http://www.nba.com/history/commissioners.html (last visited Nov. 16, 2002).

[20] FORTUNATO, *supra* note 18, at 14-17.

[21] ELDON L. HAM, THE PLAYMASTERS: FROM SELLOUTS TO LOCKOUTS – AN UNAUTHORIZED HISTORY OF THE NBA 19-43 (2000).
[22] FORTUNATO, *supra* note 18, at 17.
[23] *Id.*
[24] HAM, *supra* note 21, at 45.
[25] FORTUNATO, *supra* note 18, at 24.
[26] *Id.*
[27] *Id.* at 25.
[28] HAM, *supra* note 21, at 45.
[29] *Id.* at 47.
[30] *Id.* at 55.
[31] *Id.*
[32] Robertson v. NBA, 72 F.R.D. 64 (S.D.N.Y. 1976).
[33] Robertson v. NBA, 389 F.Supp. 867, 892 (S.D.N.Y. 1975). *See also* HAM, *supra* note 21, at 68.
[34] Monroe, *supra* note 19.
[35] John Hareas, *Coast to Coast: The NBA Expands, in* THE OFFICIAL NBA ENCYCLOPEDIA 74 (Jan Hubbard, ed., 2000).
[36] *Id.*
[37] *NBA Battles Bootleg Merchants*, CANADIAN PRESS, July 4, 1994.
[38] FORTUNATO, *supra* note 18, at 26.
[39] Superstations are "television stations whose over-the-air signals are retransmitted by satellite to cable TV systems around the country, and then by cable to cable TV subscribers." *See NBA and Chicago Bulls settle antitrust lawsuit over WGN telecasts of Bulls games*, ENT. L. REP., Dec. 1996.
[40] WGN v. NBA, 754 F.Supp. 1336 (N.D. Ill. 1991), 961 F.2d 667 (7th Cir. 1992).
[41] *NBA and Chicago bulls settle antitrust lawsuit over WGN telecasts of Bulls games*, ENT. L. REP., Dec. 1996.
[42] *See NFL and NBA Properties Win Trademark and Counterfeiting Claims*, ENTERTAINMENT LAW REPORTER, Oct. 1999; Richard Sandomir, *The Economics of a Sports Cliché*, N.Y. TIMES, June 22, 1993, at D1; *NBA Battles Bootleg Merchants*, Canadian Press, July 4, 1994.
[43] 105 F.3d 841 (2d Cir. 1997).
[44] Charley Rosen, *League of His Own: Commissioner David Stern turned a sagging NBA into the world's most recognizable sports league*, SPORT, July 1997, at 42.

[45] Edwin S. Desser Dep. at A-535, March 25, 1996. NBA v. Motorola, 939 F.Supp. 1071 (S.D.N.Y. 1996), 105 F.3d 841 (2d Cir. 1997).

[46] Douglas T. Kirk Dep. at A-857, March 28, 1996. *NBA.*

[47] Kirk Dep. at A-856. *See also* Exhibit 117, Memo on New Media, at A-1103.

[48] Exhibit 117, Memo on New Media, at A-1106-08.

[49] Edwin S. Desser Dep. at A-642, April 2, 1996. *NBA.*

[50] Bryan L. Burns Dep. at A-844, April 1, 1996. *NBA.*

[51] Exhibit 119, New Policy Regarding Electronic Media and SportsTicker, at A-1091.

[52] Brian McIntyre Dep. at A-825-26, April 3, 1996. *NBA.*

[53] *See* http://www.sportsticker.com. SportsTicker, now owned by ESPN, delivers instant scores, breaking sports news, statistics, previews, recaps and features, gathered by more than 700 event-site reporters. It is also the official statistician for many minor sports leagues, but not for the NBA. The official statistician of the NBA is a company known as Elias.

[54] Edwin S. Desser Dep. at A-552, March 25, 1996. *NBA.*

[55] Edwin S. Desser Dep. at A-636, April 2, 1996.

[56] Douglas T. Kirk Dep. at A-858, March 28, 1996.

[57] Edwin S. Desser, Reply Aff. at A-1137, April 1996.

[58] *Id.* at A-1140.

[59] SportsTrax User's Guide For Basketball, at A-253-70.

[60] *Id.*

[61] John Dewan Aff. at A-364, April 5, 1996.

[62] *See* Stephen Chase Dep. at A-732-52, April 1, 1996; James Lampariello Dep. at A-684-99, March 29, 1996; Adam David Smith Dep. at A-768-89; and James Winzig Dep. at A-713-22, April 1, 1996. *NBA.*

[63] John Dewan Aff. at A-369, April 5, 1996.

[64] Edwin S. Desser Dep. at A-589-90, March 26, 1996.

[65] Two freelancers were assigned to each game to track shots made and attempted, fouls, clock updates. John Dewan Aff. at A-361-62, April 5, 1996.

[66] Randall Dean Dep. at A-834, April 3, 1996.

[67] Edwin S. Desser Dep. at A-603, March 26, 1996.

[68] Plaintiff's brief at 12, footnote 6, NBA v. Motorola, 105 F.3d 841 (2d Cir. 1997).
[69] NBA v. Motorola, 939 F.Supp. 1071, 1085-86 (S.D.N.Y. 1996).
[70] *See* 17 U.S.C. §301 (Foundation Press 2000).
[71] *See* ROCHELLE COOPER DREYFUSS & ROBERT ROSENTHAL KWALL, INTELLECTUAL PROPERTY: CASES AND MATERIALS ON TRADEMARK, COPYRIGHT AND PATENT LAW 520 (1996).
[72] Plaintiff's brief at 29, NBA v. Motorola, 105 F.3d 841 (2d Cir. 1997).
[73] *Id.* at 25-6. Despite congressional records that indicate Congress intended for INS-like claims to stand after passage of the 1976 Copyright Act, Motorola went as far as to argue that "it is at best doubtful" that INS would survive preemption. Motorola wrote: "Although that language standing alone suggests that INS itself survived preemption while other misappropriation claims did not, floor debate on the bills clouded the issue even with respect to INS. . . . [S]ubsequent Supreme Court decisions, namely Feist and Bonito Boats, strongly suggest that INS would not be endorsed by the Supreme Court today." *See* Defendant Motorola's brief at 42.
[74] Defendant Stats' brief at 15; and Defendant Motorola's brief at 18-30.
[75] DREYFUSS & KWALL, *supra* note 71, at 522.
[76] For a discussion of the protections for game broadcasts, see Chapter Four.
[77] Defendant Stats' brief at 30, and Defendant Motorola's brief at 44-46. NBA v. Motorola ,105 F.3d 841 (2d Cir. 1997).
[78] Plaintiff's brief at 16.
[79] Bryan L. Burns Dep. at A-844, April 1, 1996. *NBA*.
[80] *Id.* at 19-22.
[81] *Id.* at 22.
[82] Defendant Stats' brief at 31.
[83] The Supreme Court wrote of INS and AP: "The parties are competitors in the gathering and distribution of news and its publication for profit in newspapers." 248 U.S. 215, 216 (1918). The Court also wrote "the parties are competitors in this field," 248 U.S. at 235.
[84] Plaintiff's brief at 6.
[85] Defendant Stats' brief at 31-32. *NBA*.
[86] *Id.* at 37.

[87] Plaintiff's brief at 4.

[88] *Id.* at 37.

[89] *Id.* at 37-43. A prior restraint is a government restriction on expression before publication and is generally unconstitutional under the First Amendment. *See* BLACK'S LAW DICTIONARY 1212 (7th ed. 1999).

[90] Under the First Amendment, any regulations of expression based on the content of what is said are unconstitutional, unless the regulation is based on a compelling state interest and is narrowly tailored. *See* BLACK'S LAW DICTIONARY 1212 (7th ed. 1999).

[91] Plaintiff's brief at 41.

[92] Defendant Motorola's reply brief at 20 (citations omitted). *See also* Defendant Stats' reply brief at 23.

[93] Defendant Stats' brief at 43.

[94] 433 U.S. 562 (1977).

[95] Defendant Stats' brief at 38.

[96] The NBA, however, did not counter the defendants' arguments on the basis of acceptable time, place, and manner restrictions. It simply argued that the First Amendment did not apply to the issues in the case.

[97] 939 F.Supp. 1071, 1097 (S.D.N.Y. 1996).

[98] *Id.*

[99] *Id.* at 1105.

[100] *Id.* at 1075.

[101] *Id.* at 1105.

[102] *Id.* at 1107.

[103] *Id.* at 1098-1104.

[104] 512 U.S. 753 (1994). In *Madsen*, the U.S. Supreme Court upheld an injunction keeping protestors 36 feet from the entrance to an abortion clinic. The Court ruled that the injunction allowed protestors to communicate their messages in an area visible to patients and clinic workers.

[105] 939 F. Supp. at 1087.

[106] *Id.*

[107] 105 F.3d, 854, 841 n. 10 (2d Cir. 1997).

[108] *Id.* at 846.

[109] *Id.* at 849.

[110] *Id.* at 851.

[111] *Id.* at 850.

[112] "Extra elements" have included state law contract claims, *see* ProCD v. Zeidenberg, 86 F. 3d 1447 (7th Cir. 1996); Selby v. New Line Cinema, 96 F.Supp. 2d 1053 (C.D. Cal. 2000), Wrench v. Taco Bell Corp., No. 1:98-CV-45, 1998 US Dist. LEXIS 12710 (W.D. Mich. June 18, 1998), Lennon v. Seaman, 63 F.Supp.2d 428 (S.D.N.Y. 1999); state unfair competition statutes, *see* ETS v. Simon, 96 F.Supp.2d 1081 (C.D. Cal. 1999); and breaches of trust, *see* A. Brod Inc. v. SK&I Co., L.L.C., 998 F.Supp. 314 (S.D.N.Y. 1998).

[113] 105 F.3d at 845.

[114] *Id.* at 853.

[115] *Id.*

[116] *Id.* at 854.

[117] *Id*

[118] Although the *INS* Court did not explicitly label the elements of a misappropriation claim, it addressed the boundaries. The Court said that the new misappropriation tort was a result of: (1) the AP's significant labor and investment in the news; (2) the great value of its news for the short period after it was published; (3) INS's "reaping where it had not sown" by free-riding on AP's investment in the news; (4) the competition between AP and INS; and (5) the harm INS would cause to AP's business by such actions.

[119] The Second Circuit's decision in *NBA* was Shepardized through March 2004.

[120] 73 F.Supp. 2d 1044 (E.D. Mo. 1999).

[121] NBA v. Motorola, 105 F.3d at 845, 852 (2d Cir. 1997).

[122] 73 F.Supp. 2d at 1050.

[123] 339 F.3d 530 (7th Cir. 2003).

[124] *Id.* at 534.

[125] *Id.*

[126] *Id.*

[127] 170 F.Supp. 2d 974 (E.D. Cal. 2000).

[128] *Id.* at 977.

[129] 117 F.Supp. 2d 1322 (M.D. Fla. 2000)

[130] *Id.* at 1329.

[131] This incomplete record, the court said, prevented it from issuing an injunction to stop what Morris described as anticompetitive practices. *See Id.* at 1328.

[132] 235 F.Supp. 2d 1269, 1279 (M.D. Fla. 2002).

[133] 364 F.3d 1288, 1292-93 (11th Cir. 2004)

[134] 124 F.Supp.2d 836 (S.D.N.Y. 2000).

[135] *Id.* at 847.

[136] 248 U.S. 215, 263-64 (1918).

[137] Motorola collected NBA scores for its pager system through a network of reporters who watched the games on television or listened to them on the radio. This, the NBA court said, did not constitute free-riding because it was different from taking the scores directly from an NBA stats service. *See* 105 F.3d at 854.

[138] 117 F.Supp. 2d 1322, 1326 (M.D. Fla. 200).

[139] *Id.* at 1327.

[140] *Id.*

[141] "Without a more complete factual record before it, however, the Court cannot presently determine the extent to which Defendant's incentive to produce and operate RTSS (the PGA's scores system) would be undermined if Plaintiff were allowed to free-ride on its investment." *Id.* at 1329.

[142] 235 F.Supp.2d 1269, 1279 (M.D. Fla. 2002).

[143] 364 F.3d 1288 (11th Cir. 2004).

[144] No. 97 Civ. 1190 (S.D.N.Y. 1997).

[145] "Framing" is a reference to a "formatting device that allows a Web page to be viewed in separate, independently scrollable windows. Since each frame houses it own HTML document, frames allow multiple documents to be viewed within a single browser window." Webmonkey Glossary, *at* http://hotwired.lycos.com/webmonkey/glossary/frame.html.

[146] No. 97 Civ. 1190 at ¶39 (S.D.N.Y. 1997).

[147] 117 F.Supp. 2d at 1329.

[148] 73 F.Supp. 2d at 1050.

[149] 105 F.3d at 853, n. 8 (emphasis added).

[150] *Id.* (emphasis added).

[151] "Without a more complete factual record before it, however, the Court cannot presently determine the extent to which Defendant's incentive to produce and operate RTSS (its own scores service) would be undermined if Plaintiff were allowed to free ride on its investment." 117 F.Supp.2d at 1329.

[152] David Tomlin considers the issue from the plaintiff's perspective: "[A] plaintiff is now required somehow to produce real

evidence to support a hypothetical, i.e., if the defendant's actions were permissible, the public would be deprived of our product." Tomlin claims this is unreasonable because "competition should not have to be lethal to be unfair." See David H. Tomlin, *Sui Generis Database Protection: Cold Comfort for "Hot News,"* COMM. LAW, Spring 2001, at 19.

[153] 248 U.S. at 241 (emphasis added).
[154] 105 F.3d at 852 (emphasis added).
[155] 73 F.Supp.2d at 1050 (emphasis added).
[156] 105 F.3d at 845.
[157] Although the *INS* Court did not explicitly label the elements of a misappropriation claim, it addressed the boundaries. The Court said that the new misappropriation tort was a result of: (1) the AP's significant labor and investment in the news; (2) the great value of its news for the short period after it was published; (3) INS's "reaping where it had not sown" by free-riding on AP's investment in the news; (4) the competition between AP and INS; and (5) the harm INS would cause to AP's business by such actions.

CHAPTER 6

[1] LAWRENCE LESSIG, CODE AND OTHER LAWS OF CYBERSPACE 223 (1999).
[2] 105 F.3d 841, 845 (2d Cir. 1997).
[3] JESSICA LITMAN, DIGITAL COPYRIGHT 79 (2001).
[4] H.R. 3261 108th Cong. (2003).
[5] 248 U.S. 215, 241 (1918) (emphasis added).
[6] 105 F.3d 841, 852 (2d Cir. 1997) (emphasis added).
[7] 73 F.Supp.2d 1044, 1050 (E.D. Mo. 1999) (emphasis added).
[8] 170 F.Supp. 2d 974 (E.D. Cal. 2000).
[9] *Id.* at 977.
[10] *Id.*
[11] Wendy J. Gordon, *Asymmetric Market Failure and Prisoner's Dilemma in Intellectual Property*, 17 U. DAYTON L. REV., 863-85(1992), summarized by J.H. Reichman & Pamela Samuelson, *Intellectual Property Rights in Data?* 50 VAND. L. REV. 51, 141 (1997).
[12] Reichman & Samuelson, *supra* note 11, at 143.

Bibliography

American Law Institute, *Restatement (Third) of Unfair Competition*. St. Paul, Minn.: American Law Institute Publishers, 1995.

Arbittier, Niki. "The Business of Sports: The Evolution of Intellectual Property Law Away From International News Service v. Associated Press," *Temple Environmental Law & Technology Journal* 17 (1998): 43-70.

Associated Press, *Law of the Associated Press, Volumes 1-2*. New York: Associated Press, 1914-19.

Associated Press. *M.E.S. His Book*. New York: Harper & Brothers Publishers,1918.

Band, Jonathan, Response to the Coalition against Database Privacy Memorandum, *The Computer & Internet Lawyer* 21 (May 2004): 7.

Band, Jonathan and Makoto Kono. "The Database Protection Debate in the 106th Congress," *Ohio State Law Journal* 62 (2001): 869-878.

Baron, Paula. "Back to the Future: Learning from the Past in the Database Debate," *Ohio State Law Journal* 62 (2001): 879-931.

Bastian, Michael J.. "Protection of 'Noncreative' Databases: Harmonization of United States, Foreign and International Law," *Boston College International and Comparative Law Review* 22 (1999): 425-463.

Benkler, Yochai. "Free as the Air to Common Use: First Amendment Constraints on Enclosure of the Public Domain," *New York University Law Review* 74 (1999): 354- 444.

Benkler, Yochai. "Constitutional Bounds of Database Protection: The Role of Judicial Review in the Creation and Definition of Private Rights in Information," *Berkeley Technology Law Review* 15 (2000): 535-602.

Black's Law Dictionary (7th ed.). St. Paul, Minn.: West Publishing Co., 1999.

Blanchard, Margaret. "The Associated Press Antitrust Suit: A Philosophical Clash Over Ownership of First Amendment Rights." *Business History Review* 61, (Spring 1987): 43-88.

Blondheim, Menahem. *News Over the Wires: The Telegraph and the Flow of Public Information in America, 1844-1897*. Cambridge, MA: Harvard University Press,1994.

Bott, Cynthia M. "Protection of Information Products: Balancing Commercial Reality and the Public Domain," *University of Cincinnati Law Review* 67 (1998): 237-264.

Bowker, Richard Rogers. *Copyright: Its History and Its Law*. Boston: Houghton Mifflin Company, 1912.

Boyarski, Jason R. "The Heist of Feist: Protection for Collections of Information and the Possible Federalization of 'Hot News,'" *Cardozo Law Review* 21 (1999): 871-925.

Carlson, Oliver, and Ernest Sutherland Bates. *Hearst: Lord of San Simeon*. New York: The Viking Press, 1936.

Chambers, John Whiteclay II.*The Tyranny of Change: America in the Progressive Era*. New Brunswick, NJ: Rutgers Unversity Press, 2000.

Cloud, Barbara. "News: Public Service or Profitable Property." *American Journalism 13* (Spring 1996):140-156.

Conley, John M. et al. "Database Protection in a Digital World," *Richmond Journal of Law and Technology* 6 (1999); available from http://www.richmond.edu/jolt.

Cooper, Kent. *Kent Cooper and The Associated Press*. New York: Random House, 1959.

Crockett, Roger O. and Peter Elstrom. "How Motorola Lost Its Way," *Business Week*, 4 May 1998, 140.

Djavaherian, David. "Hot News and No Cold Facts: NBA v. Motorola and the Protection of Database Contents," *Richmond Journal of Law and Technology* 5 (1998); available from http://www.richmond.edu/jolt.

Dreyfuss, Rochelle Cooper and Robert Rosenthal Kwall. *Intellectual Property: Cases and Materials on Trademark, Copyright and Patent Law*. Westbury, N.Y.: The Foundation Press, 1996.

Drone, Eaton S. *A Treatise on the Law of Property in Intellectual Productions in Great Britain and the United States*. So. Hackensack, NJ: Rothman Reprints, 1972 (c1879).

Epstein, Richard. "International News Service v. Associated Press: Custom and Law as Sources of Property Rights in News," *Virginia Law Review* 78 (1992): 85-128.

Ferris, William G. *The Grain Traders: The Story of the Chicago Board of Trade*. East Lansing, MI: Michigan State University Press, 1988.

Fortunato, John A. *The Ultimate Assist: The Relationship and Broadcast Strategies of the NBA and Television Networks*. Cresskill, N.J.: Hampton Press, 2001.

Freno, Michael. "Database Protection: Resolving the U.S. Database Dilemma with an Eye Toward International Protection," *Cornell International Law Journal* 34 (2001): 165-225.

Fujichaku, Rex Y., "The Misappropriation Doctrine in Cyberspace: Protecting the Commercial Value of 'Hot News,'" *University of Hawaii Law Review* 20 (1998): 421- 476.

Gomez, Frank. "Copyright: preemption – misappropriation (Washington Post v. Total News, Inc.)," *Berkeley Technology Law Journal* 13 (1998): 21-34.

Ginsburg, Jane. "No 'Sweat?' Copyright and Other Protection of Works of Information After Feist v. Rural Telephone," *Columbia Law Review* 92 (1992): 338-388.

Goldman, Sheldon, and Thomas P. Jahnige. *The Federal Courts as a Political System*. New York: Harper & Row, 1976.

Goldstein, Paul. *Copyright, Patent, Trademark and Related State Doctrines*. Westbury, New York: The Foundation Press, 1997.

Gordon, Wendy J. "On Owning Information: Intellectual Property and the Restitutionary Impulse," *Virginia Law Review* 78 (1992): 149-281.

Gordon, Wendy J. "Asymmetric Market Failure and Prisoner's Dilemma in Intellectual Property" *University of Dayton Law Review* 17 (1992): 853-869.

Gramling, Oliver. *AP: The Story of News*. New York: Farrar & Rinehart, 1940.

Ham, Eldon L. *The Playmasters: From Sellouts to Lockouts – An Unauthorized History of the NBA*. Lincolnwood, Ill.: Contemporary Books, 2000.

Gray, C. Boyden, Jamie Gorelick and Randoph D. Moss. "Memorandum on the Legal Need for H.R. 3261, the "Database and

Collections of Information Misappropriation Act" *The Computer & Internet Lawyer* 21 (May 2004): 5.

Karjala, Dennis. "Misappropriation as a Third Intellectual Property Paradigm," *Columbia Law Review* 94 (1994): 2594-2609.

Keller, Bruce. "Condemned to Repeat the Past: The Reemergence of Misappropriation and Other Common Law Theories of Protection for Intellectual Property" *Harvard Journal of Law and Technology* 11 (1998): 401-428.

Kennedy, David M. *Progressivism: The Critical Issues*. Boston: Little, Brown and Company, 1971.

Klein, Louis. "Copyright — Misappropriation Doctrine: National Basketball Association v. Motorola, Inc.: Future Prospects for Protecting Real-Time Information," *Brooklyn Law Review* 64 (1998): 585-625.

Knights, Peter R. "The Press Association War of 1866-1867." *Journalism Monographs* 6, (December 1967): 1-57.

Kolko, Gabriel. "The Triumph of Conservatism." In *Progressivism: The Critical Issues,* edited by David M. Kennedy,109-21. Boston: Little, Brown and Company, 1971.

Lessig, Lawrence. *The Future of Ideas: The Fate of the Commons in a Connected World*. New York: Random House, 2001.

Lessig, Lawrence. *Free Culture: How Big Media Uses Technology and the Law to Lock Down Culture and Control Creativity*. New York: The Penguin Press, 2004.

Litman, Jessica. "The Public Domain," *Emory Law Journal* 39 (1990): 965 – 1023.

Litman, Jessica. *Digital Copyright*. Amherst, N.Y.: Prometheus Books, 2001.

Loy, Joseph A. "Recent Development: Database and Collections of Information Misappropriation Act of 2003: Unconstitutionally Expanding Copyright Law?" *N.Y.U. Legislation and Public Policy* 7 (2003/2004): 449-464.

McCarthy, J. Thomas. *McCarthy on Trademarks and Unfair Competition, Fourth Edition*. St. Paul, MN: West Group, 2002.

Myers, Gary. "The Restatement's Rejection of the Misappropriation Tort: A Victory for the Public Domain," *South Carolina Law Review* 47 (1996): 673-707.

Note. "Nothing But Internet," *Harvard Law Review* 110 (1997): 1143-1160.

Nasaw, David. *The Chief: The Life of William Randolph Hearst.* Boston: Houghton Mifflin Company, 2000.

Nims, Harry D. *The Law of Unfair Competition and Trademarks, Fourth Edition.* New York: Baker, Voorhis, 1947.

Olson, Dale P. "Common Law Misappropriation in the Digital Era," *Missouri Law Review* 64 (1999): 837-911.

Patterson, Lyman Ray. *Copyright in Historical Perspective.* Nashville: Vanderbilt University Press, 1968.

Pollack, Malla. "The Right to Know?: Delimiting Database Protection at the Juncture of the Commerce Clause, the Intellectual Property Clause and the First Amendment," *Cardozo Arts and Entertainment Law Journal* 17 (1999): 47-145.

Poole, Alex. "Six-Sigma: Communication's Perfect Role," Strategic Communication Management (Feb.-March 2000): 34.

Posner, Richard A. "Essay: Misappropriation: A Dirge," *Houston Law Review* 40 (2003): 621-641.

Raskind, Leo J. "The Misappropriation Doctrine as a Competitive Norm of Intellectual Property Law," *Minnesota Law Review* 75 (1991): 875-906.

Reichman, J.H., and Pamela Samuelson. "Intellectual Property Rights in Data?" *Vanderbilt Law Review* 50 (1997): 51-109.

Rose, Mark. *Authors and Owners: The Invention of Copyright.* Cambridge, Mass.: Harvard University Press, 1993.

Rosewater, Victor. *History of Cooperative News-gathering in the United States.* New York: D. Appleton and Company, 1930.

Samuels, Edward. *The Illustrated Story of Copyright.* New York: St Martin's Press, 2000.

Samuelson, Pamela. "Digital Information, Networks and the Public Domain, Duke University Conference on the Public Domain," November 9-11, 2001; available from http://www.law.duke.edu/pd.

Sanks, Terry M. "Database Protection: National and International Attempts to Provide Legal Protection for Databases," *Florida State University Law Review* 25 (1998): 991-1016.

Schwarzlose, Richard. *The Nation's Newsbrokers, Volume 1.* Evanston, IL: Northwestern University Press, 1989.

Schwarzlose, Richard. *The Nation's Newsbrokers, Volume 2.* Evanston, IL: Northwestern University Press, 1990.

Sease, Edmund. "Misappropriation is Seventy-Five Years Old; Should we Bury it or Revive it?" *North Dakota Law Review* 70 (1994): 781-808.
Semonche, John. *Keeping the Faith: A Cultural History of the U.S. Supreme Court.* Lanham, MD: Rowman & Littlefield, 1998.
Sester, Dennis. "Motorola: A Tradition of Quality," *Quality* (Oct. 2001): x-x.
Sheldon, Charles H. *The American Judicial Process.* New York: Dodd, Mead, 1974.
Sklar, Martin. *The Corporate Reconstruction of American Capitalism, 1890-1916: The Market, the Law, and Politics.* Cambridge: Cambridge University Press, 1988.
Stone, Melville E. *Fifty Years as a Journalist.* Garden City, NY: Doubleday, Page & Company, 1921.
Sullivan, Paul W. "News Piracy: Unfair Competition and the Misappropriation Doctrine," *Journalism Monographs* 56 (1978): 1-31.
Tessensohn, John. "The Devil's in the Details: The Quest for Legal Protection of Computer Databases and the Collections of Information Act, H.R. 2652," *Idea* 38 (1998): 439-490.
Tomlin, David H. "Sui Generis Database Protection: Cold Comfort for 'Hot News,'" *Communication Law* 19 (Spring 2001): 15-20.
Urofsky, Melvin I. "Proposed Federal Incorporation in the Progressive Era." In *Growth of the Regulatory State, 1900-1917: State and Federal Regulation of Railroads and Other Enterprises*, edited by Robert F. Himmelberg, 304-27. New York: Garland Publishing, 1994.
Walsh, John E., and William P. Coon. "Motorola's Attempts to Increase Market Share and Profits in Japan," *International Business Case Studies For the Multicultural Marketplace*, edited by Robert T. Moran, David O. Braaten, & John E. Walsh, Jr., 210-226. Houston: Gulf Publishing, 1994.
Winkler, John K. *William Randolph Hearst: A New Appraisal.* New York: Hastings House, 1955.
Winter, Jay and Blaine Baggett. *The Great War and The Shaping of the 20th Century.* New York: Penguin Studio, 1996.
Wolken, Jeffrey C. "Just the Facts, Ma'am. A Case for Uniform Federal Regulation of Information Databases in the New Information Age," *Syracuse Law Review* 48 (1998): 1263-1305.

Index

Agnew, Fred, 52-59
Antitrust law, 21-22, 25, 34-36
ASCAP, 97
Associated Press, 6-8
   see also *INS v. AP*
   birth, 16
   Western Associated Press, 17-20, 35
      bylaws, 18-22, 61
      board of directors, 20
Associated Press vs. KVOS, 86-88

Basketball Association of America, 128
Board of Trade v. Dow Jones Co., 112
Brandeis, Louis, Justice, 78
Broadcasting v. Idaho Microwave, 100

Cable television, 100-102

Cable Vision, Inc. v. KUTV Inc., 101
CBS v. Melody Recordings, 105
Cheney Bros. v. Doris Silk Corp., 87
Chicago Board of Trade, 44-45
Cleveland News, 15, 52-62
Coble, Howard (R.-NC), 10-11
Commercial immorality, 92-93, 97
Compco Corp v. Daybright Lighting, Inc. 99-107, 164
Cooper, Kent 25, 52, 59, 161
Copyright law 4-6, 38-42, 106, 109-111
Craig, Daniel, 17
Cushing, Benjamin 52, 55

Database legislation 10-11, 167-170
Due process, for corporations, 33-34

eBay 2
Erie Railroad v. Tompkins, 98
"extra element," 115-117

Feist v. Rural Telephone 4-6, 113-115
Financial Information v. Moody's Investors Service, 113
First Amendment, 141-144
Fred Wehrenberg Circuit of Theatres v. Moviefone, 149, 167
Free-riding element, 151-153

Galvin, Christopher, 126-127
Galvin, Paul V., 124-125
Galvin, Robert, 125-126
Gannett v. Rock Valley Community Press, 117-119
Goldstein v. California, 105-107, 164
Gordon, Wendy, 168
Greeley, Horace, 16
Grosscup, Peter, 22-24, 46

Hearst, William Randolph, 26-32, 161
Herald Publishing Co. v. Florida Antennavision Inc., 102
Hot news doctrine, 3
  elements, 85
  intepretation, 85-121
  origins, 8-9, 15-48
  parameters, 160-170
  relevance today, 12

Independent News v. Williams, 108
International News Service, 25-32
International News Service v. AP, 6-8, 14, 49-83, 134-136
Inter-Ocean Publishing Co. v. AP, 21

KVOS, 88-90

Lessig, Lawrence, 162
Liberty v. Eastern Tape, 104
Litman, Jessica, 166
Loeb v. Turner, 95

Mayer v. Josiah Wedgwood & Sons, 115
Mercury Record v. Economic Consultants, 106-107
Metropolitan Opera Association v. Wagner-Nichols Recorder Corp., 92
McKevitt v. Pallasch, 149
misappropriation, *see hot news doctrine*
Morris Communications Corp. v. PGA Tour, Inc., 150
Motorola, 124-127, 162
Mutual Broadcasting System, Inc. v. Muzak Corp., 95

National Basketball Association, 128-132, 162
NBA v. Motorola, 9-10, 13, 123-157, 165-170
National Exhibition Company v. Fass, 95

Index

NFL v. Governor of the State of Delaware, 118
National Telegraph v. Western Union, 23-24, 46
National Telephone Directory Co. v. Dawson Mfg Co., 86
New York American, 50, 61
Newspapers, 2, 39-41

O'Brien, Larry, 130

Piracy 1-14, 50-60
    of cable signals, 100-102
    of newspapers, 88-90
    of radio recordings, 93-97
    of sports broadcasts, 91-95
    of tapes, 103-107
Preemption, 110-117, 137-139, 144
Pollstar v. Gigmania, 149, 167
Pottstown Daily News v. Pottstown Broadcasting, 107
Pro CD v. Zeidenberg, 116

Reichman, Jerry, 169
Recording Industry of America, 1
radio, 86-97
RCA Mfg Co. v. Whiteman, 91

Samuelson, Pam, 169
Scholastic v. Stouffer, 150
Sears Roebuck Co. v. Stiffel Co., 99-107, 164
Sports, 93-97, 132-137
SportsTrax, 128-132
Standard & Poor's Corp v. Commodity Exchange, 112

Stern, David, 130-131
Stone, Melville, 20, 23-25, 50-53, 59

Tape Industries Association of America v. Younger, 104
Tape recordings, 103-107
Telegraph, 16-17
Teleprompter Corp. v. CBS, 102
threat element, 153-155
Ticker cases, 43-47
Twentieth Century Sporting Club, Inc. v. Transradio Press Service, 93

unfair competition, 36-38, 63, 67, 84, 92, 98-100,
United Artists v. Fortnightly, 102
United Press, 19-20
Universal City Studios v. The T-shirt Gallery, 116
Uproar Co. v. National Broadcasting, 92
USGA v. St. Andrews Systems, 118

Voter News Service, 2

Waring v. WDAS Broadcasting Station Inc., 91
Washington Post v. Total News, 152
Watterson, Henry, 19

Zacchini v. Howard, 143